A History of
Psychology in Letters

A History of Psychology in Letters

Ludy T. Benjamin, Jr.

Texas A&M University

WCB Brown &
Benchmark

Book Team

Editor *Michael Lange*
Developmental Editor *Sheralee Connors*
Production Coordinator *Deborah Donner*

P U B L I S H E R S
A Division of Wm. C. Brown Communications, Inc.

Vice President and General Manager *Thomas E. Doran*
Executive Managing Editor *Ed Bartell*
Executive Editor *Edgar J. Laube*
Director of Marketing *Kathy Law Laube*
National Sales Manager *Eric Ziegler*
Marketing Manager *Carla Aspelmeier*
Advertising Manager *Jodi Rymer*
Managing Editor, Production *Colleen A. Yonda*
Manager of Visuals and Design *Faye M. Schilling*
Production Editorial Manager *Vickie Putman Caughron*
Publishing Services Manager *Karen J. Slaght*
Permissions/Records Manager *Connie Allendorf*

Wm. C. Brown Communications, Inc.

Chairman Emeritus *Wm. C. Brown*
Chairman and Chief Executive Officer *Mark C. Falb*
President and Chief Operating Officer *G. Franklin Lewis*
Corporate Vice President, Operations *Beverly Kolz*
Corporate Vice President, President of WCB Manufacturing *Roger Meyer*

Cover and interior design by Morris Lundin

The credits section for this book begins on page 211 and is considered an extension of the copyright page.

Library of Congress Catalog Card Number: 91–78195

ISBN 0–697–12980–2

Printed in the United States of America by Wm. C. Brown Communications, Inc., 2460 Kerper Boulevard, Dubuque, IA 52001

10 9 8 7 6 5 4 3 2 1

Table of Contents

Preface vii

Chapter 1   John Locke as Child Psychologist 1

Chapter 2   Why Did Charles Darwin Delay in Publishing
             His Theory? 14

Chapter 3   John Stuart Mill and the Subjection of Women . . . 26

Chapter 4   An American in Leipzig 39

Chapter 5   The Struggle for Psychology Laboratories 53

Chapter 6   A Woman's Quest for Graduate Education 65

Chapter 7   William James and Psychical Research 77

Chapter 8   Edward Bradford Titchener's Experimentalists 93

Chapter 9   John B. Watson's Behavioral Psychology 108

Chapter 10   Psychology and "Feeblemindedness" 121

Chapter 11   Sigmund Freud and Carl Jung in America 131

Chapter 12   Coleman Griffith as Sport Psychologist 143

Chapter 13   The Migration of Gestalt Psychology 153

Chapter 14   A Social Agenda for American Psychology 165

Chapter 15   B. F. Skinner's Experimental Analysis of Behavior . 177

Chapter 16   Abraham Maslow's Research on Good
             Human Beings 190

References 205
Credits 211
Index 213

Preface

The idea for this book grew out of my undergraduate and graduate courses on the history of psychology—courses I have been teaching for more than 20 years. Almost from the beginning of my teaching, I have used letters of individuals, famous in the history of psychology, to supplement my lectures: letters from John Stuart Mill describing his views on the sexes, letters from Charles Darwin concerning his quandary over losing credit for his theory of species evolution, and letters between Sigmund Freud and Carl Jung discussing their trip to the United States in 1909 and their hopes for the future of psychoanalysis in America. As it became apparent that students liked this material, I added more of it to my courses. I have even begun to use it in my introductory psychology course as a supplement to lectures on conditioning, personality theory, and motivation. Students greatly enjoy these letters and have consistently rated them among the most favorable aspects of my courses. Consequently, this book is intended to make this kind of material readily available to students and instructors. Students should find this book easy to read, very interesting, and helpful in their understanding of the development of the discipline of psychology.

This book is not a textbook in the history of psychology; instead, it is intended as a supplement to a textbook in history of psychology courses or to a textbook in introductory psychology courses. See Tables 1 and 2 for a suggested matching of the chapters of this book with those commonly found in texts in the history of psychology and in introductory psychology.

This book is an annotated compilation of the private ideas of individuals who have been important in the development of psychology. Individuals were selected for this book in order to cover a broad spectrum of psychology with regard to time period and subfield of psychology.

TABLE 1
Using This Book for a History of Psychology Course

History of Psychology Textbook Chapter	Corresponding Chapter in This Book
Empiricism	1. John Locke 3. John Stuart Mill
Evolution/Functionalist Antecedents	2. Charles Darwin
Wundtian Psychology or American Functionalism	4. James McKeen Cattell
Beginnings of American Psychology	5. Harry Kirke Wolfe 6. Mary Whiton Calkins
Functionalism	7. William James
Structuralism	8. Edward B. Titchener
Behaviorism	9. John B. Watson
Mental Testing or Applied Psychology	10. Henry H. Goddard 12. Coleman R. Griffith
Psychoanalysis	11. Freud and Jung
Gestalt Psychology	13. Koffka, Kohler, & Lewin
Psychology in the Post Schools Era	14. Society for the Psychological Study of Social Issues
Neobehaviorism	15. B. F. Skinner
Humanistic Psychology	16. Abraham Maslow

Inclusion does not imply that these persons were the *most* significant figures in psychology. Although that criterion is followed where possible, some significant figures were excluded because no letters exist for them, or because it was not possible to secure permission for publication of their letters. Others were excluded because the content too closely paralleled other letters in the collection.

Where possible, only letters have been used. However, in several cases journal entries or notebooks have been used where letters are not readily available. The letters and journal entries in several of these

TABLE 2
Using This Book for an Introductory Psychology Course

Introductory Psychology Textbook Chapter	*Corresponding Chapter in This Book*
Introduction (history, approaches, methods)	4. Cattell in Leipzig 5. Struggles for Laboratories 8. Titchener's Experimentalists 13. Gestalt Psychology
Physiological Psychology	2. Darwin and Evolution
Sensation and Perception	7. James and Psychical Research
Learning	9. Watson's Behaviorism 15. Skinner's Operant Psychology
Cognition	7. James and Psychical Research 12. Griffith and Sport Psychology 13. Gestalt Psychology
Motivation and Emotion	16. Maslow's Self Actualization
Development	1. Locke as Child Psychologist
Gender (Sex Roles and Differences)	3. Mill and Subjection of Women 6. Calkin's Quest for Graduate Education
Personality	16. Maslow's Self Actualization
Psychological Testing/Intelligence	10. Goddard and Feeblemindedness
Abnormal Psychology and Treatment	11. Freud and Jung in America
Social Psychology	14. Founding of SPSSI
Applied Psychology	12. Griffith and Sport Psychology

chapters are now in print, although in a few chapters they represent letters that were scattered across several published sources and have been integrated here for our purposes. The inclusion of these letters in this book reflects the permission of literary heirs and publishers as noted in the acknowledgments. In many chapters, the letters are previously unpublished. These have been taken from several archival collections and are reprinted here with permission.

Each chapter typically features the letters of a single individual, although there are several exceptions. The letters or notes for each chapter were selected according to a particular theme, for example, William James's involvement in psychical research, Charles Darwin's delay in publishing his *Origin of Species,* James McKeen Cattell's work as a graduate student in the earliest psychology laboratory in the 1880s, and B. F. Skinner's use of his science in his everyday observations.

Every chapter begins with a brief essay intended to set the stage for the letters. Then the letters are presented in sequence, usually chronologically, with brief footnotes where needed. Footnotes have been kept to a minimum so as not to distract the reader from the flow of the letters. Finally, each chapter ends with an annotated bibliography that adds explanation to the chapter's content, and this section can also be used as a guide to sources of further information for interested readers.

Correspondence and personal journals are the backbone of the individual manuscript collections that make up archives today such as the Archives of the History of American Psychology at the University of Akron. The richness of these unpublished accounts provides historians with valuable insights into the published records. The items collected in this book offer the reader a glimpse of the wealth of personal histories that underlies the development of modern psychology. It is hoped that readers will be stimulated to go beyond the brief treatments presented here and read further in the published letter collections of the shapers of psychology.

Finally, I want to acknowledge the very helpful assistance of David Baker, University of North Texas; Thomas K. Fagan, Memphis State University; Joel Garcia, University of St. Thomas; Joyce Hemphill, College of St. Francis; Terry J. Knapp, University of Nevada; Peggy Pittas, Lynchburg College; Elizabeth Scarborough, Indiana University at South Bend; and W. Scott Terry, University of North Carolina in reviewing drafts of this book. Because I have not always followed the advice of the scholars, they cannot be held responsible for any faults in the final product. I am certain, however, that this book is significantly better because of their counsel.

Finally, I am especially grateful to Priscilla Benjamin for preparing the index to this book and for her valuable assistance throughout this project.

Ludy T. Benjamin, Jr.

Chapter 1

John Locke as
Child Psychologist

For more than 20 years, John Locke (1632–1704) studied the question of how the mind works. During that time he wrote and rewrote his most important contribution to psychology, finally published in 1690 as *An Essay Concerning Human Understanding*. This book began a philosophical movement, important to the emergence of scientific psychology, known as British empiricism, which rejected the idea of innate knowledge and argued instead that all ideas were derived from experience. Locke's significance for modern psychology is, according to Edna Heidbreder (1933), that he

> . . . stands at the starting-point of two movements. One, a line of critical inquiry carried on by Berkeley, Hume, and Kant, led to the destruction of the old rational psychology, that system of thought which, claiming a knowledge of the soul that was based on intuition and deduction, held that its knowledge was demonstrable as absolutely valid. The other was a more positive movement, which, expressing itself partly in the common-sense philosophy of the Scottish school, and partly in the teachings of the British associationists, led to a psychology that, though it was empirical as opposed to rational, stopped just short of becoming experimental. (pp. 40–41)

Resurrecting Aristotle's notion of *tabula rasa*, Locke described how experience would write on the blank slate, thus filling the mind with its ideas. Locke argued that although all ideas were derived from experience, they were not necessarily derived from direct sensory experience. Some ideas were the products of reflection, what Locke called the internal operations of the mind. For Locke, there were two kinds of ideas. Simple ideas could be the result of direct sensory experience or reflection. Yet complex ideas could only come from reflection.

Earlier philosophers had focused attention largely on the content of mind—*what* the mind knows. Although he recognized the importance of studying content, he was more interested in *how* the mind knows; that is, how ideas, both simple and complex, were acquired.

As a boy, Locke was tutored at home by his father, a country attorney. At the age of 20 he went to Oxford University where he studied medicine, philosophy, and meteorology, earning his baccalaureate (1656) and master's (1658) degrees. Although Locke never practiced as a physician, he had completed his medical studies. He remained at Oxford off and on for the next 25 years until he was expelled in 1684 by an order of King Charles II. Locke was in hiding in Holland at the time of the Royal order, because he was suspected of being part of a plot against the King. Although he probably was not part of the movement against Charles II, he may have played a political role in the bloodless Revolution of 1688 that placed William of Orange on the throne (Cranston, 1957).

After the revolution, Locke was able to return to England, where he spent the last 15 years of his life in government work and writing. These were very productive years for Locke as an author, who had actually published very little before this time partly due to political fears about the fate of his manuscripts should he try to publish them. Certainly the social and political themes surrounding the revolution shaped many of his ideas (see Moore-Russell, 1978). In addition to the *Essay*, which appeared in 1690, he also published his most famous political work, *Two Treatises on Government*, in that same year. Parts of that document would later be incorporated into the American *Declaration of Independence*. His long-time interests in religious tolerance led to two other important works being published during this time: *Letters on Tolerance* (1689–1692) and *The Reasonableness of Christianity* (1695).

One of Locke's lesser known works began as a series of letters to Edward and Mary Clarke, written when he was in self-exile in Holland. Edward Clarke was an attorney who owned an estate near Somerset where Locke's family lived. Clarke had married Locke's cousin, Mary Jepp. Edward Clarke and Locke became very close friends and Locke took considerable interest in the Clarke children, especially the oldest boy, Edward (referred to as "master" in most letters), and one of the two daughters, Elizabeth, whom he affectionately called his "mistress."

When the Clarkes asked for advice on educating their son, Locke was pleased to oblige, often writing lengthy epistles. He saved drafts of these and used them to write *Some Thoughts Concerning Education*, which was published in July, 1693. This book illustrates Locke's belief in environment as a critical determinant of individual potential, an idea that was consistent with the rest of his empiricist psychology.

The letters reprinted in this chapter are all from Locke to Edward Clarke, with one exception, that being a single letter to his cousin, Mary Clarke. The later letters (not reprinted here) deal with the education of young Edward, for example, how to teach mathematical concepts and when Latin and Greek should be learned. However, the earlier letters focus more on general advice about child rearing. The opening letter offers advice on the importance of good physical health, whereas the final letter provides a strategy for extinguishing crying behavior. In between are some delightful accounts on how to raise boys versus girls, advice drawing both on Locke's medical training and his empiricist views of psychology. He reminds the Clarkes that it is advice from a life-long bachelor with no children of his own. Surely Locke was not the first, nor will he be the last, child expert without children.

To Edward Clarke, July 9, 1684

. . . 1. *Mens sana in corpore sano*[1] is a short but full description of the most desirable state we are capable of in this life. He who has these two has little more to wish; and he that wants either of them will be but little the better for anything else. Men's happiness or misery is for the most part of their own making. He whose mind directs not wisely will never take the right way; and he whose body fails his mind will never be able to march in it. I confess there are some men's constitutions of body and mind so vigorous, and well framed by nature, that they shift pretty well without much assistance from others; by the strength of their natural genius, they are, from their cradles, carried towards what is excellent. But those examples are but few, and I think I may say of all the men we meet with, nine parts of ten, or perhaps ninety-nine of one hundred, are what they are, good or evil, useful or not, by their education. 'Tis that which makes the great difference in mankind. The little and almost insensible impressions, on our

---

1. A sound mind in a sound body.

tender infancies, have very important and lasting influences; and there it is, as in the fountains of some rivers, where a gentle application of the hand turns the flexible waters into channels that make them take quite contrary courses; and by this little impression given them at the source they come to arrive at places quite distant and opposite.

2. I imagine the minds of children are as easily turned this or that way as water itself; and I think [with parents should be] their first care. . . . But though this be the principal part, and our main care should be about the inside, yet the clay tenement is not to be neglected. I shall therefore begin with the case, and consider first the health of the body, as that which perhaps you may rather expect, from that study I have been thought more peculiarly to have applied myself to; and that also which will be soonest dispatched, as lying, as I imagine in a very little compass.

3. How necessary health is to our business and happiness, and how necessary a strong constitution, able to endure hardships and fatigue, is to one that will make any figure be anything considerable in the world, is too obvious to need any proof.

4. Your son seems to me to be of as strong principles of nature as any child I have seen, so that one and the hardest part touching the body is spared. We need not trouble ourselves how to invigorate a weak or mend a faulty constitution. We have nothing to do but to preserve a good one, and help it to continue suitable to so promising a beginning; and that perhaps might be dispatched all in a word, by bidding you use him as you see one of our ordinary tenants does his children.

5. But because that perhaps may seem to you a little too spare, and to your Lady a little too hard, . . . who will be ready to say, 'tis apparent he has no children of his own, I shall explain myself a little more particularly, laying this down in the first place as a general and certain observation for Madam to consider of, viz. that most children's constitutions are either weakened or spoiled by cockering and tenderness. I say not this to accuse her, for I think her not guilty, but to fortify against the silly opinions and discourses of others.

6. The first thing then to be had a care of is, that he be not too warmly clad or covered in winter or summer. The face is no less tender than any other part of the body when we are born. 'Tis use alone hardens it, and makes it more able to endure the cold. . . .

7. I think it would also be of great advantage to have his feet washed every night in cold water, and to have his shoes so made that they may leak and let in water whenever he treads on any marshy place. Here, I imagine, I shall have both Mistress and maids about my ears. One perhaps will think it too filthy, and the other too much pains to make his stockings clean. But yet truth will have it, that his health is much more worth than all this little ado, and ten times as much more. Must my young master never dirty his shoes? and if it cost the wash of a pair of stockings or two more in a week the trouble may be borne and the thing be worth it, if we consider how mischievous and mortal a thing taking wet in the feet proves often to those who have been bred nicely. When a fever or consumption follows from just an accident, for wet in the feet will sometimes happen, then will he wish he had, with the poor people's children, gone barefoot, and so 'scaped the danger and perhaps death which a little unhappy moisture in his feet hath brought upon him; whilst the hardened poor man's son, reconciled by custom to wet in his feet by that means, suffers no more by it than if his hands were put in water. And what is it, I pray, that makes this great difference between the hands and the feet, but only custom? And I doubt not, but if a man from his cradle had been always used to go barefoot, but to have his hands close wrapped up constantly in thick mittens and handshoes[2] over them; I doubt not, I say, but such a custom would make taking wet in the hands as dangerous to him, as now taking wet in their feet is to a great many others. To prevent this, I would I say have him wear leaking shoes, and his feet washed every night in cold water, both for health and cleanliness sake. But begin first in the spring with luke warm water, and so colder and colder every night till in a few days you come to perfectly cold water, and so continue. For it is to be observed in this and all other alterations from our ordinary way of living, the change must be made by gentle and insensible degrees; and so we may bring our bodies to any thing without pain and without danger.

To Edward Clarke, December 22, 1684

. . . I am glad you approve of my . . . method for keeping your son from being costive without giving him physique. I believe you

---

2. The Dutch term for gloves.

will finde it effectuall, and I thinke it a thing of great moment to
my health, therefor I recommend it to you for your own practise as
well as for your son. Though I tend the young sprout yet I would
have the old stock also preserved as long as I could. . . . for I find
the penny post way has lost several of my letters which came safe
to London, for though I care not who sees what I write, yet I
would have those also see it to whom I write it, especially what
cost me some pains in writeing, and I thinke may be of some use
to those I send it, as I hope this discourse concerning your son
will be, or else I would not give you the trouble to read nor my
self to write so much on that occasion. If your Lady approve of it
when she sees it I will then obey her commands in reference to
her daughters, where in there will be some though noe great difference, for makeing a litle allowance for beauty and some few
other considerations of the sort . . . of training of boys and girles
especially in their younger years I imagine should be much the
same. But if my way satisfie her concerneing my young master I
doubt not but I shall also be thought by her noe lesse carefull of
my prety litle mistris, but pray let me hear from you concerning
this matter as soon as you can for if my rules have any advantage
in them . . . [they] are to be put in practise as soon as children
begin to speake and therefor noe time is to be lost.

To Edward Clarke, January 24–February 3, 1685

I am glad to hear by yours of 20th Jan. that my opinion on
children has at last come to hand. But I hope you have ere this
received a more perfect copy [of the portion] lost I took care to
send you. Indeed I was in some trouble for several days [in trying
to] find the original copy and so being [thereby able] to retrieve it
again. For if I were to be hindered at this rate I could not write to
you on the same subject again anything you or I could with patience read, because whenever I should set myself to write my
thoughts would hunt in my memory for what pleased me when I
writ before, and not in any reason whereby I should be able to
make nothing of it. I am glad also to find by yours of 16th Jan.
that it so well pleases both you and Madam. But yet though one
can but be satisfied that what one does proves acceptable to a
friend one loves, yet I once more beg you to look on it as a discourse that fell into your hands by chance and to have no consideration of the author but of your son in the case, for I had much

rather you should find me in a mistake than commit any yourself by my advice in a business of such concernment to you as is the right ordering of your son. . . .

I must therefore desire you to excuse my silence till I get a little leisure to talk to her concerning my pretty little Miss and her other daughter, wherein if I can satisfy her as well as she persuades me I have about her son I shall think myself very happy. And since you continue to think my old bachelor's advice concerning your son's education as he [proceeds] is worth the having, you may be sure that I who so forwardly thrust myself into this affair will not be backward to go on now you desire it. . . . The next thing therefore to be done is to observe his temper whether bold or timorous, careless or curious, steady or unconstant, friendly or churlish, etc., for your having once established your authority and got the ascendant over him, the next thing must be to bend the crooks the other way if he have any in him, and apply proper methods to his peculiar inclinations. Pray tell me in your next whether his cap was left off and whether his feet have been washed every night in cold water as I advised in the beginning of summer, and how it has succeeded with him. . . .

To Mary Clarke, January 28—February 7, 1685

. . . To make some acknowledgment, 'tis fit I acquit myself of my promise to you in reference to my little mistress . . .[and] you will think that speaking with [the sincere] affection I have for the softer sex I shall not think of any rougher usage than only what [her sex] requires. Since therefore I acknowledge no difference of sex in your mind relating . . . to truth, virtue and obedience, I think well to have no thing altered in it from what is [writ for the son]. And since I should rather desire in my wife a healthy constitution, a stomach able to digest ordinary food, and a body that could endure upon occasion both wind and sun, rather than a puling, weak, sickly wretch, that every breath of wind or least hardship puts in danger, I think the meat drink and lodging and clothing should be ordered after the same manner for the girls as for the boys. There is only one or two things whereof I think distinct consideration is to be had. You know my opinion is that the boys should be much abroad in the air at all times and in all weathers, and if they play in the sun and in the wind without hats and gloves so much the better. But since in your girls care is to be taken too of their beauty as much as health will permit, this in them must have some restriction, the more they exercise and the more they are in the air the better health they will have, that I am sure; but yet 'tis fit their tender skins should be fenced against the busy sunbeams, especially when they are very hot and piercing: to avoid this and yet to give them exercise in the air, some little shady grove near the house would be convenient for them to play in, and a large airy room in ill weather: and if all the year you make them rise as soon as it is light and walk a mile or two and play abroad before sun-rising, you will by that custom obtain more good effects than one; and it will make them not only fresh and healthy, but good housewives too. But that they may have sleep enough, which whilst they are young must not be scanty, they must be early to bed too.

Another thing is, that of washing their feet every night in cold water and exposing them to the wet in the day. Though my reason is satisfied that it is both the healthiest and safest way, yet since it is not fit that girls should be dabbling in water as your boys will be, and since perhaps it will be thought both an odd and new thing, I cannot tell how to enjoin it. This I am sure I have seen many a little healthy [child do in] winter, and I think that had I a daughter I should order water to be put in her [shoes] when she put them on, and have her feet well washed in cold water. But this must not be begun at any time of the year, but in the hot weather in May, and then begin only with one dabble the first morning, two the next, and so on. . . .

Their heads, I think, should never be covered, nor their necks within doors, and when they go abroad the covering of these should be more against the sun than the cold. And herein you may take notice how much it is use that makes us either tender or hardy, for there is scarce a young lady so weak and tender who will not go bare in her neck without suffering any harm at a season when if a hardy strong man not used to it should imitate her it would be intolerable to him, and he would be sure to get a cold if not a fever.

Girls should have a dancing master at home early: it gives them fashion and easy comely motion betimes which is very convenient, and they, usually staying at home with their mothers, do not lose it again, whereas the boys commonly going to school, they lose what they learn of a dancing master at home amongst their ill-fashioned schoolfellows, which makes it often less necessary because less useful for the boys to learn to dance at home when little: though if they were always to play at home in good company I should advise it for them too. If the girls are also by nature very bashful, it would be good that they should go also to dance publicly in the dancing schools when little till their sheepishness were cured; but too much of the public schools may not perhaps do well, for of the two, too much shamefacedness better becomes a girl than too much confidence, but having more admired than considered your sex I may perhaps be out in these matters, which you must pardon me.

This is all I can think of at present, wherein the treatment of your girls should be different from that I have proposed for the boys. Only I think the father [ought] to strike very seldom, if at all to chide his daughters. Their governing and correcting, I think, properly belongs to the mother. . . .

To Edward Clarke, August 22–September 1, 1685

Your son's temper by the account you give of it is I find not only such as I guessed it would be, but such as one would wish, and the qualities you already observe in him require nothing but right management whereby to be made very useful.

Curiosity in children is but an appetite after knowledge, and therefore ought to be encouraged in them, not only as a good sign, but as the great instrument nature has provided, to remove that ignorance they brought into the world with them, and which without this busy inquisitiveness would make them dull and useless creatures. The ways to encourage and keep it active and vigorous are, I suppose, these following:

1st. Not to check or discountenance any inquiries he may make, or suffer them to be laughed at; but to answer all his questions and explain matters he desires to know, so as to make them as much intelligible to him, as suits the capacity of his age and knowledge. But confound not his understanding with explications or notions that are above it, or with the variety or number of things that are not to his present purpose. Mark what it is he aims at in the question, and when you have informed and satisfied him in that, you shall see how his thoughts will proceed on to other things, and how by fit answers to his enquiries he may be led on farther than perhaps you could imagine. For knowledge to the understanding is as acceptable as light to the eyes; and children are pleased and delighted with it exceedingly, especially if they see that their enquiries are regarded, and that their desire of knowing is encouraged and commended. And I doubt not but one great reason why many children abandon themselves wholly to silly play, and spend all their time in trifling, is, because they have found their curiosity baulked and their enquiries neglected. But had they been treated with more kindness and respect, and their questions answered as they should to their satisfaction, I doubt not but they would have taken more pleasure in learning several things, and improving their knowledge, wherein there would be still newness and variety, which they delight in than in returning over and over to the same playthings.

2nd. To this serious answering their questions, and informing their understandings in what they desire, as if it were a matter that needed it, should be added some ways of commendation. Let others whom they esteem be told before their faces of the knowledge they have in such and such things; and since we are all even from our cradles vain, and proud creatures, let their vanity be flattered with things that will do them good; and let their pride set them to work on something which may turn to their advantage. Upon this ground you shall find that there can not be a greater spur to anything you would have your son learn or know himself, than to set him upon teaching it his sisters.

3rd. As children's enquiries are not to be slighted, so also great care is to be taken, that they never receive deceitful and eluding answers. They easily perceive when they are slighted or deceived, and quickly learn the trick of neglect, dissimulation, and falsehood which they observe others to make use of. We are not to entrench upon truth in our conversation, but least of all with children. Since if we play false with them, we not only deceive their expectation, and hinder their knowledge, but corrupt their innocence, and teach them the worst of vices. They are travellers newly arrived in a strange country of which they know very little: we should therefore make conscience not to mislead them. And though their questions seem sometimes not very material, yet they should be seriously answered; for however they may appear to us to whom they are long since known, enquiries not worth the making, they are of moment to them who are wholly ignorant. Children are strangers to all we are acquainted with, and all the things they meet with are at first unknown to them, as they were to us; and happy are they who meet with kind people, that will comply with their ignorance, and help them to get out of it. . . .

4th. Perhaps it may not, however, be amiss to exercise their curiosity concerning strange and new things in their way, on purpose that they may enquire and be busy to inform themselves about them; and if by chance their curiosity leads them to ask what they should not know, it is a great deal better to tell them plainly, that it is a thing that belongs not to them to know, than to pop them off with a falsehood, or a frivolous answer. . . .

One thing I have observed in children, that when they have got possession of any poor creature, they are apt to use it ill, and they often torment and treat ill very young birds, butterflies, and such other poor things, which they got into their power, and that with a seeming kind of pleasure. This, I think, should be watched in them, and if they incline to any such cruelty they should be taught the contrary usage. For the custom of tormenting and killing of beasts will by degrees harden their minds even towards men, and they who accustom themselves to delight in the suffering and destruction of inferior creatures, will not be apt to be very compassionate or benign to those of their own kind. Our law takes notice of this in the exclusion of butchers from juries of life and death. Children, then, should be taught from the beginning not to destroy any living creature unless it be for the preservation and advantage of some other that is nobler. And, indeed, if the preservation of all mankind as much as in him lies, were the persuasion of every one, as it is indeed the true principle of religion, politics and morality, the world would be much quieter and better natured than it is. . . .

To Edward Clarke, February 8, 1686

. . . Your children have had such good success in that plain way, that if reason had nothing to say for it, yet our own experience ought to make you exactly follow it. I had within this very month occasion to observe a child under an year [so often given] sugar candy to please him, that at last nothing but what was very sweet [was desired by him] [There was] nothing but perpetual crying and bawling, and the child from his hunger and craving after sweet things was perpetually uneasy. I told his mother she giving him those licorish things to quiet him when he cried was but the way to increase it, [un]less she could resolve to feed him wholly with them, which would certainly destroy his health; and that the only cure was to endure for a day or two his crying without appeasing [his desires. After] some time, finding that ill increased by those ways that at present [permitted the] child [to gratify his] appetite, she resolved to take away from him at once all sweet things, and when he cried [to give him] nothing but what she judged wholesomest and best for his health. This made him impatient the first day, but when he saw he got not his desire by crying he left it off, and in two or three days, he, that before could not be quieted, when he saw either sugar, or sugar candy, or apples until they were given to him, so that they were fain carefully to hide them from him, was brought by this means, when apples or the like which he loved came in his way, only to show his desire of them, but not to cry for them, and this in a child wanting one or two of twelve months old. Which example confirms me in the opinion you know I am of, that children find the success of their crying, and accordingly make use of it to have their will sooner than is usually imagined; and that they should be accustomed very early not to have their desires [always granted], and that they should not be indulged in the things they cry for, where they were not absolutely necessary.

You will find one part of this paper filled with the continuation of my opinion in reference to your son. It breaks off abruptly for want of room. But the remainder you shall have whenever you desire it; and when I know how far our rules have been put in practice, and with what success, or what difficulties have hindered. I shall in my next also add what may be convenient, or upon trial you have found deficient, or perhaps impracticable in what I have formerly writ on this occasion. For it often happens that the speculations which please a contemplative man in his study are not so easy to be put in use out of it. If also his particular temper or inclination require any further peculiar application, that also shall be considered. In the meantime I wish you, your Lady, and little ones perfect health and happiness. . . .

John Locke Bibliography

Cranston, M. (1957). *John Locke: A Biography*. Boston: Longmans Green.
A very readable and comprehensive biography of Locke's life.

de Beer, E. S. (Ed.). (1976–1989). *The Correspondence of John Locke*, *Volumes 1–8*. New York: Oxford University Press.
This is the most complete collection of Locke letters, containing all 3,648 known to exist. Isaac Newton is among the many correspondents in this collection. The correspondence with Edward Clarke is one of the most extensive in the collection and numbers more than 200 letters.

Locke, J. (1690). *An Essay Concerning Human Understanding*. (1975 edition) Oxford: Clarendon Press.
Locke's psychological treatise that marked the formal beginnings of British empiricism.

Locke, J. (1693). *Some Thoughts Concerning Education*. (1964 edition) Woodbury: Barron's Educational Series.
This book was written from the drafts of letters to Edward and Mary Clarke regarding the rearing and education of their son. The letters cited in this chapter provide part of the basis for Locke's book on education.

Moore-Russell, M. E. (1978). The philosopher and society: John Locke and the English revolution. *Journal of the History of the Behavioral Sciences*, *14*, 65–73.
Illustrates the impact of the social and political times on Locke's writings, particularly on the *Essay*.

Morris, C. R. (1931). *Locke, Berkeley, Hume*. Oxford: Clarendon Press.
A brief treatment of the lives of these three empiricist philosophers and a comparison of their theories of knowledge and knowing.

Petryszak, N. G. (1981). Tabula rasa—its origins and implications. *Journal of the History of the Behavioral Sciences*, *17*, 15–27.
Discusses Locke's use of the concept of tabula rasa to resolve the conflict between belief in divine determination and belief in individual freedom.

Chapter 2

Why Did Charles Darwin Delay in Publishing His Theory?

Many scholars consider Charles Darwin's book, *On the Origin of Species* (1859), to be the most influential book published in the last 400 years. This theory of the evolution of species by means of natural selection has had profound impact on many fields of study from art to zoology, and psychology is no exception.

The word "evolution" has taken on a very different meaning since Darwin and is a word that often evokes spirited discourse, if not outright vociferous attacks. Darwin did not use that word anywhere in the 429 pages of his *Origin of Species*. Yet a form of the word appears as the final word in the book. After meticulously building his case for natural selection in species change, Darwin (1859) ends his book with the following sentence:

> There is grandeur in this view of life, with its several powers, having been originally breathed by the Creator into a few forms or into one; and that, whilst this planet has gone cycling on according to the fixed law of gravity, from so simple a beginning endless forms most beautiful and most wonderful have been, and are being evolved. (p. 429)

Part of the mystique of this important book is that Darwin delayed the publication of his ideas about species change for nearly 20 years. Why did he wait so long to tell the world about such a revolutionary idea?

Charles Darwin (1809–1882) joined a British scientific expedition at the age of 22. As naturalist aboard the ship H. M. S. *Beagle*, he sailed around the world for 5 years, observing and collecting many mineral, plant, and animal forms. From these extensive studies he published several books, including the five-volume work entitled *Zoology of the Voyage of H.M.S. Beagle.* The voyage changed Darwin's life and, subsequently, the world. Yet he literally almost missed the boat.

The young Darwin was contacted in August of 1831 by John Stevens Henslow, a professor of botany with whom Darwin had worked when he was a student at Cambridge University. Henslow told him about a scientific voyage being planned by the British Admiralty, with Captain Robert Fitzroy in command of the Beagle. The expedition was to include a naturalist, and Fitzroy had wanted Leonard Jenyns to accept the position. When Jenyns declined, it was offered to his brother-in-law, Henslow. Henslow also declined and contacted his former student. Darwin was eager to accept this opportunity; however, his father, Robert, opposed the trip. He argued that the position could not be much of an opportunity if so many naturalists were turning it down. He also worried that the voyage would interfere with Darwin's preparation for a career as a minister, and he encouraged his son to get on with his life and to avoid forays that seemed somewhat frivolous. Darwin, a dutiful son, wrote to Henslow to say that although his father had not forbade him to accept the position, that in good conscience he could not go against his father's wishes. However, a few days later Darwin's uncle persuaded Darwin's father that the voyage was an important opportunity, and so Robert Darwin withdrew his objections. Darwin hurriedly wrote to the admiralty to ask if the position was still available. And thus he embarked on the remarkable 5-year sea voyage, which was supposed to last only 2 years (see Burkhardt, et al, 1985, pp. 127–136).

Upon his return, Darwin pondered the data that he had collected from the *Beagle's* voyage, attempting to make sense of the species variations and specializations that he had observed. In 1838 he read Thomas Malthus's essay on population (1789), which argued that the world's food supply increased arithmetically while the population increased geometrically, a condition that guaranteed starvation and competition. From Malthus's idea, Darwin recognized the fact of survival of the fittest. He began to construct a theory of the transformation of species based on the principle of natural selection. The initial account of the theory was written in 1842 as a manuscript of 35 pages and was expanded to approximately 230 pages in 1844. Portions of that manuscript were shared with several of Darwin's fellow scientists and friends, particularly Charles Lyell, an eminent geologist, and Joseph Hooker, a distinguished botanist.

As early as 1844 Darwin knew he was working on a theory of great importance. At that time he made arrangements with his wife for publication of the manuscript should he die before having the chance to reveal his theory to the world. Still, he did not publish his theory, nor did he seem to have any plans to do so. Indeed, 15 more years would pass before Darwin would actually publish this work, and even then he did so with some reluctance.

Why did Darwin delay the publication of his theory? There are many answers to that question, some more plausible than others. A number of these answers are summarized and analyzed in an article by historian Robert Richards (1983).

Some Darwin scholars, such as Howard Gruber and Stephen Jay Gould, have argued that Darwin was very much aware of the social consequences of his theory, which linked humans with the rest of the animal kingdom. The theory supported a philosophy of materialism that "assumed the rise of human reason and morality out of animal intelligence and instinct" (Richards, 1983, p. 47). Thus Darwin may have been waiting for a *Zeitgeist* more favorable to his theory.

Perhaps Darwin was just exceptionally meticulous as a scientist. He formulated his theory in 1838 and then spent the next 20 years collecting information that would support the theory and trying to account for those facts that might seem to reject it. Some facts proved especially problematic, for example, accounting for the development of instincts in worker bees that were sterile. Richards believes that this concern over the explanatory power of the theory is the most plausible reason for the delay.

Darwin's friends urged him to publish his ideas before someone else published a similar theory and thus gained priority. Yet Darwin seemed in no hurry. Then on June 18, 1858, a package arrived at his home that would turn his world upside down. It was a manuscript from Alfred Russel Wallace (1823–1913), a fellow British naturalist, who outlined a theory very similar to that of Darwin.

Could Darwin honorably publish his theory now that Wallace had sent him this manuscript? As a scientist, Darwin believed that truth was his goal, not fame. But Darwin was also human and his letters to his friends, Hooker and Lyell, reveal the great conflict he felt upon receiving Wallace's manuscript. He wanted to behave honorably in this matter but in doing so he might lose credit for 20 years of painstaking work. Darwin's terrible dilemma is played out in the letters that follow.

To Joseph D. Hooker, January 11, 1844

Besides a general interest about the southern lands, I have been now ever since my return engaged in a very presumptuous work, and I know no one individual who would not say a very foolish one. I was so struck with the distribution of the Galapagos organisms, &c. &c., and with the character of the American fossil mammifers, &c. &c., that I determined to collect blindly every sort of fact, which could bear any way on what are species. I have read heaps of agricultural and horticultural books, and have never ceased collecting facts. At last gleams of light have come, and I am almost convinced (quite contrary to the opinion I started with) that species are not (it is like confessing a murder) immutable. Heaven forfend me from Lamarck nonsense of a "tendency to progression," "adaptations from the slow willing of animals," &c.! But the conclusions I am led to are not widely different from his; though the means of change are wholly so. I think I have found out (here's presumption!) the simple way by which species become exquisitely adapted to various ends. You will now groan, and think to yourself, "on what a man have I been wasting my time and writing to."

To Emma Darwin,[1] July 5, 1844

I have just finished my sketch of my species theory.[2] If, as I believe that my theory is true & if it be accepted even by one competent judge, it will be a considerable step in science.

I therefore write this, in case of my sudden death, as my most solemn & last request, which I am sure you will consider the same as if legally entered in my will, that you will devote 400£ to its publication & further will yourself, or through Hensleigh,[3] take trouble in promoting it.—I wish that my sketch be given to some competent person, with this sum to induce him to take trouble in its improvement. & enlargement.—I give to him all my Books on Natural History, which are either scored or have references at end to the pages, begging him carefully to look over & consider such passages, as actually bearing or by possibility bearing on this

---

1. Emma Wedgwood (1808–1896) married Charles Darwin in 1839.

2. The sketch to which he refers is the 230 page essay on the origin of species.

3. Hensleigh Wedgwood (1803–1891) was Darwin's first cousin and brother-in-law. Darwin's mother was also a Wedgwood.

subject.—I wish you to make a list of all such books, as some temptation to an Editor.

With respect to Editors.—Mr. Lyell would be the best if he would undertake it: I believe he w^d find the work pleasant & he w^d learn some facts new to him. As the Editor must be a geologist, as well as Naturalist.

To *Leonard Jenyns,*[4] *October 12, 1844*

I have continued steadily reading & collecting facts on variation of domestic animals & plants & on the question of what are species; I have a grand body of facts & I think I can draw some sound conclusions. The general conclusion at which I have slowly been driven from a directly opposite conviction is that species are mutable & that allied species are co-descendants of common stocks. I know how much I open myself, to reproach, for such a conclusion, but I have at least honestly & deliberately come to it.

I shall not publish on this subject for several years—At present I am on the geology of S. America. I hope to pick up from your book, some facts on slight variations in structure or instincts in the animals of your acquaintance.

To *Leonard Jenyns, November 25, 1844*

With respect to my far-distant work on species, I must have expressed myself with singular inaccuracy, if I led you to suppose that I meant to say that my conclusions were inevitable. They have become so, after years of weighing puzzles, to myself *alone;* but in my wildest day-dream, I never expect more than to be able to show that there are two sides to the question of the immutability of species, ie whether species are *directly* created, or by intermediate laws, (as with the life & death of individuals). I did not approach the subject on the side of the difficulty in determining what are species & what are varieties, but (though, why I sh^d give you such a *history* of my doings, it w^d be hard to say) from such facts, as the relationship between the living & extinct mammifers in S. America, & between those living on the continent & on adjoining islands, such as the Galapagos—It occurred to me, that a collection of all such analogous facts would throw light either

---

4. Leonard Jenyns (1800–1893) was an Anglican priest and naturalist. He was the brother-in-law of John Stevens Henslow, Darwin's teacher at Cambridge University.

for or against the view of related species, being co-descendants from a common stock. A long searching amongst agricultural & horticultural books & people, makes me believe (I well know how absurdly presumptuous this must appear) that I see the way in which new varieties become exquisitely adapted to the external conditions of life, & to other surrounding beings.— I am a bold man to lay myself open to being thought a complete fool, & a most deliberate one.— From the nature of the grounds, which make me believe that species are mutable in form, these grounds cannot be restricted to the closest-allied species; but how far they extend, I cannot tell, as my reasons fall away by degrees, when applied to species more & more remote from each other.

Pray do not think, that I am so blind as not to see that there are numerous immense difficulties on my notions, but they appear to me less than on the common view.— I have drawn up a sketch & had it copied (in 200 pages) of my conclusions; & if I thought at some future time, that you would think it worth reading, I sh^d of course be most thankful to have the criticism of so competent a critic.

To Charles Lyell, June 18, 1858

Some year or so ago you recommended me to read a paper by Wallace in the *Annals*,[5] which had interested you, and, as I was writing to him, I knew this would please him much, so I told him. He has to-day sent me the enclosed, and asked me to forward it to you. It seems to me well worth reading. Your words have come true with a vengeance—that I should be forestalled. You said this, when I explained to you here very briefly my views of Natural Selection depending on the struggle for existence. I never saw a more striking coincidence; if Wallace had my MS. sketch written out in 1842, he could not have made a better short abstract! Even his terms now stand as heads of my chapters. Please return me the MS., which he does not say he wishes me to publish, but I shall of course, at once write and offer to send to any journal. So all my originality, whatever it may amount to, will be smashed, though my book, if it will ever have any value, will not be deteriorated; as all the labour consists in the application of the theory.

---

5. Alfred Russell Wallace's article appeared in an 1855 issue of *Annals and Magazine of Natural History*.

I hope you will approve of Wallace's sketch, that I may tell him what you say.

To Charles Lyell, June 25, 1858

I am very sorry to trouble you, busy as you are, in so merely personal an affair; but if you will give me your deliberate opinion, you will do me as great a service as ever man did, for I have entire confidence in your judgment and honour. . . .

There is nothing in Wallace's sketch which is not written out much fuller in my sketch, copied out in 1844, and read by Hooker some dozen years ago. About a year ago I sent a short sketch, of which I have a copy, of my views (owing to correspondence on several points) to Asa Gray,[6] so that I could most truly say and prove that I take nothing from Wallace. I should be extremely glad now to publish a sketch of my general views in about a dozen pages or so; but I cannot persuade myself that I can do so honourably. Wallace says nothing about publication, and I enclose his letter. But as I had not intended to publish any sketch, can I do so honourably, because Wallace has sent me an outline of his doctrine? I would far rather burn my whole book, than that he or any other man should think that I had behaved in a paltry spirit. Do you not think his having sent me this sketch ties my hands? . . . If I could honourably publish, I would state that I was induced now to publish a sketch (and I should be very glad to be permitted to say, to follow your advice long ago given) from Wallace having sent me an outline of my general conclusions. We differ only [in] that I was led to my views from what artificial selection has done for domestic animals. I would send Wallace a copy of my letter to Asa Gray, to show him that I had not stolen his doctrine. But I cannot tell whether to publish now would not be base and paltry. This was my first impression, and I should have certainly acted on it had it not been for your letter.

This is a trumpery affair to trouble you with, but you cannot tell how much obliged I should be for your advice.

By the way, would you object to send this and your answer to Hooker to be forwarded to me, for then I shall have the opinion of my two best and kindest friends. This letter is miserably

---

6. American botanist (1810–1888). Intimate friend of Darwin.

written, and I write it now, that I may for a time banish the whole subject; and I am worn out with musing. . . .

My good dear friend forgive me. This is a trumpery letter, influenced by trumpery feelings.

To Charles Lyell, June 26, 1858

Forgive me for adding a P.S. to make the case as strong as possible against myself.

Wallace might say, "You did not intend publishing an abstract of your views till you received my communication. Is it fair to take advantage of my having freely, though unasked, communicated to you my ideas, and thus prevent me forestalling you?" The advantage which I should take being that I am induced to publish from privately knowing that Wallace is in the field. It seems hard on me that I should be thus compelled to lose my priority of many years' standing, but I cannot feel at all sure that this alters the justice of the case. First impressions are generally right, and I at first thought it would be dishonourable in me now to publish.

To Joseph D. Hooker, June 29, 1858

I have just read your letter, and see you want the papers at once. I am quite prostrated, and can do nothing, but I send Wallace, and the abstract of my letter to Asa Gray, which gives most imperfectly only the means of change, and does not touch on reasons for believing that species do change. I dare say all is too late. I hardly care about it. But you are too generous to sacrifice so much time and kindness. It is most generous, most kind. I send my sketch of 1844 solely that you may see by your own handwriting that you did read it. I really cannot bear to look at it. Do not waste much time. It is miserable in me to care at all about priority.

The table of contents will show what it is.

I would make a similar, but shorter and more accurate sketch for the *Linnean Journal.*

I will do anything. God bless you, my dear kind friend.

I can write no more.

To Joseph D. Hooker, July 13, 1858

Your letter to Wallace seems to me perfect, quite clear and most courteous. I do not think it could possibly be improved, and I have to day forwarded it with a letter of my own. I always thought it very possible that I might be forestalled, but I fancied that I had a grand enough soul not to care; but I found myself mistaken and punished; I had, however, quite resigned myself, and had written half a letter to Wallace to give up all priority to him, and should certainly not have changed had it not been for Lyell's and your quite extraordinary kindness. I assure you I feel it, and shall not forget it. I am *more* than satisfied at what took place at the Linnean Society.[7] I had thought that your letter and mine to Asa Gray were to be only an appendix to Wallace's paper.

You cannot imagine how pleased I am that the notion of Natural Selection has acted as a purgative on your bowels of immutability. Whenever naturalists can look at species changing as certain, what a magnificent field will be open,—on all the laws of variation,—on the genealogy of all living beings,—on their lines of migration, &c., &c. Pray thank Mrs. Hooker for her very kind little note, and pray, say how truly obliged I am, and in truth ashamed to think that she should have had the trouble of copying my ugly MS. It was extraordinarily kind in her. Farewell, my dear kind friend.

To Charles Lyell, September 30, 1859

I sent off this morning the last sheets,[8] but without index, which is not in type. I look at you as my Lord High Chancellor in Natural Science, and therefore I request you, after you have finished, just to *rerun* over the heads in the Recapitulation-part of last chapter. I shall be deeply anxious to hear what you decide (if you are able to decide) on the balance of the pros and contras given in my volume, and of such other pros and contras as may occur to you. I hope that you will think that I have given the

---

7. On July 1, 1858, Charles Lyell and Joseph Hooker read three documents at a meeting of the Linnean Society of London: the manuscript that Wallace had sent to Darwin, excerpts from Darwin's essay of 1844, and a letter from Darwin to Asa Gray dated September 5, 1857. Hooker and Lyell explained the circumstances of the necessity of the joint reading. Both of the theoretical papers were published in an 1858 issue of the Linnean Society's journal.

8. The "sheets" refer to the final pages of Darwin's *Origin*.

difficulties fairly. I feel an entire conviction that if you are now staggered to any moderate extent, ·that you will come more and more round, the longer you keep the subject at all before your mind. I remember well how many long years it was before I could look into the faces of some of the difficulties and not feel quite abashed. I fairly struck my colours before the case of neuter insects.

I suppose that I am a very slow thinker, for you would be surprised at the number of years it took me to see clearly what some of the problems were which had to be solved, such as the necessity of the principle of divergence of character, the extinction of intermediate varieties, on a continuous area, with graduated conditions; the double problem of sterile first crosses and sterile hybrids, &c., &c.

Looking back, I think it was more difficult to see what the problems were than to solve them, so far as I have succeeded in doing, and this seems to me rather curious. Well, good or bad, my work, thank God, is over; and hard work, I can assure you, I have had, and much work which has never borne fruit. You can see, by the way I am scribbling, that I have an idle and rainy afternoon. I was not able to start for Ilkley yesterday as I was too unwell; but I hope to get there on Tuesday or Wednesday. Do, I beg you, when you have finished my book and thought a little over it, let me hear from you. Never mind and pitch into me, if you think it requisite; some future day, in London possibly, you may give me a few criticisms in detail, that is, if you have scribbled any remarks on the margin, for the chance of a second edition.

Murray has printed 1250 copies, which seems to me rather too large an edition, but I hope he will not lose.[9]

I make as much fuss about my book as if it were my first. Forgive me, and believe me, my dear Lyell.

Charles Darwin Bibliography

Bowlby, J. (1990). *Charles Darwin: A biography*. London: Hutchinson.
    The best of the recent biographies of Darwin, Bowlby examines the interplay of Darwin's personality, his frequent illnesses, and his work on

---

9. The publisher, John Murray, did not lose as all copies of the book were sold on the first day.

the *Origin*. The influence of Darwin's grandfather, Erasmus Darwin, is also emphasized.

Bowler, P. J. (1989). *Evolution: The History of an Idea*. Berkeley: University of California Press.
   This history of the concept of evolution focuses on the influences on Darwin and the fate of the theory in evolutionary biology.

Burkhardt, F., Smith, S., Kohn, D., & Montgomery, W. (Eds.) (1985–). *The Correspondence of Charles Darwin*. New York: Cambridge University Press.
   This outstanding series of books began publication in 1985 with the first volume containing Darwin's correspondence from 1821 to 1836. Subsequent volumes have been appearing at the rate of one each year, and will continue until all 14,000 letters are in print. Thus, this series constitutes the only comprehensive collection of Darwin letters.

Clark, R. W. (1984). *The Survival of Charles Darwin: A Biography of a Man and an Idea*. New York: Random House.
   A double biography covering Darwin's life and the life of his theory through the modern synthesis of Julian Huxley in the middle of the 20th century.

Darwin, C. R. (1859). *On the Origin of Species*. London: John Murray.
   The 1250 copies of the first printing of this book sold out on November 24, 1859, the first day the book was on sale. Many subsequent printings and editions exist, including inexpensive paperback versions. It is must reading for anyone wanting a feel for Darwin as scientist.

Darwin, F. (Ed.) (1950). *Charles Darwin's Autobiography, with His Notes and Letters Depicting the Growth of the Origin of Species*. New York: Henry Schuman.
   Edited by Francis Darwin, son of Charles Darwin, this book contains the autobiography Darwin wrote for his children, a collection of reminiscences of his father by Francis Darwin, and a selection of Darwin letters surrounding the writing and reception of the *Origin*.

Keynes, R. D. (1979). *The Beagle Record*. New York: Cambridge University Press.
   This book tells the story of the voyage of the *Beagle*. It is assembled from letters from Darwin and Robert Fitzroy (Captain of the *Beagle*), Darwin's diary, and published works about the voyage by Darwin and Fitzroy.

Ospovat, D. (1981). *The Development of Darwin's Theory*. New York: Cambridge University Press.

This book focuses on Darwin's journals, letters, and books during the years 1838–1859, emphasizing the role of natural theology in the early formulations of his theory, and the work of other naturalists in its later development, particularly the changing conception of natural selection.

Richards, R. J. (1983). Why Darwin delayed, or interesting problems and models in the history of science. *Journal of the History of the Behavioral Sciences, 19,* 45–53.

In this article, Richards discusses eight explanations for Darwin's delay in publishing the *Origin*. In doing so, he also discusses the determination of what is an interesting question in the history of science and how best to pursue the answers to such questions.

Richards, R. J. (1988). *Darwin and the Emergence of Evolutionary Theories of Mind and Behavior.* Chicago: University of Chicago Press.

This award-winning book traces the history of evolutionary thought from Lamarck to the modern theories of ethology and sociobiology, with a special emphasis on the treatment of moral behavior.

Chapter 3

John Stuart Mill and the
Subjection of Women

One of the last British philosophers in the empiricist tradition begun by John Locke was John Stuart Mill (1806–1873), whose importance for the history of psychology is considerable despite the fact that he is typically afforded the briefest of treatments in history of psychology textbooks.

John Stuart Mill was the eldest of nine children of James Mill (1773–1836), a Scottish empiricist philosopher whose contribution to the study of the formation and maintenance of associations was the description of a set of factors determining the strength and durability of associations. He was the most mechanistic of the empiricists, describing his mechanical view of the mind in his book, *Analysis of the Phenomena of the Human Mind* (1829). John Stuart Mill was raised according to that mechanistic philosophy; his father wanted him to become a reasoning machine.

J. S. Mill's early education was considerable, and he showed remarkable genius for his studies. He began a study of Greek at age 3 and Latin at age 8, and by the age of 10 had read many of the classic works in their original language. At the age of 12 he wrote a book-length history of Roman government. J. S. Mill, like his father before him, grew up without playmates other than his siblings. Because one of his duties was to tutor his younger siblings, learning occupied most of his waking hours (Packe, 1954).

James Mill was very possessive of his brilliant son and dominated him in all matters. When John, as a young adult, began to acquire friends, his father would drive them away. Such treatment led John, at the age of 21 to suffer the first of several major clinical depressions in his life. In his autobiography he wrote:

. . . my heart sank within me: the whole foundation on which my life was constructed fell down. . . . I seemed to have nothing left to live for.

At first I hoped that the cloud would pass away of itself; but it did not. . . . Hardly anything had power to cause me even a few minutes oblivion of it. . . . I sought no comfort by speaking to others of what I felt. If I had loved any one sufficiently to make confiding my griefs a necessity, I should not have been in the condition I was. I felt, too, that mine was not an interesting, or in any way respectable distress. There was nothing in it to attract sympathy. . . . My father, to whom it would have been natural for me to have recourse in any practical difficulties, was the last person to whom, in such a case as this, I looked for help. Everything convinced me that he had no knowledge of any such mental state as I was suffering from, and that even if he could be made to understand it, he was not the physician to heal it. (pp. 81–82)

His depression lasted nearly 3 years, and then he met Harriet Taylor in 1830. Thus began what Mill called "the most valuable friendship of [his] life" (p. 111).

Harriet Taylor was intelligent, vivacious, rebellious, and a romantic, and she was married to John Taylor, an insensitive man who shared none of his wife's love of music, philosophy, literature, and poetry. One of the first extended meetings between John Mill and Harriet Taylor was at a dinner party at the Taylor's. Mill was immediately taken with Taylor's intellect and beauty, and she, too, was fascinated by this man with such unconventional views on the place of women in society. There were subsequent dinners at the Taylor household and shortly Mill and Taylor began to exchange essays on marriage, divorce, women's roles, and a host of other subjects.

The frequent contacts of these two led to gossip in London society. John Taylor grew frustrated with the relationship but his wife was adamant in her insistence that it was nothing more than friendship. And so it seemed. Then in September of 1833, Mill confessed that he loved her, a sentiment she had expressed earlier to him. Apparently their friendship continued in a Platonic fashion. For a time Mill lived with the Taylors and sometimes vacationed with them, adding to the potential for public scandal (Hayek, 1951).

John Taylor died in 1849, and two years later Mill and Harriet Taylor were married. After a 20–year friendship, they enjoyed only 9 years of a very happy marriage before Harriet's death in 1858. It was during those years that Mill wrote what is arguably his most important work, *On Liberty*. It began as a brief essay in 1854 and in the ensuing years he and Taylor revised it again and again, "reading, weighing and criticizing every sentence" (Mill, *Autobiography*, p. 144), creating the small but powerful book. It was published a few months after Taylor's death and was dedicated to her:

> *To the beloved and deplored memory of her who was the inspirer, and in part the author, of all that is best in my writings—the friend and wife whose exalted sense of truth and right was my strongest incitement, and whose approbation was my chief reward—I dedicate this volume.* (On Liberty, 1858)

It had been in the midst of his friendship with Taylor that Mill had written his most important work for psychology, A *System of Logic*, which he published in 1843. In this book, Mill argued for the feasibility of a science of psychology, in his words, a "science of human nature." The possibility of such a science was a hotly debated issue during Mill's time, as many agreed with August Comte that there could be no science of the mind because the mind could not study its own processes (see Heyd, 1989). Although Mill acknowledged that psychology was, in his time, an inexact science, he believed that it was as precise as some sciences, such as astronomy, and worthy of study. Mill did not propose an experimental science of mind, but he did offer a methodological approach to an empirical one relying on ad hoc analysis. There is some evidence that Wilhelm Wundt was strongly influenced by Mill's views on a science of psychology, particularly his ideas of mental chemistry (similar to Wundt's later notion of creative synthesis).

Of Mill's 13 books published during his lifetime, his last one was undoubtedly one of the most meaningful for him. Written in 1861, as he was coming out of the depression caused by the loss of his wife, the book was not published until 1869. Entitled *The Subjection of Women*, the book was a treatise that described the status of women in society, argued for equality of the sexes, and offered a plan of political action to bring about such equality. The book was a culmination of 30 years of discussions between Mill and Taylor and has become one of the classic texts in the history of feminist thought.

The letters in this chapter focus on Mill's views on women and also provide a glimpse of his relationship with Harriet Taylor. That relationship had a strong base of shared interest in intellectual pursuits, but perhaps of greater importance for Mill, it afforded him the only affection he was to experience in his life.

To Taylor, (?) 1832

She to whom my life is devoted has wished for written exposition of my opinions on the subject which, of all connected with human Institutions, is nearest to her happiness. . . .

. . . [the] question of marriage cannot properly be considered by itself alone. The question is not what marriage ought to be, but a far wider question, what woman ought to be. Settle that first and the other will settle itself. Determine whether marriage is to be a relation between two equal beings, or between a superior & an inferior, between a protector and a dependent; & all other doubts will easily be resolved.

But in this question there is surely no difficulty. There is no natural inequality between the sexes; except perhaps in bodily strength; even that admits of doubt: and if bodily strength is to be the measure of superiority, mankind are no better than savages. Every step in the progress of civilization has tended to diminish the deference paid to bodily strength, until now when that quality confers scarcely any advantages except its natural ones: the strong man has little or no power to employ his strength as a means of acquiring any other advantage over the weaker in body. Every step in the progress of civilization has similarly been marked by a nearer approach to equality in the condition of the sexes; & if they are still far from being equal, the hindrance is not now in the difference of physical strength, but in artificial feelings and prejudices.

If nature has not made men and women unequal, still less ought the law to make them so. . . .

The first and indispensable step . . . towards the enfranchisement of woman, is that she be so educated, as not to be dependent either on her father or her husband for subsistence: a position which in nine cases out of ten, makes her either the plaything or the slave of the man who feeds her, & in the tenth case, only his humble friend. Let it not be said that she has an equivalent and compensating advantage in the exemption from toil: men think it base & servile in men to accept food as the price of dependence, & why do they not deem it so in women? solely because they do not desire that women should be their equals. Where there is strong affection, dependence is its own reward: but it must be voluntary dependence; & the more perfectly voluntary it is, the more exclusively each owes every thing to the other's affection & to nothing else,—the greater is the happiness.

Taylor to Mill, (?) 1832

If I could be Providence for the world for a time, for the express purpose of raising the condition of women, I should come to you to know the *means*—the *purpose* would be to remove all interference with affection, or with anything which is, or which even might be supposed to be, demonstrative of affection. In the present state of women's mind, perfectly uneducated, and with whatever of timidity & dependence is natural to them increased a thousand fold by their habit of utter dependence, it would probably be mischievous to remove at once all restraints, they would buy themselves protectors at a dearer cost than even at present— but without raising their natures at all.

Whether nature made a difference between men & women or not, it seems now that all men, with the exception of a few lofty minded, are sensualists more or less—women on the contrary are quite exempt from this trait, however it may appear otherwise in the cases of some. It seems strange that it should be so, unless it was meant to be a source of power in semi-civilized states such as the present—or it may not be so—it may be only that the habits of freedom & low indulgence on which boys grow up and the contrary notion of what is called purity in girls may have produced the appearance of different natures in the two sexes. As certain it is that there is equality in nothing now—all the pleasures such as they are being men's, & all the disagreeables & pains being women's, as that every pleasure would be infinitely heightened both in kind & degree by the perfect equality of the sexes. Women are educated for one single object, to gain their living by marrying. . . . To be married is the object of their existence and that object being gained they do really cease to exist as to anything worth calling life or any useful purpose. One observes very few marriages where there is any real sympathy or enjoyment or companionship between the parties. The woman knows what her power is and gains by it what she has been taught to consider 'proper' to her state. The woman who would gain power by such means is unfit for power, still they do lose this power for paltry advantages and I am astonished it has never occurred to them to gain some larger purpose; but their minds are degenerated by habits of dependence.

Taylor to Mill, September 6, 1833

I am glad that you have said it[1]—I am *happy* that you have—no one with any fineness & beauty of character but must feel compelled to say *all*, to the being they really love—while there is reservation, however little of it, the love is just *so much* imperfect. There has never, *yet*, been entire confidence around us. The difference between you and me in that respect is, that I have always *yearned* to have your confidence with an intensity of wish which has *often*, for a time, swallowed up the naturally stronger feeling—the affection itself—you have not given it, not that you wished to reserve—but that you did not *need* to give—but not having that need of course you had no perception that I had & so you had discouraged confidence from me 'til the habit of *checking first thoughts* has become so strong that when in your presence timidity has become almost a *disease* of the nerves. . . .

Yes—these circumstances *do* require greater strength than any other—the greatest—that which you have, & which if you had not I should never have loved you, I should not love you now.

Editor's Note: *In 1840, Mill began corresponding on a regular basis with August Comte. Eventually their letters turned to a discussion of the place of women in society, an issue on which they differed considerably. In 1844, Mill gave the drafts of his letters and the copies of Comte's letters to Taylor for her reading. Her reaction, which was painful to Mill, is printed below.*

Taylor to Mill, (?) 1844

These have greatly surprised and also disappointed me, & also they have pleased me, all this regarding your part in them. Comte's is what I expected—the usual partial and prejudiced view of a subject which he has little considered. . . . If the truth is on the side I defend I imagine C. would rather not see it. . . .

---

1. This letter is in response to a letter from Mill, which is not extant. Scholars are in agreement that in his letter, Mill had finally been able to tell Taylor that he was in love with her.

I am surprised in your letters to find your opinion undetermined where I had thought it made up—I am disappointed at a tone more than half-apologetic with which you state your opinions. & I am charmed with the exceeding nicety elegance & fineness of your last letter. Do not think that I wish you had said *more* on the subject, I only wish that what was said was in the tone of conviction, not of suggestion.

This dry sort of man is not a worthy coadjutor & scarcely a worthy opponent. With your gift of intellect of conscience & of impartiality is it probable, or is there any ground for supposing, that there exists any man more competent to judge that question than you are?

You are in advance of your age in culture of the intellectual faculties, you would be the most remarkable man of your age if you had no other claim to be so than your perfect impartiality and your fixed love of justice. These are two qualities of different orders which I believe to be the rarest & most difficult to human nature. . . .

I now & then find a generous defect in your mind or your method—such is your liability to take an over large *measure* of people . . . having to draw in afterwards—a proceeding more needful than pleasant.

Editor's Note: *The following statement was written by Mill in anticipation of his marriage to Taylor. The wedding occurred on April 21, 1851.*

Mill, March 6, 1851

Being about, if I am so happy as to obtain her consent, to enter into the marriage relation with the only woman I have ever known, with whom I would have entered into that state; and the whole character of the marriage relation as constituted by law being such as both she and I entirely and conscientiously disapprove, for this among other reasons, that it confers upon one of the parties to the contract, legal power and control over the person, property, and freedom of action of the other party, independent of her own wishes and will; I, having no means of legally divesting myself of these odious powers (as I most assuredly would do if an engagement to that effect could be made legally binding on me), feel it my duty to put on record a formal protest against the existing law of marriage, in so far as conferring such powers;

and a solemn promise never in any case or under any circumstances to use them. And in the event of marriage between Mrs.
Taylor and me I declare it to be my will and intention, and the
condition of the engagement between us, that she retains in all
respects whatever the same absolute freedom of action, and freedom of disposal of herself and of all that does or may at any time
belong to her, as if no such marriage had taken place; and I absolutely disclaim and repudiate all pretence to have acquired any
rights whatever by virtue of such marriage.

Mill to Archdeacon John Allen, May 27, 1867

I do not anticipate that women would be made less valuable
in the home by having their minds directed to the great concerns
of mankind, but quite the contrary wherever men's minds are em-
ployed as much as they ought to be on those great concerns.

Neither do I think that the adaptation of the work of each
person to his or her special endowments and position is a thing to
be preappointed by society. I believe that perfect freedom will ad-
just these things far better than any general regulation can.

Perhaps I do not differ so much from you as you suppose as to
what is likely to be permanently the main occupation of a very
great majority of women. But I do not think that the majority
should give laws to the individual action of the minority.

I do not undervalue "what teachers of religion can effect," I
rate it most highly; but what they *do* effect I rate very low. An
example of what they might do has been given lately by the Independent Church at Totnes in severely rebuking those of its members who have been implicated in bribing, and only not expelling
them from communion because they expressed the deepest peni-
tence and determination never to offend in that manner again.
This gave me the rare satisfaction of finding an existing Church,
or branch of a Church, who are actually Christians.

Editor's Note: *The following excerpts of letters from Mill are in response
to letters he received after the publication of* The Subjection of Women
(1869).

Mill to Alexander Bain,[2] July 14, 1869

The most important thing women have to do is to stir up the zeal of women themselves. We have to stimulate their aspirations—to bid them not despair of anything, nor think anything beyond their reach, but try their faculties against all difficulties. In no other way can the verdict of experience be fairly collected, and in no other way can we excite the enthusiasm in women which is necessary to break down the old barriers. This is more important now than to conciliate opponents. But I do not believe that opponents will be at all exasperated by taking this line. On the contrary, I believe the point has now been reached at which, the higher we pitch our claims, the more disposition there will be to concede part of them. All I have yet heard of the reception of the new book confirms this idea. People tell me that it is lowering the tone of our opponents as well as raising that of our supporters. Everything I hear strengthens me in the belief, which I at first entertained with a slight mixture of misgiving, that the book has come out at the right time, and that no part of it is premature.

One effect which the suffrage agitation is producing is to make all sorts of people declare in favour of improving the education of women. That point is conceded by almost everybody, and we shall find the education movement for women favoured and promoted by many who have no wish at all that things should go any further. The cause of political and civil enfranchisement is also prospering almost beyond hope. You have probably observed that the admission of women to the municipal franchise has passed the Commons, and is passing the Lords without opposition. The Bill for giving married women the control of their own property has passed through the Commons, all but the third reading, and is thought to have a good chance of becoming law this session.

---

2. Alexander Bain (1818–1903), one of the British associationists, was a frequent correspondent with Mill. Bain's contributions to psychology included: *The Senses and the Intellect* (1855), *The Emotions and the Will* (1859), *Mind and Body* (1872), and his founding of the first psychological journal, *Mind*, in 1876.

Mill to John Nichol,[3] August 18, 1869

I have been long without acknowledging your letter of 20th July, because there were several points in it on which I wished to make some remarks, and I have not had time to do this sooner. Even now I am unable to do it at any length. You have, I doubt not, understood what I have endeavoured to impress upon the readers of my book, that the opinions expressed in it respecting the natural capacities of women are to be regarded as provisional; perfect freedom of development being indispensable to afford the decisive evidence of experiment on the subject: and if, as you truly say, conventionalities have smothered nature still more in women than in men, the greater is the necessity for getting rid of the conventionalities before the nature can be manifested. I have, however, thought it indispensable to weigh such evidence as we have and examine what conclusions it points to, and I certainly think that, in all matters in which women do not entirely lean upon men, they have shown a very great command of practical talent. . . .

I thought it best not to discuss the questions of marriage and divorce along with that of the equality of women; not only from the obvious inexpediency of establishing a connection in people's minds between the equality, and any particular opinions on the divorce question, but also because I do not think that the conditions of the dissolubility of marriage can be properly determined until women have an equal voice in determining them, nor until there has been experience of the marriage relation as it would exist between equals. Until then I should not like to commit myself to more than the general principle of relief from the contract in extreme cases.

Mill to G. Croom Robertson,[4] August 18, 1869

. . . The most important of your points is the suggestion of a possible turning of what is said about the usefulness of the present feminine type as a corrective to the present masculine, into an argument for maintaining the two types distinct by difference of training. You have yourself gone into considerations of great importance in answer to this argument, all of which I fully accept. I

---

3. Professor at the University of Glasgow.

4. Robertson, a philosopher, was one of the editors of the journal, *Mind*.

should add some others to them, as, *first*, it is not certain that the differences spoken of are not partly at least natural ones, which would subsist in spite of identity of training; *secondly,* the correction which the one type supplies to the excesses of the other is very imperfectly obtained now, owing to the very circumstance that women's sphere and men's are kept so much apart. At present, saving fortunate exceptions, women have rather shown the good influence of this sort which they *might* exercise over men, than actually exercised it.

Mill to Mrs. Beecher Hooker, September 13, 1869

. . . You have perceived, what I should wish every one who reads my little book to know, that whatever there is in it which shows any unusual insight into nature or life was learnt from women—from my wife, and subsequently also from her daughter.

What you so justly say respecting the infinitely closer relationship of a child to its mother than to its father, I have learnt from the same source to regard as full of important consequences with regard to the future legal position of parents and children. This, however, is a portion of the truth for which the human mind will not, for some time, be sufficiently prepared to make its discussion useful.

But I do not perceive that this closer relationship gives any ground for attributing a natural superiority in capacity of moral excellence to women over men. I believe moral excellence to be always the fruit of education and cultivation, and I see no reason to doubt that both sexes are equally capable of that description of cultivation. But the position of irresponsible power in which men have hitherto lived is, I need hardly say, most unfavourable to almost every kind of moral excellence. So far as women have been in possession of irresponsible power, they too have by no means escaped its baneful consequences.

Editor's Note: *The following letter was written in response to a letter from a woman (unidentified) who, after reading* The Subjection of Women *asked Mill's advice on whether she should divorce her husband on grounds of incompatibility.*

Mill to unidentified woman, May 1, 1870

You greatly overrate the qualities required for writing such books as mine, if you deem them to include that of being a competent adviser and director of consciences in the most difficult affairs of private life. And even a person qualified for this office would be incapable of fulfilling it unless he possessed an intimate knowledge of the circumstances of the case, and the character of the persons concerned. It would be a long and a difficult business to define, even in an abstract point of view, the cases which would justify one of two married persons in dissolving the contract without the consent of the other. But as far as I am able to judge from your own statement, yours does not appear to be a strong case, since your husband has still an affection for you, and since you not only do not complain of any ill treatment at his hands, but have so much confidence in his goodness and high feeling, as to feel sure that even in case of your leaving him without his consent, he would not seek to withhold any of your children from you.

If I could venture to give any opinion, it would be that if the only bar between you and such a man is a difference in your "ways of thinking and feeling," unfortunate as such a difference is in married life, the mutual toleration which we all owe to those who sincerely differ from us forms a basis on which the continuance of your union may be made endurable, and the differences themselves, when nothing is done to exasperate them, may, as is usually the case between persons who live intimately together, tend gradually to an approximation.

John Stuart Mill Bibliography

Elliot, H. S. R. (Ed.) (1910). *The Letters of John Stuart Mill* (Vols. I–II). New York: Longmans Green.
    The most complete collection of Mill's letters, except that it excludes the correspondence with Harriet Taylor (see Hayek, 1951). The majority of letters printed in this chapter are from this collection.

Hayek, F. A. (1951). *John Stuart Mill and Harriet Taylor: Their Friendship and Subsequent Marriage*. Chicago: University of Chicago Press.

    This book reprints all of the known correspondence between Taylor and Mill, as well as many other letters relevant to their relationship.

Heyd, T. (1989). Mill and Comte on psychology. *Journal of the History of the Behavioral Science, 25,* 125–138.

    Contrasts the psychological views of Mill and Comte in terms of their sociopolitical and pragmatic orientations, noting that their systems are not entirely exclusive of one another.

Mill, J. S. (1885). *The Subjection of Women*. New York: Holt. (Original work published 1869)

    Mill's classic feminist treatise.

Mill, J. S. (1900). *A System of Logic, Ratiocinative and Inductive, Being a Connected View of the Principles of Evidence and the Methods of Scientific Investigation* (8th ed.). New York: Harper. (Original work published 1843)

    Mill's textbook that defined his vision of a science of human nature.

Mill, J. S. (1969). *Autobiography*. Boston: Houghton Mifflin. (Original work published 1873)

    This book was published posthumously, largely with the help of Helen Taylor, Mill's step-daughter. Although there is much of interest in this book, Mill's descriptions of his depressions are particularly moving.

Neff, E. (1924). *Carlyle and Mill: Mystic and Utilitarian*. New York: Columbia University Press.

    One of Mill's most interesting friendships was that with Thomas Carlyle (1795–1881), British essayist and historian. Carlyle's most famous work was a three-volume history of the French Revolution published in 1837. The first draft of that work was destroyed by Mill when he accidentally placed the manuscript with some papers to be burned. Neff's book is a fascinating account of the often turbulent relationship between the two and its tragic end.

Packe, M. (1954). *The Life of John Stuart Mill*. New York: Macmillan.

    Arguably the most comprehensive and scholarly biography of Mill to date.

Chapter 4

An American in Leipzig

James McKeen Cattell (1860–1944) was among the most important psychologists of his day and a key figure in the development of American psychology as a science. He coined the term "mental test," established the Psychological Corporation as the principal publisher of psychological tests and founded the psychology laboratories at the University of Pennsylvania (1887) and Columbia University (1890) where he trained a number of doctoral students who would make important contributions to psychology (for example, Robert Woodworth, Edward L. Thorndike, Harry Hollingworth).

Cattell's honors were many including his selection, in 1901, as the first psychologist admitted to the prestigious National Academy of Sciences and his election as President of the Ninth International Congress of Psychology, in 1929, the first international psychology congress to be held in the United States. Arguably Cattell's most important contribution to psychology was his editorship of the journal *Science* from 1894 until his death in 1944. He used his position as editor to promote the image of psychology among the natural sciences, and there is no denying that it significantly enhanced psychology's visibility and status among the older sciences.

Cattell was born in Easton, Pennsylvania, home of Lafayette College, where his father was president from 1863 until 1883. The Cattell family was well-educated, ambitious, well-connected politically and socially, and financially successful.

After his graduation from Lafayette College in 1880, Cattell pursued additional study for a time in Germany, but returned in 1882 when he received a fellowship to study with G. Stanley Hall (1844–1924) at Johns Hopkins University. There he began his work on the measurement of mental processes. However, he and Hall soon clashed, and the incident resulted in Hall's withdrawal of his fellowship (see Ross, 1972). Feeling anger and resentment toward Hall, Cattell returned to Germany for a second time to pursue a doctorate in psychology in Wilhelm Wundt's (1832–1920) laboratory at the University of Leipzig, arriving there in November, 1883. Cattell graduated from Leipzig in 1886, the first American to earn a doctorate from Wundt with a dissertation in the new science of psychology.

At the time of Cattell's arrival at Leipzig, Wundt's fame as a psychologist was already well established. Students from a number of countries came to Leipzig to study with Wundt, including 16 Americans for whom Wundt served as the major professor (Benjamin, Durkin, Link, Vestal, and Acord, 1992). Many of these Americans described Wundt as an excellent mentor and a gifted lecturer. Consider the following passage from one of those students:

> *Clad in a conventional black frock-coat and black trousers, he [Wundt] would steal into his great lecture hall, attended by his famulus [assistant], as if he wished to avoid observation. As soon as his familiar figure appeared, applause in the form of shuffling feet on the part of his hundreds of students would greet him. . .*
>
> *Utterly unmoved, as if he had not heard us, Wundt would glide to his place on the dais, assume his accustomed position, fix his eyes on vacancy and begin his discourse. There could not be a better scientific lecturer. Without a scrap of writing, he would speak for three-quarters of an hour so clearly, concisely, and to the point, that, in listening to him, one would imagine one were reading a well-written book in which the paragraphs, the important text of the page, the small print, and the footnotes were plainly indicated. Wundt told no stories, gave few illustrations, scorned any attempt at popularity. His only thought was to deal with the topic of the day as thoroughly and as exhaustively as the time permitted. . . . With all this, he was followed almost breathlessly, sometimes by eight hundred students, and, if the lecture had been unusually amazing, they would burst into spontaneous applause. As unconscious as at the beginning, Wundt would glide from the hall, and another great and unforgettable experience of life had ended. (Worcester, 1932, p. 90)*

Throughout his career at Leipzig, Wundt remained one of the university's most popular lecturers. Finding a room large enough to hold his classes was a perennial problem.

Apparently Cattell did not hold Wundt in the same esteem as did his other students. His letters express doubts about Wundt's abilities as a scientist and the value of his work. The letters that follow are excerpts from the Cattell letters published by historian Michael Sokal (1981). The originals are part of the Cattell Papers in the Manuscript Division of the Library of Congress in Washington, D.C. All letters, except one, are from Cattell to his parents, whom he typically addressed as "Dear Mama and Papa." The one exception is a letter to Cattell from his father, William Cattell.

These letters were written during Cattell's years as a student at Leipzig with Wundt, 1883 to 1886. They give considerable insight into Cattell's personality and his working relationship with Wundt. They portray Cattell as self-centered, arrogant, disrespectful of others, and supremely confident. In contrast, they show Wundt as a flexible mentor and not as the autocrat that some historians of psychology have portrayed him to be. These letters also give an idea of what it was like to be a student in the beginning days of the new science of psychology.

Readers of the Cattell letters are often dismayed at Cattell's egotistical manner. But perhaps he could not have played his important entrepreneurial role in psychology without such an inflated ego. He transferred his belief in himself to his belief in psychology, predicting it would ultimately be the most important of the sciences. He spent most of his life promoting that vision. As noted earlier, his position as editor of *Science* afforded him a unique opportunity to portray the new science of psychology to the better established physical sciences. That visibility was critical for psychology's growth as a science in the early part of the 20th century.

Journal entry, November 23, 1883

To think of it; here I am in Leipzig! We sailed from N.Y. on the Servia Wed. Oct 31st arriving in Liverpool early Friday morning (the 9th). The ship was tossed about somewhat but it was a pleasant passage for this time of year. I was only sick two days. . . .

I know as yet nothing about the university . . . I will hear Wundt . . . I must work harder than I have since my freshman year in college. My program is to study mostly empirical psychology, reading a little on the history of philosophy. I want to work on Lotze, translating his Psychologie & writing some review, and to work and write on stimulants & my Baltimore experiments.

To *parents, December 30, 1883*

Tomorrow afternoon Prof. Wundt is going to explain to Berger and me an "Arbeit"[1] with which Berger[2] expects to pass his examination. If we get valuable results they will be published under our two names. I am getting a piece of apparatus made, which I have invented in order to carry on the work I began in Baltimore. I have written to Dr. Hall, hinting that I would like to have my notes and papers. I am not anxious that he should publish a paper, which would give him credit, which he does not deserve. If magazine editors do not see fit to print my work under my name it need not be published at all. It looks as though I had found several serious mistakes in results published by Wundt, but of this I cannot be sure until I make further experiments. I will have to work hard during the rest of the semester as I am moving on a number of different lines having little in common. Experimental psychology lies about as far apart from philosophy as chemistry from Greek.

To *parents, January 6, 1884*

I am working hard and I think successfully. There were four of us, working at a subject in experimental psychology, I being the last to join, and one, who was to publish the results under his name, having been working on the subject for about a year. I told you Wundt was going to give Berger and me a subject; we were pleasantly surprized when he told us that we could keep on with the same work, that the others had not been very successful, and would have to take up a new and less important subject. This was of course quite a compliment to us. We hope to have results worth publishing in two or three months. It would be quite nice for me to be the joint author of a German paper. We work every day and very hard. Day before yesterday we worked, with only twenty minutes intermission, from eight in the morning until after seven in the evening. We have a room to ourselves, and can come when

---

1. Literally meaning "work," it refers here to a research problem.
2. Gustav Oscar Berger was a German student and friend of Cattell.

we please and do what we please. Besides the work given us by Wundt, we are making some experiments I suggested, and which we hope will give interesting results. Of course I have lots of other work before me. I can now continue my Baltimore experiments, and must do a good deal of preparatory study before I will be ready to translate Lotze's psychology.

To parents, January 20, 1884

I spend four mornings and two afternoon's working in Wundt's laboratory. I like Berger very much, he works hard, has good ideas and—what is equally important—is ready to follow my good ideas. He does most of the averaging & table-making, which is no small or easy work. On the whole I like Wundt, though he is inclined first to disparage our ideas and then adopt them, which is rather agravating. It is of course possible that we may not get along well together, as differences of fact and opinion will occur, and I dont know how to give up when I think I'm right. German Professors are not used to "indocile" students, as it usual here in the Professor's presence to "hold

Awe-striken breaths at a work divine."

But as I said I respect and like Wundt, and as he mostly lets us alone every thing may move along smoothly. Our work is interesting. If I should explain it to you you might not find it of vast importance, but we discover new facts and must ourselves invent the methods we use. We work in a new field, where others will follow us, who must use or correct our results. We are trying to measure the time it takes to perform the simplest mental acts—as for example to distinguish whether a color is blue or red. As this time seems to be not more than one hundredth of a second, you can imagine this is no easy task. In my room I am continuing my Baltimore experiments, and here too I measure times smaller than 1/1000 of a second. With all this and my lectures I have as you may suppose but little time for reading or writing.

To James McKeen Cattell from his father, William Cattell January 27, 1884

I address you this separate letter, because your mother & I have had our anxiety as to your relations with Prof. Wundt much increased by yr references to him in yr last letter. If in this matter

I trusted alone to my own judgment, so often clouded of late with groundless apprehensions, it might seem as if I was giving myself needless anxiety. But dear Mama, from yr very first reference to Prof. W. & without a word from me, has felt intensely anxious & has often expressed her great apprehension lest, instead of securing him as a friend you w^d say or do something that w^d first alienate him & then (alas! Such is human nature in the best of men) lead him to place something in yr way—Of course on other grounds than any personal reason, such as want of "docility" &c—

I fear you cannot understand how deeply we feel this danger. Both of us are distressed at the very thought of your having—even if you are in the right—a repetition of the ill feeling wh. it is evident was brought about between some of the authorities & yrself at Balt.—We both fear you are not as cautious in this matter as you should be. You speak in yr letter of not being able to accept the views of the German Professors as to their students being "docile"—but in the very kind letter you rec^d fr. Dr. Hall he used this very word with ref. to you:—he was favorably impressed with yr abilities & had the highest expectations of what you c^d have accomplished had you only been more "docile"—Parental partiality is proverbially blind, especially where a son is so loving & thoughtful & dutiful as you are: yet dear Mama & I cannot but fear that there is some real ground for apprehension here; that what you may regard as "independence," or even "self-respect" in yr relations to yr Professors, we shd call by another word;—and I should be wanting in parental love & faithfulness if I did not earnestly warn you against it—*for your own sake*. . . .

So my dear son let me beg you to act with great circumspection in all your relations to the Professors for our sakes as well as your own. You write of having found errors in some of Prof. W's published investigations. If he is really wrong & you have discovered it, to publish this with becoming modesty when you are no longer under his instructions will of course do you honor. *Now* it is dangerous ground. No matter if Prof. W. is convinced that he is wrong; it will require great tact for you to let him & others know it without wounding his amour propre: and engendering unkind feelings towards you. And no honor that you could get from any such correction of his errors could possibly compensate for the loss of his kindly personal interest in you. It w^d be far better for you, while a student, to be as "docile" as the most exacting Professor could demand.

I have written you a long letter—& yesterday & today have been poor days with me:—but dear Mama was anxious that I sh^d write. She has read what I have already written and says it expresses just what she feels. I know you will appreciate our devoted love for you that leads me to call yr attention to this matter, & to urge you to act with great caution—for yr own sake as well as ours.

May God ever bless you my dear son.

To parents, February 6, 1884

I thank you, Papa, for your letter anent [concerning] my relations with Wundt and other people. No one, not even I myself, has my welfare so much at heart as you and Mama, and by following your advice I would probably always be more successful and happy than in following my own impulses. The only question is whether a life of uniform success and happiness would not be as undesirable as it is impossible. I admire men who struggle, and suffer, and fail, rather than those who are always comfortable and in a good humor. It is perhaps better to fight one's way through life, than to slip through. As to this special case my relations with Wundt could not be pleasanter, nor do I see any reason why they should change. Both Berger and I intend to take our Dr.'s degree here, and would not want to get into trouble with Wundt.

To parents, October 16, 1884

I got my largest piece of apparatus from the machinist's today.[3] I feel like an author with his first book. The machine is really a great advance on methods heretofore used. I imagine Prof. Wundt would give $500 if he had it four years ago—or indeed so much if he had himself thought of it now. I shall set up my elements tomorrow, and have things in working order. It is very much better having my apparatus in my room.[4] In the first place every-thing is in good order, I shall never be disturbed, and it is far more

---

3. The apparatus was a gravity chronometer, a device to measure time in 1/1000ths of a second.

4. Wundt allowed Cattell to move his experiments from the Psychology Laboratory to his apartment.

convenient. But there are two greater advantages even than these. There will arise no difference of opinion between Prof. Wundt and myself, and Prof. Wundt will not be give credit for half the work.

To Wundt from Cattell, approx. October 25, 1884

I should like to present as a thesis in application for the degree of doctor of philosophy an essay on Psychometry, or the time taken up by simple mental process. I am well aware that this subject is too large and difficult for me to thoroughly investigate as a university student, but I trust I shall be able to prepare an acceptable thesis by giving (1) a brief summary of the work which has been done in this field. (2) a fuller account of experiments I myself have made and the results reached (3) the subjects which seem to me to need investigation.

I give below an imperfect analysis, of the factors on which the reaction time depends, underlining with blue ink the subjects on which I have worked, and with red ink those which I should like to investigate this winter.

Reaction Time

Analysis.

The sense stimulus. Sound, Light, Touch (touch proper, electric shock, temperature) Taste, Smell.

Sound—loudness, pitch, timbre
Light—intensity, color (saturation)
Touch proper—force, kind
Electric shock—intensity   momentary
Temperature—degree (heat & cold)   continuous
Taste—intensity, variety
Smell—intensity, variety

Sense organ, nerve, and muscle.   { normal / abnormal }

Sense organ & efferent nerve used—touch on lip and back, light image on yellow or field of indirect vision, taste on lip of tongue or palate.

Muscle & efferent nerve used, finger, wrist, foot.

The Subject (physiological / psychological)

Sex, Age, Temperament, Character, Mental Acumen, Physical power, Avocation.

The Same Individual

Normal
Abnormal

Normal

Mental State— } Fresh, wearied, interested, indifferent, dull, excited
Physical State } Eating, Sleep, exercise, temperature, weather (saturation & electric condition)

Attention–Practice–Fatigue

Attention { voluntary
caused (signal, distraction &c)

Practice } { series
Fatigue } day
continuous

Abnormal

Physical (pain or disease)
Mental (distress, elation, or disease) { natural.
(insanity) artificial.

artificial, by use of drugs, alcohol, ether, caffein, morphine, &c.

To parents, October 28, 1884

The lectures began yesterday. I have already heard the most important of them and the light is too bad to admit of taking notes. I am very busy, and as I want to work in the morning and evening, ought to take exercise in the afternoon. The air is so bad, as to be really injurious. In Prof. Wundt's lecture room there are packed some three hundred men—the ceiling is low and not a crack is left open. For all of which reasons I shall attend but few lectures. German students in their last year scarcely ever hear any.

To parents, October 29, 1884

At four I heard Prof. Wundt lecture on Ethics.

After the lecture he talked to me for three quarters of an hour and was extremely pleasant. In the paper I gave him on Saturday, I classified the work I have done, and propose doing this winter under four heads. Prof. said he would accept any one of these as a doctor's thesis, but recommended one as especially original.[5] He said he would accept this for his "Philosophische Studien."[6] This offer is all the more of an honor from the fact that scarcely any of the work has been done—he must therefore have considerable confidence in me. He said he would let me use the set up type for printing my doctor's thesis, which would make it comparatively inexpensive. He also said he hoped when I printed work in English I would send him a translation for his "Studien". He is going to come to see me.

To *parents, November 6, 1884*

Prof. Wundt came to see me this morning. He stayed three quarters of an hour and was very cordial, as he has always been recently. He has treated me very nicely, considering that I have called his attention to mistakes in his work, and have left his laboratory, where he would much rather have had me stay. That he has acted this way is not only plesanter for me, but also better for him. If, as many would have done, he had insisted that my corrections were wrong and my work of no account, and had put obstacles in the way of my setting up my own laboratory, the facts would not have been changed; but I would have published sometime or other my work in a way not pleasant to him. As it is he offers to print my work in his own magazine and is in every way pleasant and obliging. I shall therefore probably correct his work in a way that will be almost a compliment, and I shall be considered a pupil of his, and he will be given credit for what work I print now or later.

He praised today my arrangement of apparatus highly, and will copy it in some respects for his institute. He also offered to accept as my doctor's thesis and print in his "Studien" the work I began in Baltimore. This I have been working on and can easily finish by Christmas. So I could probably get my degree the first of August. In six months I could study up enough Philosophy, physics,

---

5. The topic was association.

6. Wundt's journal, which he had founded in 1881.

and biology or mathematics, I imagine. Still unless there is some special reason for this I would rathor finish up all my experimental work by August, then come home to see you, and return and pass the examination in the Winter. Besides the division of my work above mentioned—which is on the Time of Simple Mental Processes—there are three others. The Association time, which Prof. Wundt recommended for a doctor thesis and offered to accept for his Journal. This is scarcely begun. Then there is a good deal of work already done on the Reaction Time—this is what Berger and I worked on last winter. Fourthly there is work on the Legibility of letters, words and phrases, practically the most interesting and valuable of all. I have quite a good deal of work on this, but there is any amount more to be done.

To parents, January 16, 1885

Prof. Wundt lectured yesterday and today on my subject—I suppose you won't consider it egotistical when I say that I know a great deal more about it than he does, but you will be surprised when I say that half of the statements he made were wrong. I cannot understand how he is willing to give as positive scientific facts the results of experiments which he knows were not properly made. I could write a paper on these two lectures most damaging to Prof. Wundt. It is to be hoped for his sake as well as mine that he passes me in the examination on philosophy.

To parents, January 22, 1885

I worked in Wundt's laboratory this afternoon probably for the last time. Berger has enough material for his thesis—he is to hand it in next month. I have no doubt but that it will be accepted, and if so mine will be as a matter of course. Wundt's laboratory has a reputation greater than it deserves—the work done in it is decidedly amateurish. Work has only been done in two departments—the relation of the internal stimulus to the sensation, and the time of mental processes. The latter is my subject—I started working on it at Baltimore before I had read a word written by Wundt—what I did there was decidedly original. I'm quite sure my work is worth more than all done by Wundt & his pupils in this department, and as I have said it is one of the two department on which they have worked. Mind I do not consider my work of any special importance—I only consider Wundt's of still less. The subject was first taken up by Exner, and Wundt's continuation of it has no originality at all; and being mostly wrong has done more harm than good.

To parents, February 13, 1885

As I told you I was invited by Prof. Wundt to supper with other members of the laboratory. I cant say that I enjoy such things, I have no special reverence for any one I know personally, and it gives me no special delight to hear Wundt talk about the opera and such like. Mrs Wundt is however nice and Prof. Wundt seems to like me and to appreciate my phenomenal genius.

To parents, June 13, 1885

I called on Mrs. Wundt this morning—she is very nice, as I have told you. The professor also came in to see me—I am going to row them up to Connewitz some day next week. There are two bright children—a girl of eight, and boy of six. Prof. Wundt is coming to see me tomorrow. I am invited to dinner at Prof. Heinze's the day after—so you see I am on excellent terms with my professors. Indeed I imagine—though I have often been told the contrary—that I am quite clever in getting along with all sorts and conditions of people. The only question is how far it is manly—or worth the while—to spend ones life playing a part or rather a dozen different parts.

To parents, November 14, 1885

I received today both "Brain" and the "Studien" with my paper.[7] My work is of considerable importance, and some parts of it are very easy to understand and of general interest. I think it would be well if you get it noticed in the papers, quoting possibly some paragraphs. Indeed it might not be impossible and might be worth the while to get it reprinted in one of our papers—the Sunday Tribune for example. I shall myself send copies to some journals (mostly European) and to some people—I shall not however send any to Philadelphia, Princeton or Bethlehem.

---

7. Cattell's paper, "The Inertia of the Eye and Brain," appeared in Wundt's journal in German and in the English-language journal, *Brain*.

A paper like this gives me a very secure place in the scientific world, makes me equal with any American living. One likes however to be given credit for what one has done even by people who know nothing about the work. I scarcely know why we like to be praised by fools, but we do. Still there is some reason in my case. I may want a position or a wife, and certainly do want to be able to pick out the people I associate with.

James McKeen Cattell-Wilhelm Wundt Bibliography

Baldwin, B. T. (1921). In memory of Wilhelm Wundt by his American students. *Psychological Review, 28,* 153–188.
　　Upon Wundt's death in 1920, a number of his American students contributed to a collection of memories about him. Cattell's recollections of Wundt are part of this tribute.

Blumenthal, A. L. (1975). A reappraisal of Wilhelm Wundt. *American Psychologist, 30,* 1081–1088.
　　This article marks the emergence of a renewed interest in the work of Wilhelm Wundt and a critical examination that corrected earlier views of Wundt's psychology. Particularly significant is a section of the article that relates Wundt's ideas to contemporary psychology, notably cognitive psychology.

Bringmann, W. G., & Tweney, R. D. (Eds.). (1980). *Wundt Studies: A Centennial Collection.* Toronto: Hogrefe.
　　This book is a collection of articles commemorating the centennial of Wundt's founding of his laboratory in Leipzig in 1879. It provides extensive biographical material about Wundt, discusses the founding of the Leipzig laboratory, describes the research topics investigated in that laboratory, and provides case studies of several of Wundt's doctoral students.

Cattell, J. McK. (1885). The time it takes to see and name objects. *Mind, 11,* 63–65.
　　This article is a brief account of some of Cattell's research at Baltimore and Leipzig on the speed and nature of mental processing.

Sokal, M. M. (1971). The unpublished autobiography of James McKeen Cattell. *American Psychologist, 26,* 626–635.
　　This article is an unfinished Cattell autobiography that Sokal found in a box of unmarked papers at the Library of Congress. It is the

only extant autobiographical material of Cattell other than that contained in his letters.

Sokal, M. M. (1980). *Science* and James McKeen Cattell, 1894–1945. *Science, 209,* 43–52.
    This article describes the fifty years of Cattell's editorship of *Science* and the importance of that activity for a science of psychology.

Sokal, M. M. (1981). *An Education in Psychology: James McKeen Cattell's Journal and Letters from Germany and England, 1880–1888.* Cambridge, MA: MIT Press.
    This book is an edited collection of Cattell's letters from his graduate study in Baltimore, Germany, and England. It includes excerpts from more than 450 documents—letters and journal entries—selected from the Cattell Papers in the Library of Congress. Themes of the book include Cattell's personal development, the early development of experimental psychology, and the nature of American study in European universities in the late 19th century.

Wundt, W. (1904). *Principles of Physiological Psychology.* (E. B. Titchener, Trans.). New York: Macmillan.
    This is the first edition of Wundt's most influential work in psychology. It was a thorough compendium of the research underlying the new science of psychology. The book eventually went through five editions.

Chapter 5

The Struggle for Psychology Laboratories

In 19th century America, psychology was a subfield of philosophy, often referred to as moral philosophy. According to the moral philosophers, like James McCosh of Princeton University and Noah Porter of Yale University, psychology was the science that would reveal the nature of the soul. But it was not an experimental science, nor was it much grounded in empiricism. In fact, some historians have argued that moral philosophy was taught in colleges to counter the so-called atheistic tendencies of the British empiricists (Leahey, 1987).

These early psychologists were interested in such topics as sensory functioning, the role of experience, and the nature of will, all of which would be important areas of study in the new psychology of the 20th century. However, they were principally interested in questions of the soul—knowing right from wrong, avoiding temptation, sustaining religious faith. The 1850 edition of Webster's dictionary affirmed this view in defining psychology as "a discourse or treatise on the human soul; or the doctrine of man's spiritual nature" (p. 886). That definition persisted into the 1880s until supplanted by one that changed "philosophical discourse" to "laboratory science." It was a remarkable metamorphosis both in terms of the nature of the change and the time it took to occur.

Historians generally credit German psychologist Wilhelm Wundt with founding the first laboratory of psychology in 1879 at the University of Leipzig (see chapter 4). In this laboratory, Wundt began experimental investigations of the questions that had long been part of philosophical psychology, particularly questions of sensory functioning (an influence of the British empiricists who argued that all knowledge was acquired through the senses). Students from all over the world came to study with Wundt, including American G. Stanley Hall.

When Hall arrived in Leipzig he already had received his doctorate (under William James at Harvard University). Hall spent minimal time with Wundt, working instead with the physiologist Carl Ludwig, but he was very committed to the new scientific psychology. A few years after his return to America, Hall opened the first American psychology laboratory at Johns Hopkins University in 1883. From that point the laboratory movement quickly spread in the United States, partly stimulated by the publication of James's *Principles of Psychology* in 1890. By 1900, only 17 years after Hall had established his laboratory, there were more than 40 psychology laboratories in the United States (see Murray & Rowe, 1979).

A number of these early laboratories were founded by American students who got their doctorates with Wundt: James McKeen Cattell (University of Pennsylvania, 1887 and Columbia University, 1890), Harry Kirke Wolfe (University of Nebraska, 1889), Edward A. Pace (Catholic University, 1891), Frank Angell (Cornell University, 1891 and Stanford University, 1893), Edward Wheeler Scripture (Yale University, 1892), and George M. Stratton (University of California, 1896). And thus began the science of psychology, referred to as the "new psychology" to distinguish it from the old psychology of the moral philosophers. (See Morawski, 1988, and Danziger, 1990 for treatments of the rise of scientific psychology in America.)

Some universities embraced the new psychology and eagerly supported the development of their psychological laboratories. However, for the majority of universities the enthusiasm was less and the pace of development much slower. There were still many university scholars who believed, like August Comte, that there could never be a science of mind, that the mind was capable of studying everything except itself. Or they might have agreed with John Stuart Mill that psychology could be a science but only an empirical one, never an experimental one. Many of these late 19th-century psychology laboratories struggled against these beliefs, trying to establish their legitimacy alongside the established natural sciences.

One of the earliest of the American psychology laboratories was founded at the University of Nebraska in September of 1889. It was the sixth such laboratory to be founded and possibly the first that was exclusively devoted to laboratory instruction and research by undergraduate students. Its founder was Harry Kirke Wolfe (1858–1918) who graduated from Nebraska with his baccalaureate degree in 1880. Wolfe taught school for a few years and then went to Berlin in 1883 where he studied with Hermann Ebbinghaus and to Leipzig the following year. He received his doctorate with Wundt in 1886 conducting a study on the memory for tones for his dissertation research. Wolfe was in Leipzig with James McKeen Cattell (see chapter 4), and the two of them became the first Americans to earn psychology degrees with Wundt, Cattell finishing in April and Wolfe in August.

Wolfe returned to the United States and once again taught in the public schools for a few years before accepting a job at the University of Nebraska in 1889 as assistant professor in philosophy. He was also chair of the Philosophy Department, a dubious honor at best because he was the only member of the department. In his first year Wolfe taught a course in scientific psychology and a year-long course entitled "experimental psychology" emphasizing the methods of the new psychology that he had learned in Germany. Several senior students in this class were allowed to pursue original research for college credit.

In any account of the development of the new psychology in America, Wolfe should have an honored place. His early laboratory attracted a number of students who went on to distinguished careers in psychology. Two surveys during the 1920s ranked Nebraska third among the universities in the training of psychologists, an achievement due principally to Wolfe's dedication and inspiration as a teacher. Three of Wolfe's undergraduates (Walter Pillsbury, Madison Bentley, Edwin Guthrie) would become presidents of the American Psychological Association.

The success of his students belie the success Wolfe had in building and equipping his laboratory. His tenure as a faculty member at the University of Nebraska was a continuing struggle to convince an agriculturally-minded administration of the value of the new psychology and the need for a laboratory. The letters and other documents that follow tell the story of this struggle. It is not just Wolfe's story but more broadly is the story of psychology's early struggle for recognition as a laboratory science. These papers also give an idea of the nature of research and equipment common to the early psychology laboratories (see Capshew, 1992).

The documents in this chapter are taken from the Archives of the University of Nebraska and the personal papers of the Wolfe family.

H. K. Wolfe to Charles E. Bessey,[1] May 15, 1890

I respectfully offer the following report of the Dept. of Philosophy for the current collegiate year.

I. (a) A beginning has been made in collecting the more important works on Modern Psychology. A few recent works of Ethics and Logic have also been added to the library. The number of periodicals has increased from three to fourteen, including several foreign magazines of my own.[2]

   (b) The following illustrative apparatus is now ready for use.

   1 *Set Marshall's Physiological Charts* (13)
   1 *Synthetic preparation of the Brain*
   1 *Greatly enlarged model of the eye*
   1 *Greatly enlarged model of the ear*
   1 Stop-clock (1/4 sec)
   1 Metronome
   1 *Chronoscopograph with electrical accessories*[3]
   1 Large Seconds Pendulum (regulator of above)
   1 Oliver's Color-sense Test
   1 Helmholtz Standard color sheets
   1 Drop apparatus (Intensity of sound)[4]
   1 Revolving apparatus (memory for color)
       Several hundred hand-painted cards for testing color sense and color-memory, and for illustrating the phenomena of contrast, mixture of sensations, after images etc.
   1 Large case for preserving the instruments and materials of the Dept.
   A few drawings illustrating the development of the nervous system and sense organs

---

1. Bessey was Acting Chancellor, University of Nebraska.

2. One of those added was Wundt's journal, *Philosophische Studien*, which began publication in 1881.

3. This was a device for measuring time, probably to one thousandth of a second, and was a standard piece of apparatus for the early psychology laboratories.

4. The drop apparatus was probably an acoumeter, a device that produced sounds of differing intensity by dropping a metal ball from different heights onto a glass plate.

Attention may be called to the fact that this dept. has received *no* "Equipment fund." $217.50 "Library fund" and $100.00 "Dept. fund" have been granted.

II. The work of this Dept. ought to be chiefly scientific, but lack of equipment has compelled me to make it largely literary. A mixed system of recitation and informal lectures has been followed. The stimulation of curiosity rather than its satisfaction has been my aim. . . .

IV. The isolation of the department and the reputed difficulty of its subjects make it impossible to insist on organic development. I have in mind the following lines for extension.

(a) Two years of Psychology as *science* (Clark University, the Universities of Penn, Wis & Ind place this subject alongside the *other nat. sciences*) . . . .

I hope the scientific nature of this dept. may be recognized in the next apportionment of funds. We *need* a tone instrument, a time-sense instrument, a number of cheaper instruments . . . and *an additional room.*

H. K. Wolfe to the Regents of the University [of Nebraska], May 29, 1891

I offer the following report of the department of Philosophy for the academic year 1890–'91.

I. *Improvements* during the year

In the fall term an effort was made to begin the work in Experimental Psychology; though the lack of equipment prevented the rise of sanguine expectations. First of all a laboratory room was necessary. After consulting with one of the Regents I decided to use a part of the Library Fund of my department for fitting up an unoccupied room in the basement, and if necessary to replace the loan from the department fund of the following year. In my opinion the success of the dept. depended on the introduction of experimental work this year. About $80.00 was used in fitting up a laboratory. Most of the apparatus added during the year was made by the University mechanic, by students, or by the professor.

II. *Nature of the Work of the Department* during the year . . .
    (b) Laboratory work may be roughly grouped as follows;
(1) Measurement of simplest mental phenomena, as the
Least Observable Difference in sensations. (2)
Determination of the relation between stimulus and
sensation. (3) Testing Weber's Law. (4) Determination of
the area of extent of consciousness for simple ideas. (5)
Sense of Time. (6) Time occupied by simple mental
processes.

    Even with our crude apparatus some of the results are
very interesting and with supplementary experiments for
verification have sufficient value to warrant publication.
With some addition to our equipment these laboratory
experiments ought to offer enough new material each year
for at least one monograph worthy of publication. This,
however, would be merely incidental to the repetition of
the better known experiments in Psychophysics as scientific
discipline and as an introduction to the study of mind. . . .

IV. Plans for the future, including estimate of necessary
expenses.

    I cannot emphasize too strongly the necessity of
providing some facilities for experimental work. . . . It is
possible to build up an experimental dept. in Psychology
with little outlay. No field of scientific research offers such
excellent opportunities for original work; chiefly because
the *soil is new.* If it is not deemed advisable to encourage
original research in this line, $500.00 will provide sufficient
equipment for illustrating the most common phenomena of
our elementary course. I think this sum would enable me to
furnish work for two hours per week during the entire year.[5]

---

5. Wolfe was trying to add a two-hour per week laboratory component to the beginning course
    in psychology. Notice his use of the agricultural metaphor, something he uses in other
    letters as well. As a Land Grant college, agriculture played a significant role at the Uni-
    versity of Nebraska.

H. K. Wolfe to the Regents of the University [of Nebraska], May ?, 1891[6]

The Department of Philosophy now possesses sufficient equipment for such work as has been heretofore required. It is believed, however, that opportunity is now afforded for greatly increasing its usefulness at comparatively small expense. . . .

The scientific nature of Psychology is not so generally recognized; hence I feel justified in calling attention to two points. 1st The advantages offered by experimental Psychology, as a discipline in scientific methods, are not inferior to those offered by other experimental sciences. The measurement of the Quality, Quantity and Time Relations of mental states is as inspiring and as good discipline as the determination of, say the per cent of sugar in a beet or the variation of an electric current. The *exact* determination of *mental processes* ought to be as good *mental* discipline as the exact determination of processes taking place in matter.

2nd The study of mind is the most universally *applied* of all sciences. Because we learn so much about it from everyday experience is the reason, perhaps, that it only recently has become an "exact" science. Whatever is known of mind is especially valuable in professional life, and particularly so in that profession whose object is the *training* of mind. The science of teaching depends immediately upon the results of psychological investigation. The progressive teacher must know, not only these results and the "methods" based thereon, but also how to investigate for himself.

On the recommendation of the Faculty you have adopted an Elective Course in Pedagogics based on the study of Mind. The importance of that Course itself would justify the equipment asked for. I do not think, however, that only those expecting to teach would elect work in experimental Psychology. On the contrary there is a natural demand for such work by students of philosophical tendencies.

---

6. Likely this letter was encouraged by Chancellor Bessey who wanted Wolfe to give the Regents extra justification for his equipment requests. The reference to sugar in a beet was not just another agricultural metaphor. The University was one of several funded by the U.S. Government trying to develop an American sugar beet that would reduce American sugar imports. Consequently, the Chemistry Department at the University was very well supported.

On the whole I think it is probable that a course in experimental Psychology would be elected by as many non-professionals as elect work in some of the other departments of science.

With the following apparatus and with such books as the Library Fund will enable me to procure, I shall be able to offer a two years course in Psychology and to inaugurate the elective course in Pedagogics based thereon. [*Note: the remainder of the letter is a two-page listing of needed equipment with prices totalling $1818.00.*][7]

H. K. Wolfe to the Chancellor and Board of Regents of the University [of Nebraska], March 17, 1895

The relative growth of the department of Philosophy during the past three years has been even greater than that of the University. It is now impossible to carry the work in a manner at all creditable to the professor in charge. The demand has been created and we are not able to satisfy it as becomes a University. . . .

The equipment of psychological departments has not thus far depended upon the total revenue of the Universities. Harvard had no laboratory until ours was commenced. Indiana University with half our income has as good a laboratory as we have, while Michigan with twice our income has not half as good a beginning, though Wisconsin has made a better start than we have. The growth of the laboratory has depended upon the success of its application to the work in hand. Ours was the fifth to begin (in this country) and is not far from fifth in material equipment, while only one laboratory is helping more students. . . .

The chancellor has announced that for the next year, at least, we must be content to be a *teaching* university. I agree with him in this and with the sentiment back of it—that we must always be chiefly a teaching school. In so far as that principle *is recognized* facilities will be afforded departments in proportion of their teaching needs. . . .

7. Wolfe's class enrollments were growing at this time at a rate more than double the University's growth and in the summer of 1891 he was promoted to the rank of Professor. However, he received no equipment fund. He kept the laboratory functioning by building most of the necessary equipment himself. He also borrowed some equipment from the departments of Biology (microscopes, thermometers, and embryological specimens) and Physics (tuning forks, resonators, electric motors, magnets, and batteries). He bought some items using his own money and then overspent his departmental budget. Even without the funds, he added the two-hour laboratory to the beginning course and continued the lab for the experimental course, both of which were two-semester courses.

I know it will be impossible to furnish equipment for a second year in psychology or for special work by advanced students, though there is already demand for both. . . But I do confidently expect that means will be furnished to make my own work as effective as possible in the lines already opened.

The following items are believed to be necessary to maintain the work of philosophy at its present standard.

1. Student assistance $700.00
2. Mechanical assistance (wood & metal work)   200.00
3. Additional Equipment   500.00
4. Incidental (or current) Expenses   250.00
5. Repairs on basement rooms   65.00
6. Books, periodicals, etc.   350.00

In regard to the third item I wish to say that the lack of equipment this year has been largely made up by additional time and energy on the part of the professor, and that cannot possibly be continued another year even by working all day Sundays.[8]

H. K. Wolfe in the Psychological Review (1895)[9]

It ought to be unnecessary to describe the effects on the student of a laboratory course in psychology, and yet, like chemistry and physics and biology and zoology, this new science will have to fight for every inch of ground. . . .

A valid objection [to the psychology laboratory] is . . . the time required for this work. Better supervision is required than for laboratory work in either chemistry or physics. This demands personal attention from the instructor in psychology. I think this objection is unanswerable. If instructors in psychology are unwilling to do this kind of work, we must wait until another species of instructor can be evolved. . . .

8. This report is undoubtedly the most negative filed by Wolfe. In part it reflects a broken promise of a $1200 equipment fund from the administration in the spring of 1894. When the budget situation worsened the promised funds were withdrawn. No equipment funds were forthcoming from this request either.

9. Unable to convince the local authorities, Wolfe made his arguments public in a journal article entitled "The New Psychology in Undergraduate Work" (Wolfe, 1895). One of the arguments against funding his laboratory was that it was for undergraduate students, and there were many in psychology and other fields who believed that psychology laboratory instruction should be reserved exclusively for graduate students (see French, 1898).

Logic and metaphysics and the dictionary may be well taught without a laboratory; physiological and experimental psychology require some *things* to see and *feel*. . . .

The junior . . . comes to psychology with more or less information concerning isolated facts of several sciences. [In a] general course of physiological and experimental psychology with laboratory practice . . . the needed facts of the associated sciences will be brought together; their relations will become clear, and gradually there will grow up a rational appreciation of the interdependence of the forces of nature.

Editor's Note: *In 1897 the University of Nebraska had a new chancellor, George MacLean, who objected to Wolfe's habit of overspending his budget. He asked Wolfe to provide a written explanation of a budget deficit of $75.86.*

H. K. Wolfe to G. MacLean, March 24, 1897

. . . I do not consider these expenses as a "deficit" even in the technical use of the term. I am personally responsible for them and if the University doesn't wish to buy the articles from me when it is able to do so I shall preserve the remains as "heirlooms" in my family treasure house.

. . . As long as I work thirty five hours (35) per week with my students I shall provide any needed inexpensive article for my work without reference to the condition of my departmental fund.[10]

Epilogue

No doubt Wolfe's attitude about overspending his budget irritated MacLean who fired him at the end of 1897. More than 1,000 of the University's 1,600 students signed a petition calling for Wolfe's reinstatement, but the Regents upheld the firing.

Wolfe was replaced by Thaddeus L. Bolton, who had earned his doctorate with G. Stanley Hall. Bolton, too, was a strong advocate of the laboratory and for awhile it seemed that he might be more

---

10. The 35 hours to which Wolfe referred were his actual class and lab contact hours each week. That represented far more contact hours than was typical of the other professors. He received no teaching credit for the laboratory hours he added to his courses. Perhaps more amazing was that the students received no credit for the extra laboratory hours either. Yet enrollments in those courses continued to mushroom.

successful than Wolfe. He managed to get a commitment from the administration for seven laboratory rooms in the new physics building scheduled for completion in 1905. He proudly described his laboratory-to-be in a 1904 article in *Science* magazine. However, a few months before the building opened, the rooms were assigned to the Physics Department, and Bolton was left in his old space in the basement of the library.

After working for eight years as a school superintendent and high school principal, Wolfe was rehired at the University in 1906, and he continued his requests for laboratory support. Mostly they were ignored although he did get some minimal equipment funds, and funds for several student assistants for the laboratory. Finally, in 1916, the University announced it would build a new social sciences building. Wolfe was told to design the psychology laboratories for that building, which he did. It was his last contribution because he died in the summer of 1918 at the age of 59. His dream laboratory opened approximately 18 months later.

Psychology Laboratory Bibliography

Benjamin, L. T., Jr. (1991). *Harry Kirke Wolfe: Pioneer in Psychology.* Lincoln: University of Nebraska Press.
>   This biography describes the life of one of the earliest American psychologists and arguably the most inspirational psychology teacher of his generation.

Billia, L. M. (1909, July). Has the psychological laboratory proved helpful? *Monist*, pp. 351–366.
>   Offers a mixed view of the accomplishments of more than 25 years of the new psychology.

Bruce, R. V. (1987). *The Launching of Modern American Science, 1846–1876.* New York: Cornell University Press.
>   Traces the development of science laboratories in America in the natural sciences and their impact on the course of higher education.

Capshew, J. H. (1992). Psychologists on site: A reconnaissance of the historiography of the laboratory. *American Psychologist, 47,* 132–142.
>   Discusses the development of historical accounts of American psychology laboratories and includes an extensive bibliography of such published accounts.

Capshew, J. H., & Hearst, E. (1980). Psychology at Indiana University from Bryan to Skinner. *Psychological Record, 30*, 319–342.

A history of the Indiana psychology laboratory, founded in 1887 by William L. Bryan, a student of G. Stanley Hall.

Murray, F. S., & Rowe, F. B. (1979). Psychology laboratories in the United States prior to 1900. *Teaching of Psychology* 6, 19–21.

Brief descriptions of the founding of 44 psychology laboratories.

Raphelson, A. C. (1980). Psychology at Michigan: The Pillsbury years. *Journal of the History of the Behavioral Sciences, 16*, 301–312.

Although Pillsbury did not establish the psychology laboratory at the University of Michigan, his arrival there in 1897 marked a new era in excellence for that department. Pillsbury was one of Wolfe's undergraduate students. This article describes the growth of the Michigan department during Pillsbury's tenure as department head.

Wolfe, H. K. (1895). The new psychology in undergraduate work. *Psychological Review, 2*, 382–387.

Wolfe's rationale for providing psychology laboratory instruction for undergraduate students. See the opposing view as offered by Ferdinand C. French in the same journal (1898, 5, 510–512).

Chapter 6

A Woman's Quest for Graduate Education[1]

Mary Whiton Calkins (1863–1930) was a distinguished psychologist and philosopher of her day. She wrote a number of important books in both fields and was perhaps best known for her system of self-psychology, a belief that "psychology should be conceived as the science of the self, or person, as related to its environment, physical and social" (Calkins, 1930, p. 42).

Calkins' many accomplishments included inventing the paired-associate technique for studying learning and memory, founding the first psychology laboratory at a women's college (Wellesley College in 1891), being the first woman elected to the presidencies of the American Psychological Association (1905) and the American Philosophical Association (1918), and being elected the first honorary woman member of the British Psychological Association (1928).

Calkins was born in Connecticut but grew up in Buffalo, New York where her father was a Congregationalist minister. At the age of 19, she enrolled at Smith College where she studied the classics, especially Greek and philosophy. After graduation in 1885 she spent a year in Europe studying languages. Shortly after her return to the United States, she accepted a position at Wellesley College as a tutor in Greek.

Because of her interest in philosophy and her skills as a teacher, a colleague in the Department of Mental Philosophy suggested Calkins consider a new faculty position for someone to teach psychology. At first Calkins showed little interest; however, her colleague convinced

---

1. This chapter was written with considerable assistance from Laurel Furumoto, Professor of Psychology at Wellesley College and an outstanding scholar in the history of psychology. See the bibliography at the end of this chapter for a listing of some of her works.

her to change her mind, and the idea was presented to the president of the college who agreed and offered Calkins the position contingent upon her studying the new subject for a year (Furumoto, 1990).

In late 1888 and early 1889, Calkins sought advice from several of her former professors at Smith College: Mary Augusta Jordan, a professor of English; Harry Norman Gardiner, a professor of philosophy; and especially Charles Edward Garman, a visiting professor of philosophy (from Amherst College) who had exerted a powerful influence on her in the one course she had taken from him. Calkins asked them if they thought she needed additional study in psychology or if they thought she could satisfactorily teach the course without such work. Jordan felt she could teach without any additional formal study; Garman was less certain in his answer. By June of 1889, Calkins had decided to remain in her current teaching field, but did not close the door on the psychology opportunity.

In February of 1890, Calkins accepted the position of Instructor in Psychology at Wellesley and began to make plans for a year of graduate study in the field. She hoped she might study psychology with Garman, but he was forced to decline due to poor health. For awhile she considered going to Germany for study but she learned that many universities there would not admit women students to their degree programs. She was aware of the recent emergence of a new scientific psychology (often called "physiological psychology"), which contrasted with the old psychology of mental and moral philosophy, and she was interested in obtaining some of her training in this new field. Therefore she sought a graduate program that could offer her laboratory training in the new psychology.

In May of 1890, Calkins wrote to two professors at nearby Harvard University: William James and Josiah Royce. Both expressed interest in having her as a student but were unable to invite her because of rules against coeducation at Harvard. That decision was later reversed, and she was allowed to attend classes but could not be officially recognized as a student.

One of the first courses Calkins took was James's seminar on psychology, a class with four men. Shortly all the men dropped the course, perhaps because of the presence of a woman. In recalling this experience Calkins (1930) wrote:

> Most unhappily for them and most fortunately for me the other members of his [James's] seminary in psychology dropped away in the early weeks of the fall of 1890; and James and I were left . . .

*at either side of a library fire. The Principles of Psychology was
warm from the press; and my absorbed study of those brilliant, erudite, and provocative volumes, as interpreted by their writer, was
my introduction to psychology. What I gained from the written
page, and even more from the tete-a-tete discussion was, it seems
to me as I look back on it, beyond all else, a vivid sense of the
concreteness of psychology and of the immediate reality of "finite
individual minds" with their "thoughts and feelings." (p. 31)*

Could any student in the history of psychology have been afforded a
greater opportunity for learning?!

After a year of study with James and Royce at Harvard and with
Edmund C. Sanford at Clark University in Worcester, Massachusetts,
Calkins returned to Wellesley where she began her laboratory (with
considerable help from Sanford) and her instruction in psychology.
But after only a semester at Wellesley she began to think about further study and wrote to her psychology professors for advice. Sanford
recommended study in Europe, and mentioned that Hugo Münsterberg
(who had received his doctorate from Wundt at Leipzig) had admitted
a woman to his psychology program at the University of Freiberg in
Germany. Calkins also considered going to Cornell University where
Frank Angell, another of Wundt's doctoral graduates, had established
a new psychology laboratory. James encouraged her to delay her decision as long as possible and soon his reason became apparent: Münsterberg accepted a position at Harvard in the fall of 1892 to direct
the psychology laboratory.

Calkins applied to Harvard to study with Münsterberg, and he
strongly supported her application. Again, she was allowed to take
courses but only as a "guest;" she was not to be officially registered.
For the next three years she studied with Münsterberg, mostly on a
part-time basis while she continued her duties at Wellesley. In one of
those years, however, when she was on-leave from her college, she
worked full time in his laboratory.

In 1895 Calkins asked the Philosophy Department to give her a
doctoral examination, albeit an unofficial one. Her examining committee consisted of James, Royce, Münsterberg, and George Santayana, and others. On behalf of the committee, Royce reported to the
Harvard Corporation that the committee voted unanimously to pass
Calkins and that her performance demonstrated a scholarship that was
"exceptionally high." Thus she had completed all of the requirements
for a doctoral degree at Harvard and had the enthusiastic support of

her professors. But of course she would not be granted a doctoral degree, because she was never an official student. She was later offered a doctoral degree from Radcliffe College, Harvard's college for women. However, she refused to accept it, arguing that she had done her work at Harvard and the only appropriate degree for her was one from Harvard.

Calkins wrote that she never felt the lack of the doctoral degree hindered her in any significant way, although its absence was sometimes an "inconvenience." She certainly went on to enjoy a life of considerable scholarly accomplishment. Her story reveals some of the barriers to women of her time in pursuing graduate education. No doubt her scholarly success and her persistence helped to break down some of those barriers.

The letters in this chapter tell part of the story of Calkins' struggle. The majority are part of the Calkins Papers, which are part of the Wellesley College Archives.

Mary Augusta Jordan to Calkins, December 18, 1888

My opinion is most gladly at your disposal in the matter of your possibly teaching psychology. It seems to me that you are remarkably adapted to such work and that in the department of Philosophy in general you are sure to do your best work ever. . . . Special preparation may well afford to wait. Personally I may say that I have come in contact with few minds among women that I would as gladly see devoted to hard work as yours. . . . No class would suffer at your hands and I believe that in a few years classes would get from you what they comparatively seldom do get from teachers here—original work and a spur to original work. . . .

Calkins to Charles Garman, January 1, 1889

Do you think it right, under any circumstances for a person to undertake to teach psychology without a thorough and long preparation especially for the work?

. . . Since my senior year (1885) in Smith College, when I studied psychology under your guidance, I have not done any psychological or philosophical *study;* I have read a little in these subjects and constantly increased my interest in them. This year and last I have been teaching Greek at Wellesley and the further study of Plato has led, as it needs must, to serious thought on philosophic questions. . . .

Do you think it possible—admitting an antecedent enthusiasm for the subject that anyone with such insufficient preparation can properly teach a class?

Garman to Calkins, April 27, 1889

I remember with much pleasure the interest with which you took up the study of Psychology in the fall of 1884 and I also have distinctly in mind the success with which you dealt with the most difficult problems. It does not seem to me that you have any reason for hesitation on this question so far as your natural qualifications for teaching this study are concerned. I feel that you would be eminently successful. Now as to the particular question that you desire me to answer viz. as to the wisdom of taking the place in your college without a more extended preparation than you have already had. This is a question I do not feel able to answer. There must be considered the temper and habits of the classes. . . .

My judgment on the whole is that you had better take the risks and accept the position should it be offered to you in June. You will have all summer to study psychology and if you will not be too ambitious the first year or two and be content to take the classes over no more ground than you are familiar with, you will by that time be in a position to branch out.

Calkins to Garman, June 1, 1889

. . . but I have not wholly surrendered the hope that I may sometime be able to study and to teach psychology. Your helpful and discriminating counsel has been of utmost value to me and I shall keep your letter, with the words which I gathered up from lectures and discussions, as my guides, if ever I do enter this path.

Calkins to Garman, February 22, 1890

I am venturing now to trouble you with some questions about my study. I myself have positively decided on two points only: first, that, of all things, I wish and need to study with you; second, that some part of my work must be in the line of physiological psychology. I feel myself very presumptuous in asking whether it will be possible for you, in any measure, to direct my work. I owe to you so much of my interest in psychology, my understanding of the subject, any apprehension of its relation to the great life problems, that your personal help seems to me almost necessary, if I am to enter on work of such importance.

Harry Norman Gardiner to Calkins, May 1890

I do not know at all how to advise you or help you about your suggestion of study in Germany. Of two things only I am clear, first that you will be able to prosecute your studies to greater advantage if you have the direct inspiration of a teacher even though he may be able to teach you little or nothing, and secondly that Germany is a good place to study, if only you can find the teacher you want there. Whether you could have the privilege of attending lectures or obtaining private instruction in Psychology and Philosophy at any of the German universities . . . I do not know.

William James to Calkins, May 24, 1890

The President [Charles Eliot] writes that he "sees no way to do anything for you not even in Philosophy 20 a" [James's seminar].

It seems very hard. But he has to keep guard all along the line, and I suppose that laxity would soon produce an involuntary and unintended occupation of a great many of these higher courses by women. . . .

I can only say now that if you do come to Cambridge, I shall be most happy to help you over difficulties and give you some advice. Had I double my present strength, I should also enjoy giving you some instruction free of all duties and taxes, but I don't dare to propose any such thing, with as much work as I have, and so little ability to do it.

Believe in my sincere regret for this action of our authorities. Can't you get to Worcester almost as easily as to Cambridge? Stanley Hall's Psychological department ought to be the best in the world.

Josiah Royce to Calkins, May 27, 1890

I understand that the President [Eliot] is unwilling to have the arrangement made for your attendance of Phil 20a & b [Royce's course]. Prof. James will probably have notified you of this fact already. I need not add that I regard this official view as one of the mysteries into which no one may hope to penetrate who is not himself accustomed to the executive point of outlook. I suppose that you will understand my regret in the case for I had sincerely hoped that we could be of service to you, and I am still anxious to offer you all the aid in my power. This at any rate I may still suggest, that in case you appear in the annex[2] next year, it will cause me no small pleasure to give you such time as I can for advice in the pursuit of advanced work, to direct in a measure your reading, should you desire such aid, and to read a thesis or two of yours should you prepare such papers. . . . I need not point out that my present offer would be quite independent of official approval, which I would not need to ask.

William James to Calkins, May 29, 1890

I have been attacking the President again on the subject you know of. He tells me that the overseers are so sensitive on the subject that he dares take no liberties. He received such a "tremendous wigging" from them a few years ago for winking at just this thing, that he is forced now to be strict. They are at present in hot water about it at the medical school he himself being for the admission of women. I think that in justice to him you should know these facts.

Editor's Note: *On July 1, 1890 Wolcott Calkins sent a letter to the Harvard Corporation, the overseers, to ask that his daughter be admitted for study in Philosophy 20a and 20b. The letter was accompanied by another letter from the president of Wellesley College indicating the importance of the study at Harvard for the new subject Calkins was to teach at Wellesley. They argued that this case was special because it involved postgraduate education for someone who was already a college faculty member. Likely Calkins notified James and Royce of the appeal to the Harvard Corporation, which prompted the next two letters.*

Josiah Royce to Calkins, July 21, 1890

I am glad to know that you will be with us next year, and I shall be glad to aid in the opening to you of Phil 20, as well as in

---

2. The Harvard Annex was where Harvard professors offered classes to women students for extra money; however, the courses did not carry official Harvard credit.

the ways that I previously promised. If we do not succeed as to Phil 20, there is still, I hope, much that can be done for you.

William James to Calkins, July 30, 1890

I am heartily glad to hear what you say about the Corporation etc. It is flagitious that you should be kept out. Enough to make dynamiters of you and all women. I hope and trust that your application will break the barrier. I will do what I can.

Editor's Note: *The Corporation authorized James and Royce to allow Calkins in their classes during the coming year but it was to be understood that "by accepting this privilege Miss Calkins does not become a student of the University entitled to registration." (Corporation Records, October 1, 1890, Harvard University Archives)*

William James to Calkins, October 3, 1890

I was about to write you today anyhow to express my gladness. My students 4 in number seem of divergent tendencies and I don't know just what will come of the course. Having published my two rather fat tomes [the two volumes of his *Principles of Psychology*], I shan't lecture, but the thing will probably resolve itself into advice and possibly some experimentation. Our evening meetings have been provisionally fixed for Thursdays at 7:15. Will you please come if you can, next Thursday at seven so as to have a little talk in advance, or rather come at 1/2 past six and take tea.

William James to Calkins, August 12, 1891

. . . Your thesis [on the association of ideas] has been waiting for me all this time. I hope you don't need it before October. I can't *look* at anything psychological for a fortnight.[3] Then I shall *devour* it.

William James to Calkins, November 6, 1891

I read your thesis at last, a week ago, and have just found a moment in which to drop you a line about it. . . .

---

3. William James's desire to avoid anything psychological was no doubt due to the fact that he was spending much of his time condensing his two-volume *Principles* into what would become known as *Psychology: A Briefer Course* (1892).

The thesis has given me exquisite delight. The middle portion, with its classification and criticism gives the subject a real hitch ahead, and is luminous. It certainly ought to go to Schurman's Journal of Philosophy, and if you are too modest I will "introduce" it to him.

William James to Calkins, December 20, 1891

I have just written to Schurman, in a way that will ensure his attention. I had already done so without saying who you were.

Edmund C. Sanford to Calkins, February 16, 1892

Assuming then that you are going to study next year, should it be Cornell or Europe? I say Europe? Why? Because 1. a European PhD will do you more good I believe than an American one . . . 2. Because I doubt the kind of course you would get at Cornell, because the psychological dept there is newly organized. . . .

Josiah Royce to Calkins, February 17, 1892

I am disposed to think, from the data furnished in your letter, that you will do well, in case you can get the fellowship at Cornell, to take your next year there, as you seem inclined to do. I think it very obvious that your work will be aided by another year of study taken pretty early, after your experience as a teacher has made you alive to your most significant ideals and consequent needs, and, before you have been teaching long enough to get tolerant as a teacher is so likely to do, of the incompleteness of which at first your work makes you aware. . . .

Edmund C. Sanford to Calkins, June 25, 1892

. . . I spoke in a guarded way and without names to Dr. Scripture[4] about the chance for lady students at Yale. He . . . wrote: "I am willing to offer special advantages for the sake of having women graduate students at the start. I am quite willing to give them the same lecture and demonstration course as the undergraduates (undergraduate courses are not open you know generally) or with even greater fullness on the day before the

---

4. Edward Wheeler Scripture received his doctorate in psychology in 1891 from Wundt and established the Yale laboratory in 1892.

undergraduate lectures or on the morning before them. . . . This I am willing to do whether women are admitted to the course (undergraduate) in physiological psychology or not. I think, however, there will be no objection in case they wish to attend with the class. . . ." Please let me know when you finally make up your mind, for in the mean time (wh[ich] please do not mention) I want to use the fact that you would like to take a degree for moral effect here [Clark University].

I fear that it is for the present quite a hopeless thing to think of but I should like to have Clark give you a chance though at the same time I do not know whether it would not be pedagogically well for you to go elsewhere. You know what we are like here. . . .

Editor's Note: A decade later, long after completing her doctoral work at Harvard, Calkins wrote the following letter when she was offered a Ph.D. degree from Radcliffe.

Calkins to Agnes Irwin [Dean of Radcliffe College], May 30, 1902

I have seldom received so just, discriminating and kind a letter as yours of May 19. . . . and I am sorrier than I can tell you not to reply to it in the way which would best please you. I hope that I may make quite clear to you my reasons for declining to accept the honor of the Radcliffe doctor's degree. I . . . think it highly probable that the Radcliffe degree will be regarded, generally, as the practical equivalent of the Harvard degree and, . . . I should be glad to hold the Ph.D. degree for I occasionally find the lack of it an inconvenience; and now that the Radcliffe Ph.D. is offered, I doubt whether the Harvard degree will ever be open to women. On the other hand, I still believe that the best ideals of education would be better served if Radcliffe College refused to confer the doctor's degree. You will be quick to see that, holding this conviction, I cannot rightly take the easier course of accepting the degree. . . .

Mary Whiton Calkins Bibliography

Calkins, M. W. (1892). A suggested classification of cases of association. *Philosophical Review, 1,* 389–402.

    This is the thesis that so impressed James (see his letters of August 12 and November 6, 1891).

Calkins, M. W. (1892). Experimental psychology at Wellesley College. *American Journal of Psychology, 5,* 260–271.

    A detailed description of the experimental psychology course and laboratory that Calkins began at Wellesley.

Calkins, M. W. (1896). Association: An essay analytic and experimental. *Psychological Review Monograph Supplement Number 2,* pp. 1–56.

    This classic article describes the series of experiments that originated the paired-associate technique, which would become a major tool for studying learning and memory in the 20th century.

Calkins, M. W. (1901). *An Introduction to Psychology.* New York: Macmillan; (1909). *A First Book in Psychology.* New York: Macmillan.

    Calkins' two textbooks on psychology, which are the most complete statements of her self-psychology.

Calkins, M. W. (1930). Autobiography. In C. Murchison (Ed.), *A History of Psychology in Autobiography: Volume 1,* pp. 31–62. Worcester, MA: Clark University Press.

    Written shortly before her death, the first ten pages of this chapter are autobiographical. In the remainder Calkins devotes herself, "first, to setting forth and, secondly, to arguing for the essentials of a personalistic psychology." (p. 41)

Furumoto, L. (1990). Mary Whiton Calkins (1863–1930). In A. N. O'Connell & N. F. Russo (Eds.), *Women in Psychology: A Bio-Bibliographic Sourcebook,* pp. 57–65. New York: Greenwood Press.

    An excellent and very complete, albeit brief, treatment of Calkins' life and career. Includes a bibliography of many of Calkins' publications.

Madigan, S., & O'Hara, R. (1992). Short term memory at the turn of the century: Mary Whiton Calkins' memory research. *American Psychologist, 47,* 170–174.

    A discussion of Calkins' research on short term memory, focusing on its anticipation of contemporary work in the field. The contributions described are substantial.

Scarborough, E., & Furumoto, L. (1987). *Untold Lives: The First Generation of American Women Psychologists*. New York: Columbia University Press.
Chapter 1 deals with Calkins' quest for graduate education in psychology. This outstanding book describes the problems faced by the early women psychologists: access to graduate education, claims from family (e.g., elderly and infirm parents), marriage vs. career, evaluation of scholarly worth independent of gender, and exclusion from academic networks limited solely to men.

Chapter 7

William James and
Psychical Research

William James (1842–1910) is arguably the greatest of all figures in the history of American psychology. That reputation results, in part, from his classic book, *The Principles of Psychology* (1890), a two-volume work that set the stage for an American functional psychology. Through James's incomparable prose, the *Principles* recruited a generation of researchers to share in James's enormous promise for the new science of psychology.

James's contributions to the science of psychology were acknowledged by his peers in many ways, including his election to the National Academy of Sciences and to the presidency (twice) of the American Psychological Association. Yet a few years after the publication of the *Principles*, some of America's most prominent psychologists (e.g., James McKeen Cattell, Edward Bradford Titchener, Hugo Münsterberg) were openly concerned that James was becoming a liability for scientific psychology. That concern grew from James's identification with psychical research—particularly investigations of mediums and their abilities to communicate with spirits of the dead.

James had actually expressed interest in psychic phenomena as early as 1869 when he was only 27-years-old. However, he did not become seriously interested in the field until a trip to London in 1882–1883 exposed him to the newly established Society for Psychical Research (SPR). In that trip he met Henry Sidgwick (then president of the SPR), Frederic Myers, and Edmund Gurney, all of whom would figure prominently in James's growing interest in the topic.

In 1884, James joined the British SPR and also became a supporter of the American SPR, which was founded in Boston that same year. The following year, James met Mrs. Leonore Piper (1859–1950), a Boston medium who had already impressed some members of James's family with her abilities in contacting the spirit world. James then became seriously involved in the field, conducting a prolonged investigation of Mrs. Piper through participation in a number of seances. He reported on that work in 1886 to the American SPR and had his novelist brother, Henry, read a further report to the British SPR in 1890.

James became an active promoter of the progress of both the British and American SPRs. For the former, he was a vice-president for 18 years and served two terms as president (1894–1896). He also was a frequent contributor to the *Proceedings* of both groups, writing on such topics as clairvoyance, automatic writing, and mediumistic phenomena, such as trance, materialization, and sensory occurrences. Some of his articles were also published in popular magazines (e.g., *Scribner's*), and in these accounts he often attacked scientific psychology for its unwillingness to pursue research on psychic phenomena or at least to keep an open mind about such occurrences.

James's colleagues counterattacked him in a series of letters in Cattell's journal, *Science*, with James joining in the debate. The new psychology, which had only recently declared its independence from philosophy and which sought to improve its standing among the sciences (see Coon, 1992; Moore, 1977), was naturally concerned about James's work, which was seen as taking psychology back to the mysticism and metaphysics of its past. Some of the attacks were quite pointed and voices on both sides of the controversy expressed bitterness in their exchanges. Yet none of the criticism deterred James, who persisted in psychical research until his death.

Interests in psychic phenomena were not a sideline of James's intellectual work. Indeed, as Perry (1935) has noted, such ideas were central to his philosophy, and "from his youth James contemplated such 'phenomena' without repulsion and with an open mind" (p. 204). His final published statement on psychical research came in October, 1909, only 10 months before his death. In this *American Magazine* article he concluded his 25 years of work arguing that psychic phenomena were elusive but real, and investigatable with the methods of science. He predicted that psychical research would provide "the greatest scientific conquests of the coming generation" (James, 1909, p. 589). On that account, James was monumentally wrong.

James is often portrayed today as a figure who embraced psychology early in his life only to abandon it after 1890 for a preference for philosophy and mysticism. Certainly James said some disparaging things about science, including the new scientific psychology. Yet, although he lost faith in the promise of experimental psychology as his colleagues were practicing it, he never abandoned his belief in the scientific method and continued his version of science in his psychic investigations, despite its rejection by experimental psychology. The letters in this chapter reveal something of this important area of James's life and career, a story that is often omitted from the contemporary histories of scientific psychology.

James to Thomas Davidson, February 1, 1885[1]

As for any "anti-spiritual bias" of our Society, no theoretic basis, or *bias* of any sort whatever, so far as I can make out, exists in it. The one thing that has struck me all along in the men who have had to do with it is their complete colorlessness philosophically. They seem to have no preferences for any general *ism* whatever. I doubt if this could be matched in Europe. Anyhow, it would make no difference in the important work to be done, what theoretic bias the members had. For I take it the urgent thing, to rescue us from the present disgraceful condition, is to ascertain in a manner so thorough as to constitute *evidence* that will be accepted by outsiders, just what the *phenomenal conditions of certain* concrete phenomenal occurrences are. Not till that is done can spiritualistic or anti-spiritualistic theories be even mooted. I'm sure that the more we can steer clear of theories at first, the better.

James to Shadworth Hodgson, August 16, 1885[2]

We have been stirred up by the English Society for Psychical Research's example, to start a similar society here, in which I am somewhat interested, though less practically than I could wish. Returns come slowly—I mean stuff to inquire into comes slowly; and altogether my small experience has filled me with a prodigious admiration of the devotion and energy of Gurney, Myers, and others with you. Something solid will come of it all, I am sure.

---

1. This letter was prompted by a complaint from Davidson that the American Society for Psychical Research had an "anti-spiritual bias."
2. Hodgson was an English philosopher who was greatly admired by James.

James to Carl Stumpf, January 1, 1886[3]

I don't know whether you have heard of the London "Society for Psychical Research," which is seriously and laboriously investigating all sorts of "supernatural" matters, clairvoyance, apparitions, etc. I don't know what you think of such work; but I think that the present condition of opinion regarding it is scandalous, there being a mass of testimony, or apparent testimony, about such things, at which the only men capable of a critical judgment—men of scientific education—will not even look. We have founded a similar society here within the year—some of us thought that the publications of the London society deserved at least to be treated as if worthy of experimental disproof—and although work advances very slowly owing to the small amount of disposable time on the part of the members, who are all very busy men, we have already stumbled on some rather inexplicable facts out of which something may come. It is a field in which the sources of deception are extremely numerous. But I believe there is no source of deception in the investigation of nature which can compare with a fixed belief that certain kinds of phenomenon are *impossible*.

James to George Croom Robertson, October 4, 1886[4]

I mailed you t'other day Part II of the *Proceedings* of the American Society for Psychical Research, a rather sorry "exhibit," from the "President's" address down. There is no one in the Society who can give any time to it, and I suspect it will die by the new year.

James to Christine Ladd-Franklin, April 12, 1888[5]

Your letter interests me very much, because the account you give is similar to accounts which I have heard from others of the influence upon them of the hand of a certain Mrs. Wetherbee who is a "magnetic healer" here, and who, on members of my

---

3. Carl Stumpf (1848–1936) headed the psychology laboratory at the University of Berlin and is best known for his work on the psychology of tone. James had met Stumpf on an earlier trip to Europe.

4. Robertson was a professor of mental philosophy and logic at University College, London and the initial editor of the journal, *Mind*. He was among James's closest friends.

5. Ladd-Franklin (1847–1930) was one of the most famous of the first generation of American women psychologists who contributed substantially to the field of color perception.

wife's family, has certainly "charmed away pain" in a most surprising manner. I know Dr. Crockett also, and like him. I have had hitherto only his own accounts of his performances, not knowing any of his patients but one, on whom he failed.

But I am very dubious of the poor little Soc. for Psych. Re. accomplishing much by seeking to "investigate" these things. Of all earthly things, therapeutic effects are the hardest to run to ground, and convince a skeptic of. There will always be a dozen loopholes of escape from any conclusion about therapeutics, and the mind will take which ever one it prefers.

James to Frederic William Henry Myers, December 1890[6]

You asked for a record of my own experiences with Mrs. Piper, to be incorporated in the account of her to be published in your *Proceedings*.

I made Mrs. Piper's acquaintance in the autumn of 1885. My wife's mother, Mrs. Gibbens, had been told of her by a friend, during the previous summer, and never having seen a medium before, had paid her a visit out of curiosity. She returned with the statement that Mrs. P. had given her a long string of names of members of the family, mostly Christian names, together with facts about the persons mentioned and their relations to each other, the knowledge of which on her part was incomprehensible without supernormal powers. My sister-in-law went the next day, with still better results, as she related them. Amongst other things, the medium had accurately described the circumstances of the writer of a letter which she held against her forehead, after Miss G. had given it to her. The letter was in Italian, and its writer was known to but two persons in this country. . . .

I remember playing the *espirit fort* on that occasion before my feminine relatives, and seeking to explain by simple considerations the marvelous character of the facts which they brought back. This did not, however, prevent me from going myself a few days later, in company with my wife, to get a direct personal impression. The names of none of us up to this meeting had been announced to Mrs. P., and Mrs. J. and I were, of course, careful to make no reference to our relatives who had preceded. The

---

6. Myers (1843–1901) was a philosopher, founding member of the British SPR, and a close friend of James.

medium, however, when entranced, repeated most of the names of "spirits" whom she had announced on the two former occasions and added others. The names came with difficulty, and were only gradually made perfect. My wife's father's name of Gibbens was announced first as Niblin, then as Giblin. A child Herman (whom we had lost the previous year) had his name spelled out as Herrin. I think that in no case were both Christian and surnames given on this visit. But the *facts predicated* of the persons named made it in many instances impossible not to recognize the particular individuals who were talked about. We took particular pains on this occasion to give the Phinuit[7] control no help over his difficulties and to ask no leading questions. In the light of subsequent experience I believe this not to be the best policy. For it often happens, if you give this trance personage a name or some small fact for the lack of which he is brought to a standstill, that he will then start off with a copious flow of additional talk, containing in itself an abundance of "tests."

My impression after this first visit was that Mrs. P. was either possessed of supernormal powers, or knew the members of my wife's family by sight and had by some lucky coincidence become acquainted with such a multitude of their domestic circumstances as to produce the startling impression which she did. My later knowledge of her sittings and personal acquaintance with her has led me absolutely to reject the latter explanation, and to believe that she has supernormal powers.

I visited her a dozen times that winter, sometimes alone, sometimes with my wife, once in company with the Rev. M. J. Savage. I sent a large number of persons to her, wishing to get the results of as many *first* sittings as possible. I made appointments myself for most of these people, whose names were in no instance announced to the medium. In the spring of 1886 I published a brief "Report of the Committee on Mediumistic Phenomena" in the *Proceedings* of the American Society for Psychical Research.

I dropped my inquiries into Mrs. Piper's mediumship for a period of about two years, having satisfied myself that there was a genuine mystery there, but being over-freighted with time-consuming duties, and feeling that any adequate circumnavigation of the phenomena would be too protracted a task for me to aspire

7. Phinuit was Mrs. Piper's control, that is the spirit that communicated through her to the others involved in a seance.

just then to undertake. I saw her once, half accidentally, however, during that interval, and in the spring of 1889 saw her four times again. In the fall of 1889 she paid us a visit of a week at our country house in New Hampshire, and I then learned to know her personally better than ever before, and had confirmed in me the belief that she is an absolutely simple and genuine person. No one, when challenged, can give "evidence" to others for such beliefs as this. Yet we all live by them from day to day, and practically I should be willing now to stake as much money on Mrs. Piper's honesty as on that of anyone I know, and am quite satisfied to leave my reputation for wisdom or folly, so far as human nature is concerned, to stand or fall by this declaration.

As for the explanation of her trance phenomena, I have none to offer. The *prima facie* theory, which is that of spirit-control, is hard to reconcile with the extreme triviality of most of the communications. What real spirit, at last able to revisit his wife on this earth, but would find something better to say than that she had changed the place of his photograph? And yet that is the sort of remark to which the spirits introduced by the mysterious Phinuit are apt to confine themselves. I must admit, however, that Phinuit has other moods. He has several times, when my wife and myself were sitting together with him, suddenly started off on long lectures to us about our inward defects and outward shortcomings, which were very earnest, as well as subtle morally and psychologically, and impressive in a high degree. These discourses, though given in Phinuit's own person, were very different in style from his more usual talk, and probably superior to anything that the medium could produce in the same line in her natural state. Phinuit himself, however, bears every appearance of being a fictitious being. His French, so far as he has been able to display it to me, has been limited to a few phrases of salutation, which may easily have had their rise in the medium's "unconscious" memory; he has never been able to understand *my* French; and the crumbs of information which he gives about his earthly career are, as you know, so few, vague, and unlikely sounding as to suggest the romancing of one whose stock of materials for invention is excessively reduced. He is, however, as he actually shows himself, a definite human individual, with immense tact and patience, and great desire to please and be regarded as infallible. . . .

The most convincing things said about my own immediate household were either very intimate or very trivial. Unfortunately the former things cannot well be published. Of the trivial things, I have forgotten the greater number, but the following, . . . may serve as samples of their class: She said that we had lost recently a rug, and I a waistcoat. (She wrongly accused a person of stealing the rug, which was afterwards found in the house.) She told of my killing a gray-and-white cat, with ether, and described how it had "spun round and round" before dying. She told how my New York aunt had written a letter to my wife, warning her against all mediums, and then went off on a most amusing criticism, full of *traits vifs*, of the excellent woman's character. (Of course no one but my wife and I knew the existence of the letter in question.) She was strong on the events in our nursery, and gave striking advice during our first visit to her about the way to deal with certain "tantrums" of our second child, "little Billy-boy," as she called him, reproducing his nursery name. She told how the crib creaked at night, how a certain rocking chair creaked mysteriously, how my wife had heard footsteps on the stairs, etc., etc. Insignificant as these things sound when read, the accumulation of a large number of them has an irresistible effect. And I repeat again what I said before, that, taking everything that I know of Mrs. P. into account, the result is to make me feel as absolutely certain as I am of any personal fact in the world that she knows things in her trances which she cannot possibly have heard in her waking state, and that the definitive philosophy of her trances is yet to be found. The limitations of her trance information, its discontinuity and fitfulness, and its apparent inability to develop beyond a certain point, although they end by rousing one's moral and human impatience with the phenomenon, yet are, from a scientific point of view, amongst its most interesting peculiarities, since where there are limits there are conditions, and the discovery of these is always the beginning of explanation.

This is all that I can tell you of Mrs. Piper. I wish it were more "scientific." But, *valeat quantum!* it is the best I can do.

James to F. W. H. Myers, January 30, 1891

. . . To speak seriously, however, I agree in what you say, that the position I am now in (professorship, book published and all) does give me a very good pedestal for carrying on psychical research effectively, or rather for disseminating its results effectively. I find however that *narratives* are a weariness, and I must confess that the reading of narratives for which I have no personal responsibility is almost intolerable to me. Those that come to me at first-hand, incidentally to the census, I get interested in. Others much less so; and I imagine my case is a very common case. One page of experimental thought-transference work will "carry" more than a hundred of *Phantasms of the Living*. I shall stick to my share of the latter, however; and expect in the summer recess to work up the results already gained in an article for *Scribner's* magazine, which will be the basis for more publicity and advertising and bring in another bundle of schedules to report on at the Congress. Of course I wholly agree with you in regard to the *ultimate* future of the business, and fame will be the portion of him who may succeed in naturalizing it as a branch of legitimate science. I think it quite on the cards that you, with your singular tenacity of purpose, and wide look at all the intellectual relations of the thing, may live to be the ultra-Darwin yourself. Only the facts are *so* discontinuous so far that possibly all our generation can do may be to get 'em called facts. I'm a bad fellow to investigate on account of my bad memory for anecdotes and other disjointed details. Teaching of students will have to fill most of my time, I foresee; but of course my weather eye will remain open upon the occult world.

James McK. Cattell, Letter in Science, April 15, 1898 (v. 7, pp. 534–535)

MRS. PIPER, THE MEDIUM.

The last number of the *Proceedings of the Society for Psychical Research* contains a statement to the effect that the present writer does not pay 'the slightest attention to psychical research à la English Society;' he 'taboos it throughout, but has never even read the reports and their experiments in telepathy.' If this information were obtained by telepathy it does not increase my confidence in that method of communication. It is exactly the thirteen volumes issued by the Society for Psychical Research that seem to me to prove the trivial character of the evidence for the heterogeneous mass of material taken under the wing of the Society.

The present number of the *Proceedings* seems to me, however, of some interest in that it concludes or continues an account of the séances of Mrs. Piper, under the title, 'A Further Record of

Observations of Certain Phenomena of Trance,' on which subject
Dr. Richard Hodgson has now contributed over 600 pages. The
case of Mrs. Piper is of interest, because Professor James has said:

"If you wish to upset the law that all crows are black, you
musn't seek to show that no crows are; it is enough if you prove
one single crow to be white. My own white crow is Mrs. Piper. In
the trances of this medium, I cannot resist the conviction that
knowledge appears which she has never gained by the ordinary
waking use of her eyes and ears and wits." (SCIENCE, N.S., III.,
884.)

It is Professor James who gives dignity and authority to psychical research in America, and if he has selected a crucial case it
deserves consideration. The difficulty has been that proving innu-
merable mediums to be frauds does not disprove the possibility
(though it greatly reduces the likelihood) of one medium being
genuine. But here we have the 'white crow' selected by Professor
James from all the piebald crows exhibited by the Society.

I find, among the great number of names and initials whose
séances with Mrs. Piper are reported, five and only five well-
known men of science. The following are the concluding sen-
tences of their reports:

These elements of truth were, however, so buried in masses of
incoherent matter and positive errors as to matters in which she
tried to give information that the sense of her failure on the
whole is far stronger with me.

Even as to the fact of her being in a trance at all my impression is not strong, despite the fact that I came fully expecting to
be convinced on that point.

My state of mind, therefore, is almost the same that it was
before the sitting, *i.e.*, a condition of willing approach to any evidence on either side of the question at issue; I am only disappointed that she did not give me more data for forming a positive
opinion. I am fully aware, however, that one such sitting has very
little negative weight, considering the variations which this sort of
phenomena are subject to.

J. MARK BALDWIN.

I was struck by a sort of insane cunning in the groping of the woman after something intangible.·

It did not seem to me that she simulated a trance state. She was apparently, as far as I could judge, in some abnormal condition.

I could not discover that she hit upon anything that was connected with the handkerchief.

JOHN TROWBRIDGE.

Let me say that I have no firm mind about the matter. I am curiously and yet absolutely uninterested in it for the reason that I don't see how I can exclude the hypothesis of fraud, and, until that can be excluded, no advance can be made.

When I took the medium's hand, I had my usual experience with them, a few preposterous compliments concerning the clearness of my understanding, and nothing more.

N. S. SHALER.

Since writing the foregoing, I have gone over the notes in detail, making a memorandum of successes and failures. I am surprised to see how little is true. Nearly every approach to truth is at once vitiated by erroneous additions or developments.

J. M. PEIRCE.

On re-reading your notes I find absolutely nothing of value. None of the incidents are correct, and none of the very vague things hinted at are true, nor have they any kind or sort of relation to my life, nor is there one name correctly given.

S. WEIR MITCHELL.

Truly, "we have piped unto you, but ye have not danced."

James to the "Editor of Science*" (Cattell), Letter in* Science, *May 6, 1898, (v. 7, pp. 640–641)*

Your reference to my name in the editorial note in *Science* for April 15th, entitled 'Mrs. Piper, the Medium,' justifies me in making some remarks of my own in comment on your remarks upon Mr. Hodgson's report of her case. Any hearing for such phenomena is so hard to get from scientific readers that one who believes them worthy of careful study is in duty bound to resent such contemptuous public notice of them in high quarters as would still further encourage the fashion of their neglect.

I say any hearing; I don't say any fair hearing. Still less do I speak of fair treatment in the broad meaning of the term. The scientific mind is by the pressure of professional opinion painfully drilled to fairness and logic in discussing orthodox phenomena. But in such mere matters of superstition as a medium's trances it feels so confident of impunity and indulgence whatever it may say, provided it be only contemptuous enough, that it fairly revels in the untrained barbarians' arsenal of logical weapons, including all the various sophisms enumerated in the books. . . .

I am sure that you have committed these fallacies with the best of scientific consciences. They are fallacies into which, of course, you would have been in no possible danger of falling in any other sort of matter than this. In our dealings with the insane the usual moral rules don't apply. Mediums are scientific outlaws, and their defendants are quasi-insane. Any stick is good enough to beat dogs of that stripe with. So in perfect innocence you permitted yourself the liberties I point out.

Please observe that I am saying nothing of the merits of the *case*, but only of the merits of your forms of controversy which, alas, are typical. The case surely deserves opposition more powerful from the logical point of view than your remarks; and I beg such readers of SCIENCE as care to form a reasonable opinion to seek the materials for it in the Proceedings of the Society for Psychical Research, Part XXXIII. (where they will find a candid report based on 500 sittings since the last report was made), rather than in the five little negative instances which you so triumphantly cull out and quote.

James McK. Cattell to James, May 6, 1898 (Letter in Science, V. 7, pp. 641–642)

My note in SCIENCE was not 'editorial,' but was placed in that department of the JOURNAL for which editors take the least responsibility. I gave my individual opinion, Professor James gives his, and I fear that our disagreement is hopeless. . . .

I wrote the note with reluctance and only because I believe that the Society for Psychical Research is doing much to injure psychology. The authority of Professor James is such that he involves other students of psychology in his opinions unless they protest. We all acknowledge his leadership, but we cannot follow him into the quagmires.

James to Theodore Flournoy, February 9, 1906[8]

Yes! Hodgson's[9] death was ultra-sudden. He fell dead while playing a violent game of "hand-ball." He was tremendously athletic and had said to a friend only a week before that he thought he could reasonably count on twenty-five years more of life. None of his work was finished, vast materials amassed, which no one can ever get acquainted with as he had gradually got acquainted; so now good-bye forever to at least two unusually solid and instructive books which he would have soon begun to write on "psychic" subjects. As a *man*, Hodgson was splendid, a real man; as an investigator, it is my private impression that he lately got into a sort of obsession about Mrs. Piper, cared too little for other clues, and continued working with her when all the sides of her mediumship were amply exhibited. I suspect that our American Branch of the S. P. R. will have to dissolve this year, for lack of a competent secretary. Hodgson was our only worker, except Hyslop, and *he* is engaged in founding an "Institute" of his own, which will employ more popular methods. To tell the truth, I'm rather glad of the prospect of the Branch ending, for the Piper-investigation—and nothing else—had begun to bore me to extinction. . . .

James to Ferdinand C. S. Schiller, August, 24, 1906[10]

The ghost of dear old Hodgson is reappearing through Mrs. Piper and I am to co-ordinate his utterances and make report. *Not* convincing, to me: but baffling exceedingly. . . .

James to Charles Lewis Slattery, April 21, 1907

My state of mind is this: Mrs. Piper has supernormal knowledge in her trances; but whether it comes from "tapping the minds" of living people, or from some common cosmic reservoir of memories, or from surviving "spirits" of the departed, is a question impossible for *me* to answer just now to my own satisfaction. The

8. Flournoy, a Swiss psychologist, shared James's interest in psychic phenomena, and the two were frequent correspondents between 1890 and James's death in 1910.

9. Richard Hodgson (1855–1905), a psychologist and psychic researcher was one of the leaders of the American SPR and was involved with James in the investigation of Mrs. Piper for many years. After his death, James worked with Mrs. Piper to contact Hodgson in a series of seances James called the Piper-Hodgson control.

10. Schiller (1864–1937) was a philosopher and president of the British SPR.

spirit theory is undoubtedly not only the most natural, but the simplest, and I have great respect for Hodgson's and Hyslop's arguments when they adopt it. At the same time the electric current called *belief* has not yet closed in my mind.

Whatever the explanation be, trance mediumship is an excessively complex phenomenon, in which many concurrent factors are engaged. That is why interpretation is so hard.

James to Thomas S. Perry, January 29, 1909

I have just got off my report on the Hodgson control, which has stuck to my fingers all this time. It is a hedging sort of an affair, and I don't know what the Perry family will think of it. The truth is that the "case" is a particularly poor one for testing Mrs. Piper's claim to bring back spirits. It is *leakier* than any other case, and intrinsically, I think, no stronger than many of her other good cases, certainly weaker than the G. P. case. I am also now engaged in writing a popular article, "the avowals of a psychical researcher," for the *American Magazine*, in which I simply state without argument my own convictions, and put myself on record. I think that public opinion is just now taking a step forward in these matters . . . and possibly both these *Schriften* of mine will add their influence.

William James Bibliography

Bjork, D. W. (1983). *The Compromised Scientist: William James in the Development of American Psychology*. New York: Columbia University Press.

A look at James as artist, philosopher, and psychologist, including excellent coverage of his debates on the scientific validity of psychical research with Cattell, Münsterberg, and Titchener. The phrase "compromised scientist" has several meanings in this book, one of which refers to the perception of James's abandonment of scientific standards.

Coon, D. J. (1992). Testing the limits of sense and science: American experimental psychologists combat spiritualism, 1880–1920. *American Psychologist*, 47, 143–151.

Details the efforts of psychologists to distance themselves from pseudopsychology, particularly the claims of spiritists.

James, H. (Ed.) (1920). *The Letters of William James* (2 volumes). Boston: Atlantic Monthly Press.

This collection of James's letters was edited by his son, Henry, and selectively covers the years 1861 to 1910. The earliest of the many published collections of James letters, it contains some of the most significant pieces in James's vast correspondence, which is now housed in the archives at Harvard University.

James, W. (1890). *The Principles of Psychology* (2 volumes). New York: Henry Holt.

James's classic treatment of psychology in 1,400 pages, a book that required him 12 years to write. Many contemporary scholars in psychology regard it as the greatest book written in the history of psychology. It is must reading for any card-carrying psychologist. And it will interest students who read only a chapter or two.

James, W. (1909). The confidences of a "psychical researcher." *American Magazine*, 68, 580–589. Reprinted in Murphy and Ballou (1960) and in James (1911), *Memories and Studies* (NY: Longmans Green), under the title "The final impressions of a psychical researcher."

James's final contribution to the literature on psychical research. He laments that after 25 years he is no closer to understanding psychic phenomena than he was at the beginning of his research. Yet he forecasts a future of significant scientific advance for the field.

Le Clair, R. C. (Ed.) (1966). *The Letters of William James and Theodore Flournoy*. Madison: University of Wisconsin Press.

A collection of more than 120 letters between James and Swiss psychologist Theodore Flournoy (1854–1920) covering the years 1890 to 1910. These two men shared a number of interests, especially psychical research.

Murphy, G., & Ballou, R. O. (Eds.) (1960). *William James on Psychical Research*. New York: Viking Press.

This book is a compilation of most of James's published and unpublished writings on psychical research and includes more than 100 pages on James's investigations of Mrs. Piper. It also includes a number of letters with various correspondents on the topic.

Perry R. B. (1935). *The Thought and Character of William James* (2 volumes). Boston: Little Brown.

An early biography of James written by one of his students who later became a colleague in James's philosophy department at Harvard. Emphasizing James' role as a philosopher, it also contains many excerpts from James's letters.

Scott, F. J. D. (Ed.) (1986). *William James: Selected Unpublished Correspondence, 1885–1910*. Columbus: Ohio State University Press.
  The best of the James' letters appear in earlier collections. Still, these are of interest to anyone who enjoys the charm and vitality of James's writing.

Chapter 8

Edward Bradford Titchener's Experimentalists

Edward Bradford Titchener (1867–1927) was born in Chichester, England. After earning a master's degree at Oxford University, he went to Leipzig where he earned his doctorate in psychology with Wilhelm Wundt, graduating in 1892. He arrived in the United States that year, assuming the psychology position at Cornell University recently vacated by another of Wundt's students, Frank Angell. Titchener built his laboratory in the Leipzig tradition and soon established himself as one of the foremost psychologists in the United States. In the 35 years of his professional career he wrote more than 200 articles and books and trained more than 50 doctoral students in his brand of psychology. Many of those students would found laboratories of their own, for example, Margaret Floy Washburn at Vassar College and Walter B. Pillsbury at the University of Michigan.

Titchener named his system of psychology *structuralism* because of its emphasis on discovering the elemental structure of consciousness. Conceptually, that focus of his system was similar to one of the goals of Wundtian psychology, although Wundt never used the label structuralism to refer to his psychology (see Leahey, 1981). Titchener defined psychology in the narrowest of terms. He rejected child psychology, abnormal psychology, and any studies on animals. His experimental science was built largely on introspection, a technique that proved to be of little use in those areas of study. It was narrower still, in comparison to Wundt, because of Titchener's adherence to positivism. Whereas Wundt sought to explain consciousness by invoking some hypothetical mental processes, Titchener avoided the mentalistic dilemma by focusing his efforts on a purely descriptive science. Cornell became the stronghold for descriptive psychology, protecting its purity from the infidels that Titchener felt made up much of American psychology.

The scientific acumen of Titchener was manifested in several ways, but is nowhere more evident than in the four volumes of his *Experimental Psychology* (1901–1905). Two of the books were for the psychology instructor and two for the student. Two dealt with quantitative studies, whereas the other two focused on qualitative studies. The instructor and the student received one of each. Collectively they were known as the "Manuals" or "Titchener's Manuals." They were used to train an entire generation of American psychology students, not just those at Cornell, in the methods of this new science. Oswald Külpe, another Wundt doctoral student who frequently battled Titchener on theoretical grounds, called Titchener's *Experimental Psychology* "the most erudite psychological work in the English language" (Boring, 1950, p. 413).

Titchener was an excellent scientist, albeit narrow in scope, who sought to define experimental psychology wholly in his own terms. As the American Psychological Association (APA) grew, its membership became increasingly diverse, and its program grew to contain aspects of psychology unacceptable by Titchener's definition of experimental psychology. So in 1904 he sought to found his own society of experimental psychologists. In January of that year he sent a letter to approximately 20 colleagues whose research he considered acceptable. The group included James Angell, James McKeen Cattell, Raymond Dodge, Joseph Jastrow, Charles Judd, Hugo Münsterberg, Howard Warren, and Lightner Witmer, among others. The proposed organization was to be rather exclusive in its membership, "confined to the men who are working in the field of experimental psychology" (as Titchener defined them).

Many of those invited were troubled that this new organization might remove experimental psychology from the domain of the American Psychological Association. Angell, Jastrow, Judd, Münsterberg and others wrote to Titchener expressing their concerns over the potential conflict with the APA. Warren was upset enough about the conflict that he declined to attend the meetings of Titchener's new group for the first three years of its existence. A few complained to Titchener about the exclusion of women from the group, although one individual, Witmer, supported Titchener's policy.

Although Titchener did not receive unanimous support for his group, he received enough endorsements to found the group. Its initial meeting was held at Cornell University, hosted by Titchener. In his original letter he had implied that the group might be called the American Society for the Advancement of Experimental Psychology. A psychologist at the University of Toronto, August Kirschmann, urged Titchener to drop the word "American" from the title. In Titchener's second letter to the group that term was gone. In fact, the group never had a formal name. Instead it was always referred to as "The Experimentalists" or "Titchener's Experimentalists." Edwin G. Boring, a historian of psychology and student of Titchener's wrote that:

> "Titchener really wanted to start an informal club of experimental psychologists, an annual meeting of the heads of laboratories, who would bring with them their most promising graduate students for stimulation. He wanted oral reports that could be interrupted, dissented from and criticized, in a smoke-filled room with no women present—for in 1904, when the Experimentalists was founded, women were considered too pure to smoke. He did not achieve his goal all at once, but he worked toward it over the years" (Boring, 1967, p. 315).

Indeed, Titchener did not achieve his goal all at once. He annually struggled to make his society what he wanted. In addition to regular complaints about competition with the older APA and the exclusion of women, objections were also raised about the elitism of the group, about the definition of what research qualified as "experimental psychology," about which students were to be invited, about how many people should be invited to the meetings, and about people reading their papers instead of discussing them informally. Apparently these issues were raised at many of the annual meetings and, on occasion, dominated the meeting such that the agenda of experimental psychology became secondary. John Watson became so disenchanted with the frequent discussions of these other issues that he stopped attending.

At an APA meeting in 1922, E. G. Boring, Karl Dallenbach, (both former students of Titchener) and Samuel Fernberger discussed organizing a regular and informal discussion of experimental psychology at the annual meetings of the APA. They were worried about Titchener's reaction to the idea because he could obviously perceive it as a threat to his Experimentalists. In an effort to soften the blow, they asked Raymond Dodge to organize the first of the APA round tables. Dodge, a more senior psychologist, was a charter member of Titchener's group and a member of the APA Program Committee for 1923. Dodge wrote to Titchener to describe the idea, and his letter and Titchener's reply are included in this chapter. The APA Round Tables on Experimental Psychology did begin in 1923 and continued to be a part of the annual meetings through 1928. Attendance at the sessions was large and kept the meetings from accomplishing what the organizers had intended. Thus they ceased (Goodwin 1990).

In August of 1927, after the twenty-third annual meeting of The Experimentalists (there was no meeting in 1918 because of World War I), Titchener died of a brain tumor. His death provided an opportunity for his colleagues to reconsider the structure and content of the society. The 1928 meeting was held at Yale University as had been planned before Titchener's death. At that meeting a committee of five, chaired by Warren, was given the task of reorganization. That committee decided to add 10 others to its membership and held its next meeting at Princeton University in 1929. It was at that meeting that the Society of Experimental Psychologists was formally organized. The Committee of 15 asked 11 others to join them in the new society as charter members. Two of that number were women: June Etta Downey of the University of Wyoming and Margaret Floy Washburn of Vassar College. The new by-laws indicated that membership would be limited to those "engaged in the advancement of experimental psychology." Further, the Society was not to exceed 50 members at any time.

The Society of Experimental Psychologists still exists today as an invitation-only organization, consisting of some of the most prestigious psychologists in North America. It was, and is, an important network in the discipline of psychology. It no longer denies membership to women, but they remain a very small percentage of the membership.

The letters in this chapter tell the story of the founding of Titchener's Experimentalists. They are revealing of Titchener as psychologist and as person, and they illustrate the roles played by others important to the early development of American psychology and its organizations. Perhaps they shed some light on the continuing disagreements in psychology that lead psychologists to abandon one organization to found another.

Titchener to approximately 20 colleagues in psychology, January 15, 1904

I write to ask your assistance in the organization of an American society for the advancement of Experimental Psychology.

It is generally admitted that, in matters of Experimental Psychology, our own country stands second, if to any other, at most only to Germany. This honourable position has been won by the efforts of a relatively small body of men, working under all the disadvantages and discouragements that naturally accompany the establishment of a new method in science. There is, I hope, no serious danger that we shall ever derogate from it. But there is, I am sure, a serious need of organisation and consolidation of our present forces. Not only would the directors of laboratories benefit by interchange of ideas and discussion of programmes; but the younger men also—and this is a point upon which I desire to lay special weight—would realise, by association, the community of their interests, the common dangers to which their profession is exposed, and their responsibilities to the science

In proposing to found a new society, I have no desire to interfere in any way with the existing American Psychological Association. This association has done admirable work for American psychology at large. It is, however, evident that the opportunities which it offers for scientific and social intercourse have not met the special requirements of Experimental Psychology. If the new society is successful, I see no reason why it should not ultimately affiliate to the elder association. For the time being, however, it will be wiser, I believe, that the experimentalists act independently.

My ideas with regard to the proposed society are as follows: (1) that its membership be confined to men who are working in the field of experimental psychology, (2) that its discussions be confined to subjects investigated by the experimental method, (3) that it meet, once a year or oftener, at one of the larger university laboratories; and (4) that place and date of meeting be so chosen as to avoid conflict with the meetings of other scientific societies. The intention underlying these proposals is, very simply, that the experimentalists shall come together for a couple of days every year, to talk, think and act nothing but Experimental Psychology.

I earnestly hope that I may count upon your assistance. If I am fortunate enough to secure your general approval of the scheme, I will, later on, submit to you some further propositions of more detail.

Editor's Note: *Several of Titchener's correspondents worried about Titchener's motives in founding this new group and whether it might not seriously interfere with the American Psychological Association. Titchener answered Harvard University's Hugo Münsterberg's concerns as follows.*

Titchener to Hugo Münsterberg, February 1, 1904

For many years I wanted an experimental club—no officers, the men moving about and handling [apparatus], the visited lab to do the work, no women, smoking allowed, plenty of perfectly frank criticism and discussions, the whole atmosphere experimental, the youngsters taken in on an equality with the men who have arrived. I have waited so as not to interfere with the progress of the regular Assn. [the American Psychological Association]— which when all is said, cannot fulfill these requirements with present membership and organisation. Now, I think, the Assn. is firmly established; I cannot hurt it if I wanted to—as emphatically I do not; and there are enough men like-minded with me to make the Society or Club of experimentalists a reality. We cannot reduce exp. psych. to papers; and the Assn. is organized on a paper basis. We can't be frank if we have too many members; or if we have outsiders drifting in. We don't want officers—in science, of all things in the world! I have received good promise of support, and I hope we [can go ahead] without bothering the Assn.

Editor's Note: *Several of those who responded commented on Titchener's proposal to exclude women from the meetings.*

Edmund C. Sanford [Clark University] to Titchener, January 19, 1904

. . . The question with regard to women in the association is a poser. Several of them on scientific grounds have full right to be there and might feel hurt (in a general impersonal way) if women are not asked. On the other hand they would undoubtedly interfere with the smoking and to a certain extent with the general freedom of a purely masculine assembly. Would it be possible to give them also the chance to say whether they would like to come—assuring them by a personal note that transactions would not come off except in a partially smoke-charged atmosphere? . . .

Lightner Witmer [University of Pennsylvania] to Titchener, January 25, 1904

. . . I am quite positive in my objection to inviting women . . . I am sure from my experience, that you cannot run an informal meeting of men and women. . . . We want a small vigorous association where we can speak our minds with perfect freedom. . . . The larger and more heterogeneous the organization the more likely is vigorous discussion to be misinterpreted and to be taken as an offence by individuals who may happen to be attacked. I think that the presence of women in the organization adds greatly to this danger, owing to the personal attitude which they usually take even in scientific discussions. I favor a small association, no invited guests, and no women members.

Titchener to various colleagues, February 6, 1904

On January 15th I addressed a letter to a limited number of experimental psychologists, of whom you are one, asking them to cooperate with me in the formation of a society for the advancement of Experimental Psychology. The large proportion of favourable answers shows that the need of such an organization is keenly felt.

There seems to be a pretty general agreement, among those whose assistance is promised, that the new society should present the following features:

(1) no fees; no officers; organization as simple as possible;
(2) membership small; meetings entirely informal;
(3) for the present at least, membership confined to men;
(4) for the present at least, no affiliation to any existing society;
(5) meetings to be held at the larger university laboratories;
(6) place and date of meetings to be so chosen as to avoid conflict with the meetings of other scientific societies;
(7) special effort to be directed towards the encouragement of graduate students and the younger independent workers in Experimental Psychology;
(8) papers, demonstrations, symposia, etc., to be strictly confined to subjects investigated by the experimental method.

All these points, however, are entirely open to discussion among those who accept membership in the society.

In order that the society may have a positive starting-point, I venture to ask you to reply to the two questions printed overleaf I earnestly hope that the society may have the benefit of your assistance.

Editor's Note: *The questions on the other side of the letter were:*

(1) Are you willing to become an active member of such a society as has been described,—on the understanding that the points raised are one and all open to discussion within the society? and,

(2) Can you attend a meeting at Ithaca during the coming Easter vacation? If so, what date would best suit you? An early reply would be appreciated.

Editor's Note: *After Titchener hosted the initial meeting in 1904, subsequent meetings were held at Clark University in 1905 (E. C. Sanford), Yale University in 1906 (Charles H. Judd), the University of Pennsylvania in 1907 (Lightner Witmer), and at Harvard University in 1908 (Hugo Münsterberg). The Titchener letter that follows was intended to give Münsterberg advice on invitations and the conduct of the 1908 meeting.*

Titchener to Hugo Münsterberg, February 29, 1908

. . . Our original membership (apart from Harvard) is, I believe, as follows: Frank Angell, [Madison] Bentley, [Raymond] Dodge, [Charles] Judd, [Edward] Pace, [Walter] Pillsbury, [Edmund C.] Sanford, [Carl] Seashore, [Lightner] Witmer. The Chicago and Columbia people declined to come in. We invited [Howard] Warren and he came last year for the first time: I suppose that he and [J. W.] Baird should be counted members.

All of these men, therefore, are entitled to invitation. . . . Any further invitations are left, I believe, entirely to the discretion of the individual members. . . . You are absolutely free to invite anyone you like; and I suppose it would fall to you as chairman of the occasion, to notify [James McKeen] Cattell, [George] Stratton and James Angell, in case they cared to come or send any of their men.

I heard nothing last year of any objections to the size of the meetings: I do not think they ran over 15, and at times there were only a half dozen present. [James H.] Leuba sent in some girls [from Bryn Mawr College], whom·we promptly turned out; that was sheer misunderstanding. . . .

Editor's Note: *Christine Ladd-Franklin (1847–1930) was 20 years older than Titchener. She was an early experimental psychologist, logician, and mathematician, and in psychology was best known for her work on color vision. The following excerpts of letters illustrate her dismay at being excluded from these meetings solely on the basis of her gender. (For information on Ladd-Franklin see Cadwallader & Cadwallader, 1990 and Scarborough & Furumoto, 1987.)*

Christine Ladd-Franklin to Titchener, 1912

. . . I am particularly anxious to bring my views up, once in a while, for hand-to-hand discussion before experts, and just now I have especially a paper which I should like very much to read before your meeting of experimental psychologists. I hope you will not say nay!

Editor's Note: *Titchener's reply does not exist but apparently he denied Ladd-Franklin's request to attend, which prompted the following letter.*

Christine Ladd-Franklin to Titchener, 1912

I am shocked to know that you are still—at this year—excluding women from your meeting of experimental psychologists. It is such a very old-fashioned standpoint! [How illogical it is] that you should include in your invitation . . . the students of G. Stanley Hall, who are not in the least experimentalists and exclude the women who are doing particularly good work in the experimental laboratory of Prof. Baird. . . Have your smokers separated if you like (tho I for one always smoke when I am in fashionable society), but a scientific meeting (however personal) is a public affair, and it is not open to you to leave out a class of fellow workers without extreme discourtesy.

Mary Whiton Calkins [see Chapter 6] to Ladd-Franklin, August 14, 1912

. . . As to the experimental psychologists: I of course share your regret at their attitude toward women. In fact, I have . . . spoken of the matter in years past to Dr. Titchener and to

Dr. Münsterberg (the latter, I think favors their entrance). I feel the freer to speak because I no longer count myself an experimenter: but you, Miss [Eleanor] Gamble, Miss [Margaret Floy] Washburn, Miss [Helen Dodd] Cook, and several others should of course be invited. At the same time I doubt the wisdom of a public protest on the part of those who are shut out. It seems to be sufficiently a side-issue to be left to time or to protestants from within.

Editor's Note: *The 1914 meeting of the experimentalists was hosted by James McKeen Cattell at Columbia University in New York City, where Ladd-Franklin was living at the time.*

Ladd-Franklin to Titchener, March 21, 1914

. . . Is this then a good time, my dear Professor Titchener, for you to hold to the medaeval attitude of not admitting me to your coming psychological conference in New York—at my very door? So unconscientious, so immoral,—worse than that—so unscientific!

Titchener to Robert M. Yerkes [Harvard University], April 2, 1914

I am not sure that we had better not disintegrate! I have been pestered by abuse by Mrs. Ladd-Franklin for not having women at the meetings, and she threatens to make various scenes in person and in print. Possibly she will succeed in breaking us up, and forcing us to meet—like rabbits—in some dark place underground. . . .

Editor's Note: *Ladd-Franklin did attend one of the sessions of the 1914 Columbia meeting, perhaps at her own initiative, perhaps at the invitation of Cattell. According to E. G. Boring (1938) it marked the only attendance of women at the meetings until after Titchener's death in 1927.*

John Watson objected to Titchener's experimentalists for different reasons as the following letter shows.

John B. Watson to Howard C. Warren [Princeton University], April 14, 1916.

I have received your circular and the mileage book. I wish to thank you sincerely for the book and for the cordial invitation to come. Your memorandum, however, and certain other letters which I have received, have decided me to decline the invitation. I am going to be quite frank because I believe the ends of science and of friendship too are best conserved in that way.

Were your organization called the Titchener Club you would be acting entirely within your rights in sending out the memorandum. But this organization has called itself variously Meeting of the Experimental Psychologists, the experimentalists, etc. In other words, it is and has been a scientific gathering. In my earlier days I was more or less willing to stand for exclusiveness in science. As I grow older I get further away from this kind of thing. Every time I attend one of these meetings I am embarrassed by having to talk about the nature of the meeting, and to tell certain people that they cannot come, and I was criticized very severely for allowing too many people to come to the Baltimore meeting [hosted by Watson in 1910].

This embarrassment that I always feel in regard to these meetings takes away any pleasure that I might get from the meeting, and while I do not represent anybody but myself I seriously question the justice and wisdom of your using the term Experimental Psychologists or experimentalists. To make this organization work without hurting feelings, it should be called the Titchener Club, and invitations should be issued to join it.

Assuring both you and Titchener of my regret at not being able to see you, I am sincerely yours.

Editor's Note: *The following letters describe the emerging experimental round table sessions that were being planned for the meetings of the American Psychological Association. You should note the difference in Titchener's replies to Dodge and Boring.*

Raymond Dodge to Titchener, April 14, 1923

Several of the younger men wrote to me sometime ago asking about the possibility of an informal session at the time of the winter meeting of the American Psychological Association. I have been talking it over with a number of others who might be interested and believe such a session would enormously increase the profit of the winter meeting.

I wish you would be good enough to give me your frank reaction to the following proposals.

(1) A session open to experimentalists for the discussion of experimentali and procedures by those who are responsible for them. (2) No papers to be read that belongs (sic) to the formal session of the Association. (3) Time of the session to parallel the meetings of the psychology in clinical psychology, applied psychology, probably the last session of the meeting running over into Friday morning if there is demand for it.

I am particularly interested in getting your opinion as to how such a meeting would affect the spring meeting of experimentalists in which we are both deeply interested. I am particularly interested to know if you would attend such a meeting and lend your support. It seems to me that you would be the natural person to preside.

As member of the Program Committee I can get a place for it whenever you think it desirable and can probably arrange for such announcements as the situation would call for. . . .

Titchener to Raymond Dodge, April 19, 1923

I had heard of an idea for the establishment of an Experimental Section of the Association, but your notion of informal sessions is new to me. I do not think that you need for a moment take into account the spring meeting of the Experimentalists. We have now stood up for twenty years, and so far as I can see we are good for many years more; I doubt if any action on the part of the Association will have any effect on us. If it does then we shall deserve what we get.

I cannot say, however, that I am hopeful about your plan. For one thing, the whole atmosphere of the Association is against informality and, as you yourself say, in favor of presiding and being presided over. For another thing, an informal session, if it is to be really successful, presupposes an immense amount of hard work and unselfish work on the part of one or two members of the group; and I don't know who could be persuaded to undertake that sort of job. For a third thing, the right place for an informal experimental session is the laboratory, and the laboratory thrown open for mauling and examining. You will understand that this is simply my individual opinion, which may very well be offset by the desires and opinions of other people. Personally I have decided to leave the Association owing to the $5.00 subscription which seems to me to be preposterous. Cattell was good enough to say that the raising of the subscription would rule out the welshers, and so I mean to make myself a nucleus for the welshing group. . . .

Titchener to E. G. Boring, date unknown (quoted in Boring's letter to Karl Dallenbach, May 25, 1923)

There is a threatening complication about the Experimentalists. Dodge has decided to try to imitate us, by inaugurating a sort of round-table experimental informal conference, at the Assn. meetings.

I think . . . that we shall presently be snuffed out. We are an arbitrary and one-sexed lot; and the Assn. will give room to anybody who is a member and wants to attend, and will let women in . . . All the people whom we have offended will therefore work hard for the success of the venture; and we have offended a good many.

Editor's Note: *The 24th annual meeting of the experimentalists was to be held at Yale University in 1928. But then Titchener died on August 3, 1927.*

Roswell P. Angier [Yale University] to Raymond Dodge, November 28, 1927

The Experimentalists were, as you will remember, invited to meet at Yale next spring. Titchener's death, however, seems to several of us to have altered the situation to such an extent that it is desirable to secure the reactions of those who have longest been associated with the group to the problems of the best course to pursue in the future. Three possibilities have been suggested in informal exchange of views.

1. To hold the meeting next spring as scheduled.
2. To give up the meetings altogether.
3. To omit next spring's meeting out of respect to Titchener's memory, and then consider at leisure what to do in the future.

The various pros and cons need not be dealt with here, for they will readily occur to us who realize that Titchener not only started the meetings but was throughout their inspiration and their central figure. One suggested course may, however, be mentioned, namely, that next spring's meeting occur as contemplated and assume a character commemorative to Titchener. Some think that this would on the whole be inadvisable since eulogistic tribute would be something alien to anything that Titchener himself would have wished; and that it is too soon, on the other hand, for any of us to attempt an objective appraisal of the quality and extent of his contribution to the development of psychological thought.

Naturally Yale would be delighted to serve as host to next spring's meeting if it appears advisable on the whole to hold it; on this point, or any other phases of the matter we earnestly seek advice, and shall be grateful if you will indicate your views.

Howard C. Warren to 14 other psychologists invited to be an organizing committee for a new organization, April 11, 1928

The group of Experimental Psychologists organized by Professor Titchener held its final meeting at New Haven [Yale] last week. In view of Dr. Titchener's death, and because of the increasing attendance, it was agreed that these gatherings no longer fulfilled the purpose for which they were designed, namely, a conference of experimental investigators for intimate discussion of current laboratory problems. . . .

The [organizing] Committee will meet at Princeton next spring, at a date to be determined later. The business will include (1) a definite decision as to the character of the new organization; (2) election of members in accordance with the policy agreed upon; (3) determination of time and place of next meeting and any other matters requiring action. It is expected that in addition to the business sessions, the opportunity will be taken to discuss laboratory problems and methods.

You are requested to write to the undersigned signifying your willingness to become a member of the Committee.

Edward Bradford Titchener's Experimentalists Bibliography

Benjamin, L. T., Jr. (1977). The Psychological Round Table: Revolution of 1936. *American Psychologist, 32,* 542–549.

This article is a historical account of a secret society organized in 1936 by a group of younger psychologists who were dissatisfied with their exclusion from the membership of the Society of Experimental Psychologists. Participation in the PRT was by invitation only and psychologists were excluded when they reached the age of 40. Women were barred from participating until the early 1970s.

Boring, E. G. (1927). Edward Bradford Titchener: 1867–1927. *American Journal of Psychology, 38,* 489–506.
> Boring's obituary of his doctoral mentor.

Boring, E. G. (1938). The Society of Experimental Psychologists, 1904–1938. *American Journal of Psychology, 51,* 410–423 and (1967). Titchener's Experimentalists. *Journal of the History of the Behavioral Sciences, 3,* 315–325.
> Boring attended his first meeting of the experimentalists in 1911 (the eighth meeting). These two articles are his histories of the experimentalist meetings.

Goodwin, C. J. (1985). On the origins of Titchener's experimentalists. *Journal of the History of the Behavioral Sciences, 21,* 383–389.
> Discusses Titchener's reasons for founding the experimentalists and describes an earlier attempt in 1898 by Lightner Witmer to establish a similar group, independent of the American Psychological Association.

Leys, R., & Evans, R. B. (Eds.) (1990). *Defining American Psychology: The Correspondence between Adolf Meyer and Edward Bradford Titchener.* Baltimore: Johns Hopkins University Press.
> A collection of letters between Titchener and Meyer, one of America's most famous psychiatrists, that focuses on their markedly different views of psychology.

Scarborough, E., & Furumoto, L. (1987). *Untold Lives: The First Generation of American Women Psychologists.* New York: Columbia University Press.
> See chapter 5—"A Little Hard on Ladies: Christine Ladd-Franklin's Challenge to Collegial Exclusion," which deals specifically with the exclusion of women from Titchener's experimentalists and more broadly with the issues of collegial exclusion as a barrier for women in psychology.

Titchener, E. B. (1910). *A Textbook of Psychology.* New York: Macmillan.
> This is Titchener's textbook for the beginning psychology student, which describes his brand of psychology, known as structuralism.

Chapter 9

John B. Watson's
Behavioral Psychology

John Broadus Watson was born in 1878 in the rural community of Travelers Rest, South Carolina. After graduation from nearby Furman University, he traveled to the University of Chicago where he planned to study philosophy. He lost interest in the classes of John Dewey and turned instead to psychology where he worked with James Rowland Angell (1869–1949). Watson was also interested in biology and was influenced at the university by courses he took with Henry H. Donaldson (1857–1938) and Jacques Loeb (1859–1924).

Watson finished his doctorate in psychology at the university in 1903, with an experimental dissertation using rats and stayed on the faculty for a few years before accepting a position at Johns Hopkins University in 1908. There he continued his animal work in the psychology laboratory that G. Stanley Hall had founded 25 years earlier, the first such laboratory in America. When James Mark Baldwin, the head of the Psychology Department at Johns Hopkins, was dismissed in 1909 (following a scandal caused by his being caught in a police raid on a Baltimore bordello), Watson found himself head of the department and editor of Baldwin's journal, *Psychological Review*.

Always somewhat of a counter-conformist, Watson was greatly dissatisfied with the psychology of his day, a dissatisfaction that had begun in 1904 when he was a fledgling animal researcher at Chicago. He was concerned about the objectivity of psychology and its reliance on the method of introspection that maintained its ties to mentalism. His preference was for the controlled stimulus-response conditions of his laboratory studies with rats. In correspondence with fellow animal psychologist Robert M. Yerkes (1876–1956), Watson described his hopes for a science of psychology that would rightfully belong among the natural sciences.

After 4 years in his position as director of the Hopkins psychology laboratory, Watson apparently felt his position in psychology was secure enough to make his views known. In 1913 he published an article entitled "Psychology as the Behaviorist Views It." The article became known as the "behaviorist manifesto," and it marked the beginning of a revolution in psychology, although not an immediate rebellion (see Samelson, 1981). This brash analysis of the field of psychology began:

> *Psychology as the behaviorist views it is a purely objective experimental branch of natural science. Its theoretical goal is the prediction and control of behavior. Introspection forms no essential part of its methods, nor is the scientific value of its data dependent upon the readiness with which they lend themselves to interpretation in terms of consciousness.* (Watson, 1913, p. 158)

In this article he rebuked not only the structuralists but also the functionalists with whom he had trained. He claimed that there was really no distinction between them. Both were mired in a mentalism, in a mistaken belief that they were actually studying consciousness. In continuing his attack he wrote:

> *I do not wish unduly to criticize psychology. It has failed signally, I believe, during the fifty-odd years of its existence as an experimental discipline to make its place in the world as an undisputed natural science. . . . The time has come when psychology must discard all reference to consciousness; when it need no longer delude itself into thinking that it is making mental states the object of observation.* (Watson, 1913, p. 163)

Certainly those were brash words from someone who had received his doctorate in psychology only a decade earlier.

Watson was not alone in his dissatisfaction with the subjectivism of psychology, and his 1913 paper was by no means the initial appearance of such ideas (see O'Donnell, 1985). But behaviorism as a movement in psychology belongs to Watson. He crystallized the rumblings into a coherent whole that gained attention. The revolution started slowly but by the 1930s American psychology and behaviorism were virtually synonymous.

When Watson assumed control of the psychology laboratories at Hopkins he was responsible for both the animal labs and the human labs. He had not worked with humans before and disliked such research, recalling that he "hated to serve as a subject" (Watson, 1936, p. 276). However, when he returned from service in World War I he began a series of experiments to study motor reflexes in human infants. Undoubtedly the most famous of those experiments was the fear conditioning study of Albert B. Indeed, this study may be the most frequently cited experiment in the history of psychology (see Harris, 1979).

With a graduate student, Rosalie Rayner, Watson conditioned an 11-month-old infant, Albert B., who was initially unafraid of a white rat, to fear the rat when it was paired with a loud noise. In this study, Watson sought to demonstrate that fear could be acquired in humans as a result of conditioning, an idea he had proposed in a 1917 article. The successful results provided support for Watson's environmentalistic theory of emotions in humans and thus for his extremely environmentalistic view of all behavior. However, this experiment would be Watson's last at Hopkins. When his wife discovered his secret love affair with Rayner, their marriage ended in a scandalous divorce that occupied the pages of Baltimore newspapers. Like Baldwin before him, Watson was forced to resign his academic position in 1920.

Watson and Rayner married on New Year's Eve in 1920, one week after his divorce became final. When no other university would hire him, he went to New York City to work for J. Walter Thompson Company, an advertising firm. He was extremely successful there and was promoted to vice president of the company after only 4 years. While learning the advertising business, Watson kept spreading the gospel of behaviorism through talks on radio shows and through a number of articles in popular magazines such as *Harper's*, *McCall's*, *Cosmopolitan*, and *Collier's*. He lectured regularly at the New School for Social Research in New York and was a popular lecturer for a variety of groups, particularly women's organizations.

In 1923, Watson was flattered when Columbia University invited him to continue the promising infant research he had begun at Hopkins. The research was to be funded by the Laura Spelman Rockefeller Fund, and they strongly supported Watson's involvement in the work. Watson was unable to direct the research but he offered to consult and to participate as much as his business schedule would allow him. Watson had been particularly interested in child psychology since the birth of his first child and several of his popular articles were on this subject. The Columbia studies involved him to a greater degree in the applications of psychology to child rearing and was an impetus to writing the *Psychological Care of Infant and Child* (1928). This book, which warned parents about displaying too much affection toward their children, became a best seller as many sought to follow the child rearing advice of this charismatic and distinguished authority on psychology. There were many authorities and parents, however, who reacted quite negatively to the book. Watson (1936) later expressed regret, saying that he did not know enough to write the book.

Watson's impact on psychology was substantial, perhaps more so than any other figure in the history of American psychology. Yet the value of his legacy is debated today. In arguing for an objective science of behavior he eliminated a number of topics that have only begun to reappear in American psychology in the last 25 years, for example, consciousness, thinking, and dreaming. Some psychologists believe that Watson's philosophy was too radical, that in throwing out what he saw as bad, he also contributed to the elimination of much that was good. They argue that in the long run he inhibited psychology's progress.

Others argue that psychology's progress as a science was largely because of Watson, that he was the one figure who demanded a complete break with philosophy and the mentalistic baggage attached to it. Watsonian behaviorism strengthened the role of physiological processes in psychological explanations, expanded psychological methods, and made apparent the ties between animal and human psychology.

Watson was 80-years-old when he died in 1958. Shortly before his death he gathered all of his papers—correspondence, manuscripts, and research notes—and burned them in the fireplace of his country home. Needless to say, that act has made it difficult for scholars to examine the life of this important figure. Indeed no scholarly biography of Watson existed until 1989. The Watson letters that remain are those he wrote to others and thus have been preserved with their papers. What follows is a selection of those letters related to several of the themes in Watson's fascinating life.

Watson to Robert M. Yerkes, November 15, 1909

. . . I am glad to hear you say you seriously thought of writing a popular book. I too think it would be an interesting thing to do and it would undoubtedly excite popular interest in the subject [psychology]. If we write popular articles enough for a year or two we will be able to consolidate into book form without much effort. Harpers just accepted another of mine called "The New Science of Animal Behavior",[1] which is not so lurid as the title would seem.

Watson to Robert M. Yerkes, February 6, 1910

. . . You don't understand my position here [at Johns Hopkins University] or you wouldn't quarrel with the Harper's article. Suppose you were in charge of psychology and that all you got came about just to the extent to which you made the univ. community feel the importance of or take notice of psychology. This was the reason for the article. I am in a community which practically never heard of psychology. . . . I should be glad to get your criticisms though I don't believe we are as far apart as you seem to think.[2] I am a physiologist and I go so far as to say that I would remodel psychology as we now have it (human) and reconstruct our attitude with reference to the whole matter of consciousness. I don't believe the psychologist is studying consciousness any more than we [animal researchers] are and I am willing to say that consciousness is merely a tool, a fundamental assumption with which the chemist works, the physiologist and everyone else who observes. All of our sensory work, memory work, attention, etc. are part of definite modes of behavior. I have thought of writing . . . just what I think of the work being done in human experimental psychology. It lacks an all embracing scheme in which all the smaller pieces may find their place. It has no big problems. Every little piece of work which comes out is an unrelated unit. This might all be changed if we would take a simpler, behavior view of life and make adjustment the keynote. But I fear to do it now because my place here is not ready for it. My thesis developed as I long to develop it would certainly separate me from the psychologists—Titchener would cast me off and I fear Angell would do likewise.[3]

---

1. *Harper's*, February, 1910, pp. 346–353.

2. Yerkes, who shared Watson's concerns about the scientific status of psychology, was worried that Watson's total rejection of the acceptability of the study of consciousness was too extreme.

3. At the time of this letter the two dominant "schools" of psychology were structuralism, headed by Edward Bradford Titchener of Cornell University and functionalism, headed by James Rowland Angell of the University of Chicago.

Editor's Note: *By 1913 Watson could hold out no longer and he wrote what he thought of the contemporary work in experimental psychology. He delivered his "behaviorist manifesto" in a lecture at Columbia University in February, 1913 and published it the following month in the journal he edited,* Psychological Review. *Several years later he shifted his research from animal studies to humans, in an attempt to demonstrate the scientific power of behaviorism in that arena. After military service during World War I, Watson returned to Johns Hopkins University, where he moved his laboratory to the Phipps Clinic, and began writing a beginning textbook for psychology touting his behavioral approach* (Psychology from the Standpoint of a Behaviorist). *At this time he also began a correspondence with the English philosopher, Bertrand Russell (1872–1970), who was sympathetic to Watsonian behaviorism and spread Watson's ideas in Great Britain.*

Watson to Bertrand Russell, February 21, 1919

. . . I am writing a book on objective psychology and as I finish the chapters I get the staff to criticize the chapters. . . . I think I shall not have any trouble dealing with memory if I leave out 'recognition'. I cannot see anything in recognition, anyway, but the plain behavior fact that an individual reacts to an object as he did the day before. Of course a lot more is said about it in the various texts but I can't see that the texts lead us anywhere except into philosophy. . . . And with no disrespect to philosophy at all, I am trying to get psychology just as far away from philosophy as are chemistry and physics—which of course is not so far as the average run of chemists and physicists think it is. I make the very crude statement in the beginning of my courses always that I assume the psychologists, chemists, and physicists are beings capable of making an observation, and that the psychologist is not different from the other scientific men, i.e. that he borrows neither more nor less from philosophy than they do. I refuse then steadfastly to say anything further about the nature of a being that can make an observation. My statements are so crude in this respect that I hesitate to ask your opinion as to whether this [is] a legitimate methodological problem for a scientific man.

Watson to Bertrand Russell, October 4, 1919

. . . I am reading your article on Propositions with a great deal of interest. I think you have been more than just to me on the basis of what I have hitherto published. I am looking for my new book to be out within the next week or ten days. I shall see that you receive one of the first copies because I believe that I have made some points more clear there than in previous publications. . . .

Watson to Bertrand Russell, October 11, 1921 (written from New York City, where Watson had joined the advertising firm of J. Walter Thompson Company)

Only yesterday was I able to get your latest book [*The Analysis of Mind*]. I am delighted with it. There are many things in it, of course, that I should like pleasantly to quarrel with you about. . . .

Since my last letter to you I have left university work. You have suffered at the hands of the public, I know, so you will understand the necessity of my getting out of university work due to the publicity attached to my divorce.

I am happily at work here, and have, I think, really a wider scope for my work than I had in university circles. I am carefully putting aside my scientific impulses until I have learned the technique of business. After I have qualified as a practical man and lived down the stigma in business circles of being an academician I hope to be able to bring all my scientific interests to bear in studying some of the psychological problems underlying the industries, especially those connected with markets, salesmanship, public resistances, types of appeals, etc.

I am with a very progressive firm that feels the need of such work and gives me considerable liberty.

You certainly were more than generous to me in the book. I had not at all expected the honor of being mentioned in your preface because due to my disturbed state of mind in the spring when I was deepest in my troubles I had little spirit left to give your manuscript the reading it deserved.

Watson to Bertrand Russell, January 5, 1922

I am sending you page proof of a review of your book which has just appeared in The Dial for January 1922. I hope you will like it. I was so limited in space that I could not do it as I really cared to. I think it was terribly cheeky of me to attempt to review it at all as I wrote you once before.

Watson to Bertrand Russell, September 18, 1923

I am very sorry to say that I have no article for the new magazine. Breaking away from academic work and starting all over again in business keeps my nose pretty well to the grindstone so far as time is concerned. May I add, though, that I am enjoying my new experiences in business and find not a dull moment. . . .

Teachers College, Columbia University, has succeeded in getting together approximately $20,000 to continue the work I began on infants.[4] Because of business pressure I am not able to undertake the active work but I have secured a very competent person to carry out the daily routine of experiments. Each week I shall spend one afternoon at the little laboratory generally supervising the conduct of the experiments.

The laboratory is really an apartment situated next to a day nursery. There we have quite a bit of material which I think can be worked up in this way. I am sending you a copy of a letter I wrote about this work, giving a summary of what we plan to do.

Watson to Patty S. Hill [Professor at Teachers College, Columbia University], August 1, 1923

First and foremost, I wish to tell you how delighted I am that there is a possibility that the work on infants can be continued under your general care.

A few reflections about the matter come to me which I should like to put down in order:

1. *Physical Equipment:* I think the Manhattan Day Nursery, as we looked it over the other day, is sufficiently large to make a start in this work. I should feel badly disappointed if a plant as large as that and as well equipped as that could not be made to yield worth while results, even in a year's time. If it cannot be made to yield results, then there is something wrong with the problem or else with the investigator who is controlling the work. . . .

---

4. Columbia University received funding from the Laura Spelman Rockefeller Fund, which was a strong supporter of applied research in psychology. Watson agreed to supervise the research on preschool children so long as the experiments were applicable to child rearing. Buckley (1989) argues that Watson wanted to develop procedures "by which parents and teachers could control the behavior of children and shape the characteristics of their personalities" (p. 152).

2. *Problems:* Although the human material housed in the present plant is not ideal from a scientific perspective, because of lack of twenty-four hour control, nevertheless the conditions conform more closely to those in the home than would be the case if the plant had twenty-four hour control. Ultimately, if the infant work is to be of any distinct value to the community, its results must be capable of application in the home.

I think that even under the limitations which will surround the work there, several distinct problems can be taken up:

(a) *Thumb sucking* is almost universally prevalent. Its dangers in the way of infection, in causing poor mouth and teeth formation, and other physical ills, has been considerably emphasized especially of late. Its dangers on the psycho-pathological side, while probably far more threatening, have received little attention. I admit I haven't all the facts to back me up, but from tests which I have made I am at least willing to venture the speculation that thumb sucking breeds introversion, dependent individuals, and possibly confirmed masturbators. In your plant at the present time you have a number of infants and young children already addicted to this habit—as is also the case in about 99% of the homes in the United States! . . . I am sure methods for breaking this habit can easily be worked up. I have some vague ideas on getting control of this habit which I will be very glad to take up with the individual who is to take charge of the plant.

(b) To my mind the *uncontrollable child* (and here I mean children from two to four) has been uncontrollable through bad handling—a series of negative conditioned reflexes have been set up which could be analyzed and, I believe, removed. While the child seems to be bad tempered and to fly into a rage at everything, I feel that daily analysis of the behavior of this infant with experimentation would soon locate the basal negative conditioning which has taken place. Once located, methods should be developed for removing such conditioned responses. Connected with this general problem is the *negative reactions* (sic) to certain foods. In view of.the present convictions setting in against the theory of instincts and through my own work showing that practically all reactions of infants are positive, it is pretty evident that negative reactions in general have been built in and are not hereditary. Hence food aversions, or *aversions of any kind*, are due to bad handling. . . .

(c) *Fears:* It would not be a hard matter to sift over the children in the neighborhood and find many of them with very definite fear reactions to various types of objects. None of us, not even those who have worked most with children, has developed any method for removing them, or knows anything about the proper way of handling them. Two months' work on three children with very definite fears ought to be worth the whole cost of your equipment and expenditures for a year, because I am very sure that the problem would yield and yield quickly.

An interesting correlary (sic) would be to induce in a child a fear of an animal as I did at Johns Hopkins, and then to determine by presenting a wide range of other objects or animals the number of "transferred" fears which certainly do immediately take place. Then remove the fear of the animal and see whether at the same time the transferred fears remain or disappear.

(d) Retest the whole *range of stimuli calling out emotional reactions* and the variety of patterns so called forth.

(e) Study the problem of *incontinence* and devise method of establishing continence which can be used in the home. Earliest age at which it is profitable to begin regular system—methods of breaking up confirmed habits of incontinence in older children.

(f) Experimental study of the whole field of *masturbation*—earliest appearance—general forms of situations (irritations, etc.) possibly contributing to its initiation, etc.

(g) One of the most practical problems is to take the child which has a strong *mother or father "transference"* and study the best methods for breaking it up. At present mothers' and fathers' lives are made a burden by these transfers—they cannot get out of the sight of the child—cannot put on hat or coat without creating a disturbance. Handling transfers the right way at an early age may save the youngster a lifetime of misery.

(h)   *Teaching the child to let objects alone* without saying "don't" a million times a day. Would it not be possible to arrange a table containing interesting but not to be touched objects with electric wires so that an electrical shock is given when the table to be avoided is touched—and to have other objects, the *child's own*, on another table which can be touched with impunity? . . .

Hundreds of other problems, of course, are possible, but the above list seems to me to be most easily attacked with your present equipment. All of them are home problems as well and their solution would be of immediate practical help. . . .

In closing may I say that I feel so hopeful about this work that I shall be only too delighted to co-operate in every way I can with the staff you select.[5] I will gladly help plan, work out a more detailed program, help with ideas on apparatus and technique, spend time at the plant in the evening helping get things started, watching experiments and the like. . . .

Editor's Note: *In January of 1932, Robert Yerkes, perhaps feeling that Watson's talents were wasted in the business world, encouraged him to return to observational research. Yerkes wrote, "Surely you can sufficiently forget your behavioristic philosophy to be happier in experimentation than in generalization" (as cited in Buckley, 1989, p. 177). A portion of Watson's reply appears on the next page.*

---

5. The staff person selected to carry out the experiments at the nursery school was Mary Cover Jones (1896–1987), a student of Margaret Floy Washburn at Vassar College. Jones knew of Watson through her Vassar classmate, Rosalie Rayner, and she hoped to study with Watson at Johns Hopkins. However, his dismissal prevented that, so she enrolled in the graduate program at Columbia University instead. At the Manhattan Day Nursery School, Jones conducted her classic study of deconditioning a child's fear of rabbits (Jones, 1924). The technique she used in removing the fear is quite similar to the modern-day therapeutic technique known as systematic desensitization, and consequently Jones is recognized as one of the early pioneers in behavior therapy.

Watson to Robert Yerkes, January 22, 1932

. . . I am afraid there is too much water over the dam for me ever to be able to think of going back into observational work. In the first place all my habits and tastes are geared beyond the return I could hope for from any academic job, even assuming that any university in the country were so misguided as to offer me a job. I would not mind this a bit but I doubt if my family would understand it.

In the second place, if I ever went back I would want a real infants laboratory. . . . I should want a good staff and a lot of ground. Then I should want about fifteen years for work and never to have to publish a line or a note or to have anybody interview me on any subject whatsoever. Then if I got anything I would like to spend about five years writing it up. Then I would say to old Father Time that any time he was ready, I was.

I think I still have the guts to do this but it requires so much money that I am sure it will not come in my lifetime.

John B. Watson Bibliography

Buckley, K. W. (1989). *Mechanical Man: John Broadus Watson and the Beginnings of Behaviorism.* New York: Guilford Press.

A scholarly and very readable account of Watson's life and career that draws on his published work and unpublished materials from more than 30 archival collections.

Harris, B. (1979). Whatever happened to little Albert? *American Psychologist, 34,* 151–160.

A critical history of psychology's most famous experiment and the way it has been reported (and misreported) over the years.

Jones, M. C. (1924). A laboratory study of fear: The case of Peter. *Pedagogical Seminary, 31,* 308–315.

Jones collaborated with Watson on the deconditioning of Peter's fear of rabbits. For Jones's more personal account of this study see, Jones, M. C. (1974). Albert, Peter, and John B. Watson. *American Psychologist, 29,* 581–583.

Samelson, F. (1981). Struggle for scientific authority: The reception of Watson's behaviorism, 1913–1920. *Journal of the History of the Behavioral Sciences, 17,* 399–425.

A search for the impact of Watson's ideas shows that behaviorism gained little acceptance in the decade following the publication of Watson's manifesto.

Watson, J. B. (1913). Psychology as the behaviorist views it. *Psychological Review, 20,* 158–177.

Watson's call to arms for a behavioral psychology.

Watson, J. B. (1919). *Psychology from the Standpoint of a Behaviorist.* Philadelphia: Lippincott.

Watson's second book was a textbook for the beginning psychology course, emphasizing a behavioral approach to psychology. It was published shortly before he left academic life forever.

Watson, J. B. (1928). *Psychological Care of the Infant and Child.* New York: Norton.

Part of Watson's advice about children in this book was, "never hug and kiss them, never let them sit on your lap. If you must, kiss them once on the forehead when they say good night. Shake hands with them in the morning" (p. 81). The book represents behaviorism in its most radical form.

Watson, J. B. (1936). Autobiography. In C. Murchison (Ed.), *A History of Psychology in Autobiography,* Volume 3. Worcester, MA: Clark University Press, pp. 271–281.

In reading this, one has the impression that Watson was not very serious about providing a meaningful account of his life. It is interesting but sketchy.

Watson, J. B., & Rayner, R. (1920). Conditioned emotional reactions. *Journal of Experimental Psychology, 3,* 1–14.

The initial published account of the conditioning study of Albert B. A more popularized version appeared in *Scientific Monthly* (1921, *13,* 493–515).

Chapter 10

Psychology and "Feeblemindedness"

At the beginning of the 20th century, few Americans were involved in psychological investigations of individuals whose intelligence was below normal. As a class the mentally retarded were referred to as "feebleminded," a term of unclear reference that sometimes included all persons of below-average intelligence and sometimes referred to those just below average. These "high-grade mental defectives," as they were called, were of interest to educators because they were deemed capable of achieving reasonable functioning through appropriate training. Most prominent in this work in 1900 were A. R. T. Wylie of the Institution for the Feebleminded at Faribault, Minnesota and Will S. Monroe, a psychology professor in normal schools (colleges that trained teachers) in Massachusetts and New Jersey. However, most psychologists found this subject matter to be of no interest to them.

An exception to this rule was Henry Herbert Goddard (1866–1957) who began his career as a secondary school principal. After 6 years in that job he returned to graduate school at Clark University where he earned his doctorate in 1899 from G. Stanley Hall. For the next several years, Goddard was a faculty member at the Pennsylvania State Teachers College at West Chester.

While at West Chester, Goddard met Edward Johnstone, the director of the New Jersey Training School for Feebleminded Girls and Boys located in nearby Vineland. Goddard accepted Johnstone's invitation to visit the Vineland Training School (as it was typically called) in 1901 and made regular visits thereafter. Their discussions often focused on the growth of feeblemindedness and the general lack of information about its causes and methods for remediation.

In 1906, Johnstone invited Goddard to become the Director of Psychological Research at the Vineland School, and Goddard accepted, beginning his work there in September. One historian (Napoli, 1981) marks the significance of this appointment by calling Goddard "America's first permanent full-time psychologist who did not hold an academic appointment" (p. 17). Thus began 12 years of work at Vineland that would produce many of Goddard's contributions to psychology.

When Goddard began at Vineland he had little knowledge of how to begin a research program on feeblemindedness. His review of the psychological and educational literature convinced him that he was not alone in that ignorance. So he wrote to several psychologists and psychiatrists asking for suggestions about where he might begin. His urgent requests brought few helpful responses.

Drawing on his training at Clark, Goddard assembled a laboratory of equipment to test sensory, motor, and mental functioning in children at Vineland. Some of the apparatus he designed and had built such as an automatograph, which measured a child's ability to stand still. He worked with the attendants, asking their help in collecting data through their daily observations of the children. He even suggested keeping a record of barometric pressure and other meteorological statistics to see if weather changes were related to changes in children's moods or activities.

The daily entries in Goddard's diary of his first 2 years at Vineland illustrate the fact that he was struggling to establish a meaningful program of assessment. He was frustrated that the apparatus and testing methods so successful for studying children of normal intelligence were of little use with the Vineland children. Hearing that Europe was more advanced in this field, Goddard spent two months there in the spring of 1908 where he visited 19 institutions for the feebleminded. In Brussels, Goddard met Ovide Decroly who told him of a mental test developed in 1905 by the French psychologist, Alfred Binet. That discovery would dramatically alter the course of Goddard's career and the face of American psychology and education. Upon his return to Vineland, Goddard translated the Binet test and began to use it on Vineland children as well as children from regular schools.

In subsequent years, Goddard functioned as one of the chief promoters of the Binet scale in America. In 1910 he coined the term "moron" to refer to individuals who tested near, but below, the bottom of the range of normal intelligence. This term became part of a tripartite division of below-average intelligence devised by Goddard with "idiot" used for those with a mental age of less than 3 years, "imbecile" for those whose mental age was 3 to 7 years, and "moron" for those whose mental age ranged between 8 and 12 years. When Binet published a revision of his test in 1908, Goddard translated it and standardized it on 2,000 Vineland public school children. That work, and the subsequent efforts of Stanford University's Lewis Terman, provided the impetus for an explosion of research and application in intelligence testing in America.

Goddard remains a controversial figure today because of his strongly nativistic views of intelligence and the way his research findings were used. Goddard frequently expressed concern about the necessity of identifying the feebleminded and preventing them from harming America's "social fabric." He recommended sterilization and lifelong institutionalization for many feebleminded and cautioned against "wasted" educational efforts to try to raise the feebleminded above their genetic limitations. Although his efforts helped to convince some psychologists of the critical needs in mental retardation and the necessity for psychology to play a role in that subfield, most psychologists have been content to leave that subject to the field of education. Today the American Psychological Association (APA) has a division on mental retardation but its membership represents less than 1% of the total membership of APA.

The letters in this chapter are drawn from the Goddard Papers, which are part of the Archives of the History of American Psychology at the University of Akron. They give evidence of the difficulty Goddard had in getting his colleagues interested in mental retardation. They show the growing need in this area and a recognition of that need, yet no real efforts by psychologists to train people to work in mental retardation. As E. B. Titchener stated in the last letter, virtually everyone was willing to leave the subnormal to Goddard.

Adolf Meyer[1] to Goddard, February 8, 1906

I am delighted to hear from you that you are taking up this work [study of feeblemindedness]; I have several times thought I saw my way to take it up more carefully and certainly must do so

---

1. Adolf Meyer was one of America's leading psychiatrists. At the time of this letter he was director of New York's State Commission on Lunacy. He spent most of his career as a professor at Johns Hopkins University and director of the psychiatric clinic there.

in the near future. Each child should have a record conducted by the observer and left in the hands of the school, noting the actual facts of efficiency, and, as far as possible, any observations demanding special tests. I should advise the most direct common-sense method that has as little appearance of fussy test-work as possible, and to allow the form to grow out of what one encounters. It is naturally desirable that one should be familiar with the wider field of anomalies, but the chief thing to guard against is to pile up a lot of apparently very scientific tests which in the eyes of the teacher and any common-sense individual would appear to be top heavy, and therefore bring discredit to the movement. I shall be glad to remember your interest as soon as I shall be able to start on the thing myself; I hope that in connection with some dispensary work I shall be able to do something. I have been told that Professor Witmer[2] of Philadelphia has devoted more attention than anyone else to the study of defectives; it might be worth your while to look up his work.

G. Stanley Hall to Goddard, February 9, 1906

In response to your favor of the 2nd, would say that I have no doubt psychological study of defectives could be made valuable to the sciences [as] well as to the institution. As to lines of research one I have long greatly desired is to have a complete study of the vocabularies of higher grade idiots that develop a vocabulary, and this perhaps ought to be supplemented by a careful study of their exclamations, grunts, noises and also of their characteristic gestures.

When I visit institutions I always go away immensely impressed with the fact that here is a rich but uncultivated field, but, of course, it needs the seeing eye to glean from it. Take, for instance, the characteristic automatisms. I should think if they were indexed, each given a page, with careful notes on diurnal, mensal, annual changes in their type or in persistence, especially if suggestion or comparison could shed light on their origin, it would be interesting. I want to see comparative studies made of their nutrition, including their power to eat and feed themselves and the

---

2. Lightner Witmer (1867–1956) earned his doctorate in psychology from Wilhelm Wundt and returned to his native Philadelphia where, at the University of Pennsylvania, he opened the first psychological clinic in 1896.

nature of their appetites, especially its perversions, whether taste and smell are more or less efficient than with the normal, how metabolism takes care of the ingesta. Then there is the whole question of dress, putting it on and off, care for it, interest in it, the value of the clothes psychosis in grading. What can be done in their motor training, their musical abilities, their play? It is very easy to make such superficial suggestions. There will be nothing new to you and you can definitely extend the list.

Edmund C. Sanford[3] to Goddard, February 9, 1906

As I said the other day I am delighted to hear that there is a possibility that you may be given an opportunity to study a group of feebleminded children from the psychological point of view. I have long felt that such a study would furnish valuable results for Psychology; and I think it very probable that if the work were done by a competent pedagogue as well, he might make extremely valuable suggestions to the teachers of the feeble minded. . . .

What can be done on the pedagogical side you know better than I. On the psychological side it has seemed to me that studies of certain large and general aspects might, at the beginning, give better results than minute experimental studies carried on with all the enginery of the laboratory. Wylie I think has recently made a study of the language of such classes and probably more could be done along that line both phonetically and psychologically, i.e. as to meaning and use of words; and I think possibly studies of almost any of the categories familiar in child study, if carried out systematically in considerable number, would almost surely bring something to light. The brightest jewels in my casket, however, I believe to be these two problems, namely: the expression of emotion in the human subject—both facial and by gesture—and the fundamental human instincts. In the normal person, even in the normal child, both of these are more or less covered up by training and convention. In the feeble minded they should be, with due allowance, a good deal less obscured; and if I were going to undertake a study of that sort I think I should begin upon one or the other of these topics. But there are no end of other topics, less

---

3. Edmund Clark Sanford (1859–1924) earned his doctorate in psychology with G. S. Hall at Johns Hopkins University and joined Hall on the faculty at Clark University. He wrote the first laboratory manual for experimental psychology.

extensive and more definite than these, that would certainly repay careful investigation.

If I can give you help in any way, either by suggestion or otherwise I shall be very happy to do so. I am myself too busy to work at this topic, but I have long felt its importance, and welcome any opportunity to assist in its investigation. When I was waited on several years ago, by a representative of the Carnegie Institution, with reference to fruitful lines in Psychology, I suggested this one in particular. I also recommended it, as a particularly valuable sort of Comparative Psychology, in the address that I made as Chairman of the section in Comparative Psychology at St. Louis Congresses in 1904. I believe that it is a field that will yield valuable practical results as well as theoretical.

Witmer has conducted some sort of Psycho-Pedagogical Clinic in Philadelphia for some time. I think likely that you may get something from making connections with him if you have not done so already. Cattell also has had an advanced student[4] working upon the psychical condition of the feebleminded, and I believe that she has a book nearly ready to appear. It is risky to prophesy in science, but I think that the next ten or fifteen years will see that subject receiving very much more attention than it receives at the present time.

Fred Winslow Adams to Goddard, January 2, 1909

. . . One of my friends . . . called to see me yesterday and told me of some of the most remarkable tales about the treating of feeble minded children that I ever heard.

The man who is performing these moral miracles is Charles Morris Campbell. He is one of Albany's wealthy citizens and has taken up this work, not as a profession, but simply as a passion. His treatment is based upon a discovery of his own which he made while studying music in Italy in 1878, and he calls it muscular co-ordination. He is trying to keep the matter quiet although there was a lengthy article in the New York Sunday Herald sometime ago regarding some of his cures.

His theory is that the mind in feeble minded children is alright but the outgo and inflow are hindered by certain physical defects. For instance certain imbeciles have no calves to their legs.

---

4. This student was Naomi Norsworthy (1877–1916).

By a development of muscular exercises on the leg he develops a full normal calf with the result that the mind becomes free and intelligence is born and education may begin.

His plan is to have a physician make a thorough examination of each child and give him drawings of the physical defects when he has his treatment begun to remedy them.

He especially wants to publish a series of text books for the public schools for the correction of all physical defects and inauguration of a new system of physical culture based on muscular co-ordination.

I am going over to see him and some of his patients very soon now and will be glad to report to you what I see for myself in case you are not already familiar with his work. But as this is your special line of thought, if you had not met this man and seen his theory carried out you would be glad to come on and make me a visit as soon as you can and give this system your usual critical and careful examination.[5]

Editor's Note: *A little more than 3 years after Goddard wrote to Hall asking for help, Hall would ask Goddard's help on the same subject.*

G. Stanley Hall to Goddard, August 23, 1909

Can you tell us where we can find an expert in backward and subnormal children or if there is anybody, a young person, man preferred, who for five to eight hundred dollars can come here [to Clark University] and develop that department for a year in the hope of making themselves worth more later?

If you can make any suggestions to us as to what kinds of tests or equipment we ought to have it would be a great favor. I believe Dr. Smith,[6] to whom I turn most of them over, estimated that I had some six hundred letters, mostly from strangers, last year, making inquiries about individual children, describing their peculiarities, asking what to read, what to do, where to send them, etc. There were stammerers, epileptics, semi-idiots, children with every kind of defect, until I have almost wondered whether some energetic

---

5. F. W. Adams was Goddard's cousin and at the time of this letter was minister at the First Methodist Episcopal Church in Schenectady, New York. Goddard's lack of interest in Charles Campbell, the subject of this letter, is indicated by the fact that he wrote to his cousin 5 years *later* to inquire what he had found out.

6. Theodate Louise Smith (1859–1914) earned her Ph.D. with Hall at Clark University and remained there as lecturer in the Children's Institute. She was a major spokesperson in America for the educational philosophy of Maria Montessori.

person who could put in capital might not start somewhere near here some kind of seminary for every kind of subnormal child. . . .

Goddard to Hall, September 21, 1910

We have a number of calls and are likely to have many more in the near future for men to do psychological work either in institutions for the feebleminded or in connection with the newly formed departments for special children in the public schools. We are unable to supply people for this work, or to recommend any. I am wondering if you cannot do something at Clark to interest some of the men in this line of work so that they can take it up and thus satisfy some of the demands for this. It seems to me that if the men who are working in psychology realized the opening that there was in this line that they would several of them prepare themselves for it.

Hall to Goddard, September 23, 1910

I am tremendously interested in your letter of September 21st, as I have been in one or two previous intimations on your part and from other sources that there was a great and new field opening for experts in dealing with the feebleminded. . . If we only had a million dollars we could do a lot to spread the demand for experts into many departments of child care and welfare.

Hall to Goddard, December 2, 1910

Do you know any lady, a college graduate, with a little knowledge of psychology and if possible some experience in social work of some kind, who has cleverness, tact and sympathy enough to get into the soul of the subnormal children who are being examined here? It is sympathy and tact that we chiefly want. . . .

Goddard to Hall, December 7, 1910

Yours of Dec. 2d at hand. It is one more of a type of letter that we are frequently receiving. It is too bad that we cannot supply the demand for people to do this sort of work.

Edward Bradford Titchener to Goddard, March 1, 1911

I am just back from a western lecturing trip . . . I heard a good deal of you and your work in the western universities; I think you are making a real impression.

Personally, however, I shall leave the subnormal to you; I have come back with a very lively conviction that talent is being wasted all along the line of school and college work, and I shall try to get up a movement for the help of the supernormal child . . . The two sorts of work—if we can get ours properly started—ought to supplement each other, and not at all interfere.

Goddard Bibliography

Fancher, R. E. (1985). *The Intelligence Men: Makers of the IQ Controversy.* New York: Norton.

A historical treatment of the concept of intelligence and its measurement, including a chapter on H. H. Goddard.

Fancher, R. E. (1987). Henry Goddard and the Kallikak family photographs: "Conscious skulduggery" or "Whig history"? *American Psychologist, 42,* 585–590.

This article offers an alternative interpretation of Stephen Jay Gould's claim (see Gould reference in this bibliography) that Goddard retouched the Kallikak photos to enhance a look of retardedness. (See also the letters of reply to Fancher in the *American Psychologist,* 1988, *43,* 742–746.)

Gelb, S. A. (1986). Henry H. Goddard and the immigrants, 1910–1917: The studies and their social context. *Journal of the History of the Behavioral Sciences, 22,* 324–332.

This article discusses Goddard's testing of immigrants at Ellis Island and his views on intelligence in the context of the American public's alarm over the dangers of immigration.

Goddard, H. H. (1912). *The Kallikak Family.* New York: Macmillan.

This is Goddard's most famous book and was widely quoted as evidence of the threat to society from feeblemindedness. For Goddard, the book was important in cementing his views on the role of heredity in intelligence and for reinforcing his belief in a program of eugenics that used sterilization of the feebleminded as one way to control the spread of such "undesireables."

Goddard, H. H. (1920). *Human Efficiency and Levels of Intelligence*.
  Princeton: Princeton University Press.
  This book called for a recognition of the limitations imposed by
retardation and urged society to put its educational and training efforts
where they could be effective, avoiding waste and inefficiency in the
educational system.

Goddard, H. H. (1943). In the beginning. *The Training School Bulletin*
  (Vineland), 40, 154–161.
  This article is a reminiscence by the 77-year-old Goddard about
the beginnings of his work at Vineland.

Gould, S. J. (1981). *The Mismeasure of Man*. New York: Norton.
  A historical survey of the field of intelligence testing that is rather
critical of the work of Goddard.

Smith, D. J. (1985). *Minds Made Feeble: The Myth and Legend of the
  Kallikaks*. Rockville, MD: Aspen.
  A controversial book among historians of psychology that purports
that Goddard's research on the Kallikaks was sloppy at best or
intentionally selective at worst.

Sokal, M. M. (Ed.) (1987). *Psychological Testing and American Society,
  1890–1930*. New Brunswick, NJ: Rutgers University Press.
  This collection of articles by various historians of social science
includes substantial treatment of Goddard's work in intelligence testing.

Chapter 11

Sigmund Freud and Carl Jung in America

In 1908, G. Stanley Hall, psychologist and president of Clark University in Worcester, Massachusetts was busy planning a celebration of the 20th anniversary of Clark that would occur the following year. On December 15 he wrote to Wilhelm Wundt and Sigmund Freud (1856–1939), inviting them to speak at Clark in July. Wundt declined the invitation. He may even have wondered about such elaborate preparations at Clark, a university in its infancy, given that his own University of Leipzig was then planning to celebrate an anniversary—its 500th! Freud also declined the invitation but in February, 1909, he changed his mind when the dates of the planned Clark Conference were changed to September and the compensation offered him increased. Hall also promised him an honorary degree. It would be Freud's first and only trip to America.

In the next six months, Freud and his disciple, Carl Gustav Jung (1875–1961), often discussed America in their letters, especially after Freud learned in June that Jung had also been invited. Both viewed the invitation as important recognition for psychoanalysis and saw the visit as a golden opportunity to spread the word of psychoanalysis in the New World. But their eagerness was also tempered by some pessimism about the puritanical nature of the Americans and their willingness to embrace a theory of behavior emphasizing sexuality. Freud was both excited and anxious regarding the trip, fretting about his lecture topics and whether he should deliver the lectures in German or make the attempt to give them in English.

Freud invited another disciple, Sandor Ferenczi, to accompany him on the trip. They joined Jung in Bremen and on August 21, 1909, sailed for America on the liner, *George Washington*. They arrived in New York City on August 29. The following day A. A. Brill, an

American disciple, took Freud and his companions on a tour of the city. They visited Central Park and Chinatown in the morning and spent the afternoon at Coney Island. The next morning they toured the Metropolitan Museum of Art, a sight that Freud had looked forward to with great anticipation, principally because of the Greek antiquities in the museum's collection.

The next day Freud was taken to see his first movie, a film involving "plenty of wild chasing." Freud's reaction was described as "quietly amused" (Jones, 1955, p. 56). By this time the three Europeans were suffering from their American diet. Jung, in a letter to his wife, complained that they all had diarrhea and bad stomach aches. Freud even believed he might be having an attack of appendicitis. The three of them fasted for a day in an effort to alleviate some of the discomfort.

After touring New York City, Freud and Jung journeyed to Worcester, arriving on September 5, where they were invited to stay in Hall's home. Freud's first lecture was scheduled for two days later.

The lineup of speakers for the conference was impressive, notwithstanding the presence of Freud and Jung. It included William Stern, Adolph Meyer, Franz Boas, Herbert Spencer Jennings, and Edward Bradford Titchener. Those in attendance were a Who's Who of American psychology including William James and James McKeen Cattell.

Freud gave five lectures on successive days, at 11:00 each morning. The lectures covered his system of psychoanalysis and were delivered in German. He did not write out his lectures in advance. Instead, they were formed in the course of half-hour walks that he took with Ferenczi. No notes were used in delivering the lectures, and Freud's later published versions were derived wholly from his memory of those talks. Jung gave three lectures, also delivered in German, describing work with his word association method.

Freud was surely impressed with the attention and adulation he received. That feeling had begun on the trip over from Europe when he noticed one of the ship's stewards reading a copy of his book, The Psychopathology of Everyday Life. At the ceremony when he received his honorary doctorate, Freud was visibly moved. He thanked Hall for what he termed the "first official recognition of our endeavors" (Jones, 1955, p. 57). Freud felt he received recognition in America that was denied him in Europe. He told his biographer, "As I stepped on to the platform in Worcester to deliver my Five Lectures Upon Psycho-Analysis it seemed like the recognition of some incredible daydream;

psychoanalysis was no longer a product of delusion; it had become a valuable part of reality" (Jones, 1955, p. 59).

Although Freud and Jung relished the recognition for their work that the invitations represented, both had somewhat negative impressions of America and Americans. Some of those attitudes are revealed in the letters that follow. Nevertheless, their 1909 visit provided a substantial boost to psychoanalytic theory in America, spreading both Freudian and Jungian ideas to American followers (see Hale, 1979; Hornstein, 1992). Today psychoanalysis is more prominent in America than any other country, an occurrence that Freud and Jung would surely not have predicted. The letters that follow tell some of the story of this historic visit.

Freud to Jung, December 30, 1908

Now finally I come to the news that I have been invited by Clark University, Worcester, Mass., Pres. Stanley Hall, to deliver four to six lectures in the first week of July. They expect my lectures to give a mighty impetus to the development of psychotherapy over there. The occasion: the twentieth (!) anniversary of the founding of the university. I have declined without even consulting you or anyone else, the crucial reason being that I should have had to stop work 2 weeks sooner than usual, which would mean a loss of several thousand kronen. Naturally the Americans pay only $400 for travel expenses. I am not wealthy enough to spend five times that much to give the Americans an impetus. (That's boasting; two-and-a-half to three times as much!) But I am sorry to have it fall through on this account, because it would have been fun. I don't really believe that Clark University, a small but serious institution, can postpone its festivities for three weeks.

Jung to Freud, January 7, 1909

This is a real triumph and I congratulate you most heartily! Too bad it comes at such an inconvenient time. Perhaps you could arrange to go after the anniversary; even then your lectures would still be of interest to the Americans. Little by little your truth is percolating through to the public. If at all possible, you ought to speak in America if only because of the echo it would arouse in Europe, where things are beginning to stir too.

Freud to Jung, January 17, 1909

There is a good deal to be said about America. Jones[1] and Brill write often. Jones's observations are shrewd and pessimistic, Brill sees everything through rose-coloured spectacles. I am inclined to agree with Jones. I also think that once they discover the sexual core of our psychological theories they will drop us. Their prudery and their material dependence on the public are too great. That is why I have no desire to risk the trip there in July. I can't expect anything of consultations. Anyway I have heard nothing more from Clark University.

Jung to Freud, January 19, 1909

The Americans are a horse of a different colour. First I must point out with diabolical glee your slip of the pen: you wrote "your prudishness" instead of "their prudishness." We have noticed this prudishness, which used to be worse than it is now; now I can stomach it. I don't water down the sexuality any more.

You are probably right about the trip to America. I share Jones's pessimism absolutely. So far these people simply haven't a notion of what we're at. One of these days they will creep into a corner, prim and abashed. Nevertheless it will rub off on some of them and is doing so already, despite their audible silence. In any case the American medical material isn't up to much.

Freud to Jung, March 9, 1909

You recall that last December I received an invitation from Clark University in Worcester, Mass., which I had to decline because the festivities during which my lectures were to be delivered were scheduled for the second week in July and I would have lost too much money by the transaction. At the time you yourself regretted that I was unable to manage it. Well, a week ago a second invitation came from Stanley Hall, the president of Clark University, who at the same time informed me that the festivities had been postponed to the week of September 6. Also the travel allowance has been increased not inconsiderably from $400 to $750. This time I have accepted, for at the end of August I shall be free

---

1. Ernest Jones, a British disciple who was with Freud in America and later wrote a 3-volume biography of Freud.

and rested. On October 1 I hope to be back in Vienna. I must admit that this has thrilled me more than anything else that has happened in the last few years—except perhaps for the appearance of the *Jahrbuch*[2]—and that I have been thinking of nothing else. Practical considerations have joined forces with imagination and youthful enthusiasm to upset the composure on which you have complimented me. In 1886, when I started my practice, I was thinking only of a two-month trial period in Vienna; if it did not prove satisfactory, I was planning to go to America and found an existence that I would subsequently have asked my fiancée in Hamburg to share. You see, we both of us had nothing, or more precisely, I had a large and impoverished family and she a small inheritance of roughly 3000 fl. from her Uncle Jacob, who had been a professor of classical philology in Bonn. But unfortunately things went so well in Vienna that I decided to stay on, and we were married in the autumn of the same year. And now, twenty-three years later, I am to go to America after all, not, to be sure, to make money, but in response to an honourable call! We shall have a good deal to say about this trip and its various consequences for our cause.

Jung to Freud, March 11, 1909

I must congratulate you heartily on your American triumphs. I believe you will get an American practice in the end. My American has been behaving quite well so far. I am all agog for more news.

If you are going to America in September, I earnestly hope that you will put in a week with us here as a way-station. You will have all the holiday peace and quiet that could be wished for. We are boldly taking it for granted that you will come. After all, the road to America runs through Zürich too. (This piece of impudence was only half intentional, otherwise I would have deleted the sentence.)

Freud to Jung, June 3, 1909

I should like very much to talk with you about America and have your suggestions. Jones threatens me, not entirely without

---

2. The *Yearbook for Psychoanalysis and Research in Psychopathology*, the first journal on psychoanalysis, was planned by Freud and appeared in 1908 under Jung's editorship.

ulterior motive, with the absence of all leading psychiatrists. I expect nothing of the moguls. But I wonder if it might not be a good idea to concentrate on psychology since Stanley Hall is a psychologist, and perhaps to devote my 3–4 lectures entirely to dreams, from which excursions in various directions would be possible. Of course these questions have little practical interest in view of my inability to lecture in English.

Jung to Freud, June 12, 1909

Isn't it splendid about America? I have already booked a cabin on the G. *Washington*—unfortunately only a very expensive one was left. I shall sail with you from Bremen. Now I am in for it—what am I to say? What *can* one say of all this in 3 lectures? I'd be grateful for advice.[3]

Freud to Jung, June 18, 1909

Your being invited to America is the best thing that has happened to us since Salzburg;[4] it gives me enormous pleasure for the most selfish reasons, though also, to be sure, because it shows what prestige you have already gained at your age. Such a beginning will take you far, and a certain amount of favour on the part of men and fate is a very good thing for one who aspires to perform great deeds.

Of course your joy is now beginning to be clouded by the same concerns as mine, culminating in the question: What am I to say to those people? On this score I have a saving idea, which I shall not keep secret from you. Here it is: we can think about it on shipboard, on our long walks round the deck. Otherwise I can only refer you to the astute observation with which you yourself recently allayed *my* misgivings: that the invitation is the main thing, that the audience is now at our mercy, under obligation to applaud whatever we bring them.

---

3. Apparently Jung sent a telegram to Freud prior to this letter informing him that he too had received an invitation to speak at Clark University. Years later in his autobiography, Jung would say that he and Freud were invited at the same time. Certainly the Freud-Jung correspondence suggests that was not the case. See *Memories, Dreams, Reflections* (1961), pp. 120–121.

4. The reference is to the First Congress of Freudian Psychology, which was held in Salzburg in 1908.

A most gratifying detail is that you too are sailing on the G. *Washington*. We shall both be very nice to Ferenczi.

Jung to Freud, July 10–13, 1909

I shall then start immediately on the American lectures. I really don't know what to say. I shall start nibbling away at some corner just to see what happens. I have a vague idea of speaking first on the family constellation, second on the diagnostic significance of associations, and third on the educational questions raised by psychoanalysis. Naturally I am not a little bothered by the fact that you will be present and know all this far better than I do. I shall go through with it all the same. Once the essentials are down on paper it won't worry me in the least, and I shall be able to give my whole attention to the impressions of the voyage.

Jung to his wife, Emma, September 8, 1909 (from Worcester, MA)

. . . The people here are all exceedingly amiable and on a decent cultural level. We are beautifully taken care of at the Halls' and daily recovering from the exertions of New York. My stomach is almost back to normal now; from time to time there is a little twitch, but aside from that, my general health is excellent. Yesterday Freud began the lectures and received great applause. We are gaining ground here, and our following is growing slowly but surely. Today I had a talk about psychoanalysis with two highly cultivated elderly ladies who proved to be very well informed and free-thinking. I was greatly surprised, since I had prepared myself for opposition. Recently we had a large garden party with fifty people present, in the course of which I surrounded myself with five ladies. I was even able to make jokes in English—though what English! Tomorrow comes my first lecture; all my dread of it has vanished, since the audience is harmless and merely eager to hear new things, which is certainly what we can supply them with. It is said that we shall be awarded honorary doctorates by the university next Saturday, with a great deal of pomp and circumstance. In the evening there will be a "formal reception." Today's letter has to be short, since the Halls have invited some people for five o'clock to meet us. We have also been interviewed by the *Boston Evening Transcript*. In fact we are the men of the hour here. It is very good to be able to spread oneself in this way once in a while. I can feel that my libido is gulping it in with vast enjoyment. . .

Jung to his wife, Emma, September 14, 1909 (from Worcester, MA)

. . . Last night there was a tremendous amount of ceremony and fancy dress, with all sorts of red and black gowns and gold-tasseled square caps. In a grand and festive assemblage I was appointed Doctor of Laws *honoris causa* and Freud likewise. Now I may place an L.L.D. after my name. Impressive, what? . . . Today Prof. M. drove us by automobile out to lunch at a beautiful lake. The landscape was utterly lovely. This evening there is one more "private conference" in Hall's house on the "psychology of sex." Our time is dreadfully crammed. The Americans are really masters at that; they hardly leave one time to catch one's breath. Right now I am rather worn out from all the fabulous things we have been through, and am longing for the quiet of the mountains. My head is spinning. Last night at the awarding of the doctorate I had to deliver an impromptu talk before some three hundred persons. . . . Freud is in seventh heaven, and I am glad with all my heart to see him so. . . .

I am looking forward enormously to getting back to the sea again, where the overstimulated psyche can recover in the presence of that infinite peace and spaciousness. Here one is in an almost constant whirlwind. But I have, thank God, completely regained my capacity for enjoyment, so that I can look forward to everything with zest. Now I am going to take everything that comes along by storm, and then I shall settle down again, satiated . . .

Jung to his wife, Emma, September 18, 1909 (from Albany, NY)

. . . Two more days before departure! Everything is taking place in a whirl. Yesterday I stood upon a bare rocky peak nearly 5600 feet high, in the midst of tremendous virgin forests, looking far out into the blue infinities of America and shivering to the bone in the icy wind, and today I am in the midst of the metropolitan bustle of Albany, the capital of the State of New York! The hundred thousand enormously deep impressions I am taking back with me from this wonderland cannot be described with the pen. Everything is too big, too immeasurable. Something that has gradually been dawning upon me in the past few days is the recognition that here an ideal potentiality of life has become reality. Men are as well off here as the culture permits; women badly off. We have seen things here that inspire enthusiastic admiration, and things that make one ponder social evolution deeply. As far as technological culture is concerned, we lag miles behind America. But all that is frightfully costly and already carries the germ of the end in itself. I must tell you a great, great deal. I shall never forget the experiences of this journey. Now we are tired of America. Tomorrow morning we are off to New York, and on September 21 we sail! . . .

Jung to Freud, November 8, 1909

As a basis for the analysis of the American way of life I am now treating a young American (doctor). Here again the mother-complex looms large (cf. the *Mother-Mary cult*). In America the mother is decidedly the dominant member of the family. American culture really is a bottomless abyss; the men have become a flock of sheep and the women play the ravening wolves—within the family circle, of course. I ask myself whether such conditions have ever existed in the world before. I really don't think they have.

Freud to Jung, November 21, 1909

Stanley Hall wrote me recently: "I am a very unworthy exponent of your views and of course have too little clinical experience to be an authority in that field; but it seems to me that, whereas hitherto many, if not most pathologists have leaned upon the stock psychologists like Wundt, your own interpretations reverse the situation and make us normal psychologists look to this work in the abnormal or borderline field for our chief light." We are still very far from that in Germany. But coming from the old man such serious, thoughtful compliments are very nice.

Out of sheer gratitude I have already sent him three of the lectures and am working desperately on the last. I am making a few changes and additions, and also putting in a few defensive, or rather, aggressive, remarks. Deuticke wants to publish them in

German, but I don't know if Hall would like that, and it troubles me that there is nothing new in them.

Freud to Jung, January 13, 1910

First a few words about the last post from America, which is very rich and might give one a feeling of triumph. Apart from Putnam's[5] article, which you have already mentioned, I have received letters from St. Hall, Jones, Brill, and Putnam himself. Hall reports on the congress of psychologists at Harvard,[6] which devoted a whole afternoon to ψA, in the course of which he and Putnam gave the malignant Boris Sidis[7] a thorough trouncing. You have probably received the same news; if not, it will give me pleasure to send you the letters. The old man, who is really a splendid fellow, writes that in April he is devoting a special number of the *American Journal of Psychology* to us; it is to contain your lectures, Ferenczi's paper on dream-work in translation, the shorter paper by Jones, and perhaps also my five lectures. . . . My prophecy comes true! Our trip to America seems to have done some good, which compensates me for leaving a part of my health there.

Freud-Jung Bibliography

Cromer, W., & Anderson, P. (1970). Freud's visit to America: Newspaper coverage. *Journal of the History of the Behavioral Sciences, 6,* 349–353.
    A summary of the newspaper coverage of Freud's Clark Conference lectures drawn from two Boston and two Worcester newspapers.

Ellenberger, H. F. (1970). *The Discovery of the Unconscious.* New York: Basic Books.
    This excellent book describes the "history and evolution of dynamic psychiatry" (its subtitle), focusing on Sigmund Freud and psychoanalysis in Chapter 7 and C. G. Jung and analytical psychology in Chapter 9.

---

5. James Jackson Putnam, a professor of neurology at Harvard, was the first president of the American Psychoanalytic Association in 1911.

6. This meeting was the 18th annual meeting of the American Psychological Association.

7. Boris Sidis was director of a mental asylum in Portsmouth, New Hampshire. He was especially critical of psychoanalysis calling it a "worship of Venus and Priapus which encouraged masturbation, perversion, and illegitimacy." (Gay, 1988, p. 196)

Evans, R. B., & Koelsch, W. A. (1985). Psychoanalysis arrives in America: The 1909 psychology conference at Clark University. *American Psychologist, 40,* 942–948.

A historical account of the Clark Conference drawing heavily on archival records.

Freud, S. (1910). The origin and development of psychoanalysis. *American Journal of Psychology, 21,* 181–218.

Freud's five lectures delivered at the 1909 Clark Conference, translated by Henry W. Chase and published in G. Stanley Hall's journal.

Gay, P. (1988). *Freud: A Life for Our Time.* New York: Norton.

There are more than 100 published biographies on Freud. This one is arguably the best. It covers both the life of Freud and the evolution of his creation (psychoanalysis) in their social and intellectual climates.

Hale, N. G., Jr. (Ed.) (1971). *James Jackson Putnam and Psychoanalysis: Letters between Putnam and Sigmund Freud, Ernest Jones, William James, Sandor Ferenczi, and Morton Prince, 1877–1917.* Cambridge: Harvard University Press.

Putnam, a neurologist, has been called Freud's first American convert. As noted earlier, Putnam founded the American Psychoanalytic Association in 1911 and served as its first president. This book contains 89 letters between Putnam and Freud.

Hornstein, G. A. (1992). The return of the repressed: Psychology's problematic relations with psychoanalysis, 1909–1960. *American Psychologist, 47,* 254–263.

A history of the interface of American psychology and psychoanalysis that traces experimental psychology's strategies to discredit psychoanalysis.

Jones, E. (1953, 1955, 1957). *The Life and Work of Sigmund Freud* (three volumes). New York: Basic Books.

Ernest Jones, a long-time disciple of Freud, authored this comprehensive work that stood for nearly 30 years as the most respected treatment of Freud's life and work. Some have referred to it as Freud's "autobiography," arguing that Jones wrote it as Freud would have dictated it. There are better biographies today (e.g., Gay and Sulloway) but this one bears reading by any serious scholar of Freud.

Jung, C. G. (1910). The association method. *American Journal of Psychology, 21,* 219–269.

Jung's lectures at the Clark Conference in 1909 (which were translated by A. A. Brill), describing his use of the word association method in the study of personality.

Jung, C. G. (1961). *Memories, Dreams, Reflections*. New York: Random House.

> Jung's autobiography, edited by his secretary, Aniela Jaffe. It is supplemented by reliance on correspondence, some of which is published in appendixes.

Masson, J. M. (Ed.). (1985). *The Complete Letters of Sigmund Freud to Wilhelm Fliess, 1887–1904*. Cambridge: Belknap Press of Harvard University Press.

> A collection of 301 letters important to the development of psychoanalysis. Fliess, Freud's closest friend, was a physician in Berlin. Fliess attended several of Freud's lectures in Vienna, after which their correspondence began. The breakup of their friendship commenced in 1900, following the publication of Freud's *Interpretation of Dreams*, presumably because of Fliess's jealousy of Freud's success. The demise of their friendship was very painful for Freud.

McGuire, W. (Ed.) (1974). *The Freud/Jung Letters: The Correspondence between Sigmund Freud and C. G. Jung*. Princeton, NJ: Princeton University Press.

> The complete collection of the correspondence between Freud and his crown prince, Jung, 1906–1913. All of the Freud-Jung letters in this chapter were taken from this book. The annotations are extensive adding to the reader's understanding and pleasure.

Ross, D. (1972). *G. Stanley Hall: The Psychologist as Prophet*. Chicago: University of Chicago Press.

> An excellent biography of Hall who introduced Freud and Jung to America. See pages 381–413 for coverage of Hall's involvement in the Clark Conference and psychoanalysis.

Schultz, D. (1990). *Intimate Friends, Dangerous Rivals: The Turbulent Relationship between Freud and Jung*. Los Angeles: Tarcher.

> A fascinating account of the Freud-Jung relationship, that begins with an analysis of their childhoods. Drawing on those experiences Schultz shows what drew them together and how they were destined to be driven apart. Although there are several books on this subject, none matches this one for its use of the scholarly record.

Sulloway, F. J. (1979). *Freud: Biologist of the Mind*. New York: Basic Books.

> The first major biography of Freud written by someone outside the Freudian community of family and followers. Sulloway, a historian of science, emphasizes the influence of Darwin on Freud as the latter constructed an evolutionary theory of the mind.

Chapter 12

Coleman Griffith as Sport Psychologist[1]

✍️

When the fledgling American scientific psychology took its first infantile steps at the end of the 19th century, some of those steps were in an *applied* direction, first with regard to education and child rearing, then to business and industry via research on such topics as advertising and sales, and then to mental testing and psychotherapy. All of those early applied efforts grew to mature applied specialties that dominate psychological practice today. But not all applied specialties enjoyed continuous prosperity, as is shown in looking at the history of the psychology of sport.

Coleman Roberts Griffith (1893–1966) is an individual largely absent from the histories of American psychology. However, his name has resurfaced in the past 20 years with the growth of a new field, sport psychology. This new field has been actively pursued in other countries, especially in Europe, for several decades; however, its visibility in North America is fairly recent. Today, national and international organizations exist that bring together psychology, sport, exercise, and physical education. For example, within the American Psychological Association, members interested in the psychology of sport can belong to one of APA's newest divisions, the Division on Exercise and Sport Psychology.

Further evidence of this new psychological specialty includes a half-dozen journals established in the past 20 years to publish sport psychology research, university courses on the psychology of sport, and consulting opportunities for psychologists in the field of athletics. It is

1. I gratefully acknowledge the considerable assistance on this chapter provided by my colleague Arnold LeUnes whose work has made me aware of the importance of sport psychology and whose research in the Griffith Papers made these letters available to me.

now common to find psychologists involved in the training of Olympic athletes as well as athletes in a wide variety of professional sports.

American psychologists have been interested in sports since the beginnings of the "new" psychology in the late 1800s. The psychologist most responsible for labeling scientific psychology as the "new psychology," Edward Wheeler Scripture, studied reaction times in athletes in his Yale University laboratory in the 1890s. And later, psychologists George Patrick and Walter Miles conducted separate investigations on the psychology of football. However, for these psychologists and others, sport psychology was a passing fancy.

Coleman Griffith's involvement in sport psychology was quite different. He established a research laboratory for the psychology of athletics and for many years he studied that topic, publishing several important books. He was not only a researcher and writer but also a consultant who advised college and professional teams. He was sought after as a speaker and consultant to athletic programs and departments of physical education. Yet as a sport psychologist he worked in virtual isolation in his field; few of his psychologist colleagues showed any interest in what he was doing. And thus his contributions disappeared only to be rediscovered in the last 20 years as sport psychology emerged as a recognized applied specialty.

Griffith earned his doctorate in experimental psychology in 1920 at the University of Illinois and stayed on the faculty there until his retirement in 1953. As a graduate student in 1918, he began laboratory studies of the psychological factors involved in basketball and football, particularly regarding the processes of vision and attention. By 1920 he had moved out of the laboratory and was measuring reaction times of football players on the sidelines.

In 1920, Griffith offered a special section of his introductory psychology class for athletes "to teach the facts and principles of introductory psychology by drawing upon athletic competition rather than upon daily life for illustrative material" (Griffith, 1930, p. 35). And by 1923 this course had evolved into an entirely separate course entitled "Psychology and Athletics." This new course "sought to make a serious psychological analysis of all phases of athletic competition, to review the literature already available which bore upon such problems as skill, learning, habit, attention, vision, emotion, and reaction time, and to gain, whenever possible, such new knowledge as time and the facilities warranted" (p. 36).

Griffith's courses made him understand how much needed to be done if the relationship between psychology and athletics was to be fully understood. A well-equipped and staffed research laboratory was necessary to carry out the research agenda he envisioned. In 1925 that laboratory became a reality, thanks to the considerable support from George Huff who was Director of Physical Welfare [Physical Education] for Men at the University of Illinois. Huff believed that in building athletic teams, too much attention had been focused on physical factors such as strength and speed. Although acknowledging the importance of such motor abilities, he called for a research program that would discover the role of mental factors in athletic competition.

The new two-room laboratory opened in September of 1925 occupying more than 1,000 square feet in the newly constructed men's gymnasium. By 1930 the research completed or ongoing included studies on: a) the relation between physical exercise and learning, b) the effects of extreme physical exercise on longevity and disease resistance, c) the nature of sleep in athletes, d) methods of teaching psychological skills in football, e) measurement of physical fitness, f) the effects of emotion on learning of habits, g) muscular coordination, h) persistence of errors, i) the effects of fatigue on performance, j) measures of motor aptitude, and k) mental variables associated with excellent athletic performances.

This work led to Griffith's first publication in sport psychology, an article entitled "Psychology and Its Relation to Athletic Competition" (1924) and subsequently to his two most important books: *Psychology of Coaching* (1926) and *Psychology and Athletics* (1928). In their years of publication, both books were selected by the *Journal of Applied Psychology* as one of the 12 best books on applied psychology.

Griffith's Athletic Research Laboratory was likely the first of its kind in North America and perhaps the second one in the world. (Only one earlier laboratory, in Berlin, Germany, is known to exist.) For its first 5 years the Illinois laboratory was well supported. But soon financial pressures within the Athletic Department caused it to withdraw its funding and the lab was closed in 1932. Griffith returned to his post as Professor of Educational Psychology. He would publish a few more articles on sport psychology and in 1938 conducted a study for the Chicago Cubs professional baseball team. But his book tentatively titled *Psychology of Football,* to be co-authored with Robert Zuppke, Illinois' head football coach, would never be completed. Instead he turned his research and writing efforts toward the related field of educational psychology, publishing another four books before his retirement.

The letters in this chapter are taken from the Coleman Griffith Papers that are housed in the University of Illinois Archives. They provide a flavor of the psychological interests of this pioneer who was truly ahead of his time. Further, they give evidence of the stigma associated with applied psychology and of the suspicions the public often held about college sports, particularly football.

Griffith to Robert Zuppke, December 13, 1921

At one of our conversations during football practice the proposal was made that all prospective candidates for next year's football team should be put through an elaborate series of tests. To do this will require several weeks of preparation on my part and the expenditure of at least an hour and a half with each of the men. Because of my heavy departmental duties I cannot take the time to give these tests unless you feel I can be of genuine service to the Coaching School. You will recall that we proposed to test reaction time, memory, emotionalism, mental alertness, steadiness under emotion, rapidity of habit formation, and courage. Would it be too much to ask for your frank opinion about these tests before I begin preparation for them?

Griffith to George Huff, November 13, 1922

In working over our Announcement of Courses for next semester I am putting down Psychology 25 [Introductory Psychology], the course designed primarily for athletes. Every time I have given this course so far, I have been embarrassed by individuals coming in two or three weeks late with the excuse that they did not know about the course until too late to register regularly for it. They miss, therefore, very important reviews that are necessary to the course. Would it not be well, therefore, to have some reference in your Announcement of Courses to Psychology 25?

George Huff to Griffith, November 14, 1922

Psychology 25 is down in our curriculum as a required subject and will be announced in the time table. I believe this should do away with the trouble you have experienced in the past.

Griffith to Robert Zuppke, December 4, 1922

For the past three years you have generously given me the privilege of observing football practice at any time I have desired. I have taken advantage of this opportunity to watch you and your men as carefully as I could. During that time I have had a growing respect for your extraordinary knowledge of human nature and of the fundamental facts of psychology. In this day when there is so much cheap and naive psychologizing in athletic circles I am inclined to express my admiration for a man who knows how to avoid shoddy psychological facts and who knows, as well, how to bring to bear upon the teaching of football and the strategy of a football campaign psychological facts of the most authentic and fundamental character.

I am grateful to you for the instruction which you have given me. Our academic psychology often tends to become more artificial and distantly removed from actual life. More than once you have clothed these artificial facts with flesh and blood. You have often let me catch a glimpse of psychology as a science of actual human beings.

Please accept my thanks, not only for the privilege of seeing Illinois teams in the making, but for the instruction you have given me in my chosen field.

Robert Zuppke to Griffith, December 6, 1922

I received your letter and wish to tell you that I appreciate your kind remarks very much. I hope you can be with us in the future because I like to see you on the field.

L. M. Tobin[2] to Griffith, May 24, 1923

For the probable use in the next catalog of the four year coaching course we would like to have a description of Psychology 25. We are very sure that a description of this course in untechnical terms will be interesting to the high school graduates who see our catalog. . . .

---

2. Tobin was News Service Manager for the Illinois Athletic Association

Griffith to L. M. Tobin, May 30, 1923

Here are a few things that might be said about Psychology 25. You are probably more experienced in using untechnical terms and I give you permission, therefore, to reword wherever you want to.

Psychology 25 is a course applying the facts of psychology to all kinds of athletic competition. It is held that all games and sports call for good minds as well as for good bodies. In this course the various games are studied in the psychological aspects. The course includes such topics as learning the signal system, establishing proper habits, planning the season's campaign, developing a spirit of determination and "fight," maintaining "pep" and morale, devising and executing trick plays, selecting men for special positions on a team, learning how to control and coordinate one's muscles, developing athletic ideals and traditions, and keeping up a good spirit between the members of a team and the coach. . . .

Griffith to George Huff, November 21, 1923

I thought you would be interested to know of the general character of the Sunday services at Trinity Church a short time ago. During the morning service, Rev. Baker gave a very fine address upon some of the larger issues involved in athletic competition. He spoke, in no uncertain terms, against uninformed and unintelligent people who try to make capitol out of conference football games. He said that he saw behind such competition, a physical, mental, and spiritual value of the highest order. He spoke at length of the value of athletic ideals and traditions, of the worthwhileness of sportsmanship, cooperation, and teamwork. At no time did he resort to the unfortunate and sometimes distasteful phrases of a minister in trying to draw far fetched morals and lessons from the field of athletics.

To my mind nothing could have been finer than his address before the Homecomers. I think he made his audience appreciate, as they may never have appreciated before, the mental and spiritual things that lay behind their stadium. . . .

Griffith to Knute Rockne,[3] December 9, 1924

As you may know, I have been interested for some years in many of the problems of psychology and athletics. I am writing you now because during the past season I heard a few comments about you and your team that were of interest to my work, having always taken the point that men on a team play best when they love the game they are playing. I have said that I did not believe such a team would have to be keyed up to win its games. A team that is keyed up is bound to have a slump. Men who are always playing their best because they like the game are far more apt to go through a season without a serious slump. Now the point I am getting at is this: I have heard it said that you do not key your men up to their games: that you select such men as play the game joyously for its own sake and that you try to develop in them as much of the spirit as you can.

I am wondering if you care to tell me directly about these things? I am asking for information only because of my psychological interest in athletic sports.

Knute Rockne to Griffith, December 13, 1924

I feel very grateful to you for having written me, although I do not know a great deal about psychology.

I do try to pick men, who like the game of football and who get a lot of fun out of playing it. I never try to make football hard work. I do think your team plays good football, because they like to play and I do not make any effort to key them up, except on rare, exceptional occasions. I keyed them up for the Nebraska game this year, which was a mistake, as we had a reaction the following Saturday against Northwestern. I try to make our boys take the game less seriously than, I presume, some others do, and we try to make the spirit of the game one of exhileration (sic) and we never allow hatred to enter into it, no matter against whom we are playing.

---

3. Knute Rockne (head football coach at the University of Notre Dame) was arguably the greatest college football coach in history. A 1914 graduate of Notre Dame, he coached his alma mater's teams from 1918 through 1930. In those 13 seasons his record was 105 wins, 12 losses, and 5 ties for a winning percentage of .881, which no one has ever matched or exceeded. He died in a plane crash in 1931 at the age of 42.

Griffith to Knute Rockne, December 18, 1924

Let me thank you most heartily for your comments about the play spirit in football. If you are so inclined, I would like to hear about the plans you make for a post-season game and what efforts you have to make to re-awaken the interest of the men. I doubt very much whether teams that have to be keyed up to a game will be able to do so well weeks after the season is closed as a team which plays in the spirit in which yours seems to play. I do not mean, of course, to trouble you about this before your trip to the coast[4] but I will be most grateful for any comments you may have after you come back.

Knute Rockne to Griffith, February 10, 1925

Regarding our trip to the coast, we took it mostly in the way of a pleasure trip and an educational trip, and we made the work-outs short and snappy, so as not to make them hard work in any sense of the word. We had just one real hard workout and that was at Tucson, which served as a sort of get the boys in a mood for a game. The climate of California sort of took the resiliency and drive out of their legs before the second half began. However, the spirit of play manifested itself and the boys were so alert that they took advantage of every mistake made by Stanford. I think a keyed-up team would have been too tense and too excited to have profited by these opportunities.

From an education point of view, we had a very profitable trip and the boys missed but one day of classes.

Editor's Note: *That Coleman Griffith's sport psychology work was receiving notice is evidenced in the following telegram and two letters.*

Editor of the Yale Daily News [Yale University's student newspaper] to Griffith, April 10, 1922

It is with great interest that I read a small article on your new system of tests for athletics. At present there is so much excitement over athletics that an idea like your "Psychology of Athletics" is of particular interest.

---

4. The trip to the coast was the 1925 Rose Bowl game that Notre Dame won over Stanford University by the score of 27 to 10.

Could we expect an article from you on this subject of from five hundred to fifteen hundred words to be published in the Yale Daily News? We feel that we are able to present anything that you might have to say to a particularly interested audience and greatly to their enlightenment.

T. F. West[5] to Griffith, March 4, 1923

I understand that you have made a study of the prominent athletes of the University of Illinois to ascertain what mental traits are most useful in athletic efficiency.

Might I ask if you would give me a general outline of the scope of this study and what results you were able to obtain in connection with it. . . .

I am interested in trying to find any information which might or might not show whether there is any correlation between scholastic achievement and physical accomplishment.

U. G. Dubach [Corvallis, Oregon] to Griffith, February 14, 1924 (telegram)

ERNEST BEARG APPLYING FOR POSITION HEAD COACH OREGON AGRIC COLLEGE STOP DOES HE KNOW FOOTBALL CAN HE TEACH IT IS HE LEADER DOES HE MEET PEOPLE WELL WITH OFFICIALS HOW WOULD YOU RATE HIM FOR PHYSICAL DIRECTOR WIRE COLLECT

Griffith/Sport Psychology Bibliography

Griffith, C. R. (1923). *General Introduction to Psychology*. New York: Macmillan (2nd edition, 1928).

Based on the lectures given in Griffith's introductory psychology courses at the University of Illinois, this book has numerous examples drawn from athletics.

---

5. T. F. West was with the Department of Health Education, Detroit, Michigan Public Schools.

Griffith, C. R. (1926). *Psychology of Coaching.* New York: Scribners' Sons; and (1928) *Psychology and Athletics.* New York: Scribners' Sons.

These are the first two books on sport psychology. The earlier book is drawn largely from Griffith's observations, whereas the second book depends more heavily on the work of Illinois's Athletic Research Laboratory. Both make interesting reading in seeing how Griffith attempted to apply what he knew about psychology to the world of athletics.

Griffith, C. R. (1930). A laboratory for research in athletics. *Research Quarterly, 1,* 34–40.

Griffith's summary account of the work of the University of Illinois's Athletic Research Laboratory in its first five years and its plans for future research.

Kroll, W., & Lewis, G. (1970, January). America's first sport psychologist. *Quest,* pp. 1–4.

A brief biographical sketch of Coleman Griffith, emphasizing his work as a sport psychologist.

LeUnes, A., & Nation, J. R. (1989). *Sport Psychology: An Introduction.* Chicago: Nelson-Hall.

A readable and very comprehensive textbook on sport psychology that organizes the material along the topic areas typically covered in an introductory psychology textbook, for example, motivation, learning, and personality.

Spears, B., & Swanson, R. (1988). *History of Sport and Physical Education in the United States* (3rd edition). Dubuque, IA: Brown & Benchmark.

A history of sport in the United States, beginning with the games played by the earliest inhabitants of North America.

Note: *For the reader interested in the most recent research and applications in sport psychology see the following periodicals—the* Journal of Applied Sport Psychology *and* The Sport Psychologist.

Chapter 13

The Migration of
Gestalt Psychology

✍🏻

In 1912, Max Wertheimer (1880–1943) published a monograph on the perception of movement that was to launch a new approach in experimental psychology—Gestalt psychology. That research on apparent movement (the Phi phenomenon) was carried out at the University of Frankfurt with two graduate students, Kurt Koffka (1886–1941) and Wolfgang Köhler (1887–1967). These three would become the triumvirate of Gestalt psychology, launching their opposition to then current German psychology whose atomistic approach was antithetical to their views of consciousness. Instead of beginning with elements and trying to synthesize from those the wholes of consciousness, the Gestalt psychologists started with a phenomenological analysis of the wholes of experience and sought to determine the natural parts.

In their direct opposition to the prevailing German psychology, the Gestalt psychologists struggled to gain their place. What began as a foothold eventually supplanted the psychology derived, in part, from the ideas of Wilhelm Wundt. Evidence of this metamorphosis in German psychology was the selection of Wolfgang Köhler to head the Psychological Institute at the University of Berlin in 1921, then arguably the most prestigious position in German psychology. At the University of Berlin a fourth principal figure emerged: Kurt Lewin (1890–1947), an exceptionally creative individual who would extend Gestalt ideas into the areas of motivation, personality, and social psychology.

Americans became aware of Gestalt psychology in the 1920s from an article published by Kurt Koffka in the journal, *Psychological Bulletin* in 1922 and by a series of four articles published in the *American Journal of Psychology* in 1925. By 1924, Koffka was lecturing in America as a visiting professor at Cornell University and the University of Wisconsin. In 1927 he settled at Smith College in Massachusetts where he remained for the rest of his life. In the next decade he would watch in dismay and then in horror at the political changes in his native Germany as Adolf Hitler became chancellor of Germany in January of 1933. Two months later, Hitler had established his Nazi dictatorship.

Hitler's hatred for the Jews, a regular part of his political rhetoric, quickly became government policy. On April 1, 1933, the Nazi government called for a boycott of all Jewish businesses. The government banned Jews from holding a number of jobs such as farmer, teacher, or journalist and from holding any public office. By 1935, the Nuremberg Laws had stripped all Jews of German citizenship and had left over half of them unemployed. Even for those with money it was difficult to buy things because most shop owners would not sell to Jews. In some cities, Jews found it impossible to buy food or medicine.

As Hitler spread his Third Reich into Austria, many of the German and Austrian Jews sought refuge in other countries of eastern and western Europe and later in North America (see Cocks, 1988). Among that number were many of the Gestalt psychologists, including the founders of the movement. Wertheimer and Lewin, both of whom were Jewish, came to the United States in 1933. Köhler, who was not a Jew, joined them in 1935. These scholars left professorships in the best German universities to take lesser positions in the United States. The 1930s were hard times in the United States, the era of the Great Depression; jobs were scarce for American doctorates, much less for the wave of European immigrants. But through American friends, the Gestalt leaders were able to find academic jobs: Wertheimer at the New School for Social Research in New York City, Köhler at Swarthmore College, and Lewin at Cornell University (in the Home Economics Department) and later at the University of Iowa. Adjustment was not easy. The culture was foreign, there was a new language to learn, and the dominant school of psychology—behaviorism—was inhospitable to the phenomenological approach of Gestalt theory.

Although Gestalt psychology did not displace behaviorism, tenets of Gestalt theory became a part of the psychology of learning and perception. Lewin's work would virtually define American social psychology for the next 40 years. The Gestaltists also played a significant role in the emergence of American cognitive psychology in the 1950s. Much of the contemporary work on thinking, problem solving, language, and information processing has direct antecedents in Gestalt psychology.

The letters in this chapter were selected to portray some of the human drama involved in the Gestalt migration necessitated by the Nazi regime. The letters tell of great human determination and courage. Obviously the intellectual migration represented a windfall for the United States. The enrichment of American psychology was part of that windfall.

Kurt Koffka to Molly Harrower, March 31, 1933[1]

She writes that things are much better in Germany than they were before Hitler came to power. I can't understand that. I'm afraid it is the egotistic bourgeois point of view that judges merely on the ground of personal safety and order, unconcerned with the ideological forces behind it all, and ignorant of the actual suppression of liberty.

I wonder what her reaction will be to the boycott which is to begin tomorrow. People in Germany misunderstand foreign public opinion as always. They know that the atrocities reported in WWI were grossly exaggerated, largely invented. But they do not see that the physical violence is only a part of the causes which have stirred public opinion in the U.S. and in England. And that the fundamental causes are much deeper, and not done away with by a denial of atrocity stories. It is the discrimination against persons of other creeds and opinions which shocks the world rightly and against which it raises its voice.

Wolfgang Köhler to Ralph Barton Perry, April 1, 1933[2]

Nobody in Germany with any decency in his bones . . . knows very much about his near future. If nothing happens, I shall be in Chicago for the meeting of the American Association. . . .

As to myself, my patriotism expects the Germans to behave better than any other people. This seems to me a sound form of patriotism. Unfortunately it is very different from current nationalism which presupposes that [their] own people are right and do

---

1. Molly Harrower (1906–   ) earned her doctorate in psychology at Smith College with Koffka in 1934. She was serving a year as lecturer at the University of London when Koffka wrote her this letter. His remarks about Germany were prompted by a letter he received from a relative in Germany. The boycott to which he refers is the national boycott in Germany of all Jewish businesses scheduled to begin on April 1, 1933.

2. Perry was a professor of philosophy at Harvard University.

right whatever they are and do. However, there will still be some fight during the next weeks. Don't judge the Germans before it is over.

Wolfgang Köhler to the Deutsche Allgemeine Zeitung[3] (a Berlin newspaper), April 28, 1933

[The current rulers of Germany wonder why many valuable people have not joined the Nazi party?] Never have I seen finer patriotism than theirs.

[Regarding the dismissal of Jews from universities and other positions. . .]

During our conversation, one of my friends reached for the Psalms and read: "The Lord is my shepherd, I shall not want. . . ." He read the 90th Psalm and said, "It is hard to think of a German who has been able to move human hearts more deeply and so to console those who suffer. And these words we have received from the Jews."

Another reminded me that never had a man struggled more nobly for a clarification of his vision of the world than the Jew Spinoza, whose wisdom Goethe admired. My friend did not hesitate to show respect, as Goethe did. Lessing, too, would not have written his *Nathan the Wise* unless human nobility existed among the Jews? . . . It seems that nobody can think of the great work of Heinrich Hertz without an almost affectionate admiration for him. And Hertz had Jewish blood.

One of my friends told me: "The greatest German experimental physicist of the present time is Franck; many believe that he is the greatest experimental physicist of our age. Franck is a Jew, an unusually kind human being. Until a few days ago, he was professor at Göttingen, an honor to Germany and the envy of the international scientific community." [Perhaps the episode of Franck's dismissal] shows the deepest reason why all these people are not joining [the Party]: they feel a moral imposition. They believe that only the quality of a human being should determine his worth, that intellectual achievement, character, and obvious contributions

---

3. Henle (1978) says this was the last anti-Nazi article to be published openly under the Nazi regime. It was prompted by the dismissal of physicist James Franck from the University of Göttingen. Kohler knew the danger of writing this letter. He spent the night of April 28 playing chamber music with friends, waiting for the Nazis to arrest him. But they never came.

to German culture retain their significance whether a person is Jewish or not.

Kurt Koffka to Molly Harrower, May 10, 1933[4]

The article [Köhler's] is extremely well written, if anything could have any affect at all it would be this. Cautious, and yet brave appeal. What startled me is the introduction, in which he praises the achievement of the New [Nazi] Regime in rather glowing terms, I do not know whether this is just politics in order to give more weight to his defense of liberals, and Jews, or whether it represents his own opinion. Heider [Northampton lab psychologist Fritz Heider] showed us yesterday a clipping from a German newspaper with the names of those professors at a number of universities, who, till a final decision, have been given leave of absence. Wertheimer is of course among them. Frau Köhler wrote that Wertheimer is outside Germany at the moment.

Kurt Lewin to Wolfgang Köhler, May 20, 1933[5]

Many thanks for your article. Now, as I read through it quietly, its meaning and its nature have emerged much more clearly than the quick perusal on the trip. It is difficult to thank you adequately for this article, even face to face. But perhaps I should say how proud I am to be allowed to count among my friends one of those rare people who have demonstrated such conviction and have dared to do such a deed. Hopefully, even without words, it has become clear to you how deeply Gerti [Mrs. Gertrud Weiss Lewin] and I appreciate what you and your dear wife have done.

I've been here a few days now. But I must admit that up to now nothing has happened to change my attitude. I was a little afraid that my attitude might appear exaggerated, or a little incomprehensible, or even somewhat ungrateful. This, and my wish

---

4. The article to which Koffka refers is most likely the letter Köhler wrote for the *Deutsche Allgemeine Zeitung*. Copies of it were widely circulated outside of Germany. Koffka was concerned about some of the letter's contents and would have to wait for a later meeting with Köhler to determine the intent of such remarks.

5. This letter was found among the papers of Kurt Lewin by Miriam Lewin, his daughter. As she reports, evidently it was never mailed to Köhler. Mailing it would have been a risky act, dangerous for both writer and recipient. Lewin wrote the letter a few days after arriving back in Berlin after spending a year in the United States as a visiting professor at Stanford University.

that clarity should prevail, at least between us, almost obligates me to speak to you, although with some reluctance, about matters intimately connected to my personal future. Probably the fate of an individual Jew has never been only a personal fate. Surely it has been torn out of the sphere of the personal in our times. . . .

If I now believe there is no other choice for me but to emigrate, you will understand that this thought certainly does not come easily to me. Considerations are involved that are far removed from feeling personally hurt or a temporarily wounded pride, be such feelings ever so justified. These considerations pertain to the simplest, most elementary necessities of life.

I have said it before and would like to repeat it now: When I think of leaving my parents and relatives, of giving up the house that we built, of going out into an uncertain future, of leaving a scientific structure that would take years to rebuild, at best, then surely at the root of such a decision is not a loathing of vulgarities or the fear of personal unpleasantness, but only an overwhelmingly decisive social reality.

I think it is practically impossible for a non-Jew to gauge what being a Jew has meant for a person, even in the liberal era of the last 40 years. There have probably been very few Jewish children of any generation who have not been singled out from the natural group of their peers between their 6th and 13th year. Quite suddenly and without any kind of predictable cause, they have been beaten up and treated with contempt. Whether instigated by teachers, by students, or simply by people on the street, these recurring experiences pull the ground out from under the feet of the young child, and cut off all possibility of objective discussion or unbiased evaluation. They throw the child totally back upon its own resources. They make all natural supports appear entirely deceptive and force the young person to exist in a conflicting world of appearance and reality right from the start. Very few children are capable of surviving such disrupting experiences without suffering serious damage to their natural growth. After all, these experiences are not just casual irritations, but instead involve the very foundations of life itself on which all important decisions are based. Thus the effects are ever present. At the same time, people have demanded absolute patriotism from Jewish children quite as a matter of course. One always had to reckon with the fact that evaluations of one's own achievements would be biased to an unpredictable degree. As a result, exaggerated personal qualities, whether aggressiveness or excessive softness, were scarcely avoidable. . . .

'   The issue of German anti-Semitism is indeed a long chapter that would require an interpretation of the history of the Jews as well as of the Germans. I am quite aware that the foreign political pressures of the last 15 years have allowed primitive atavisms to surface in Germany as well as in every other people. The need for a scapegoat has become so strong that the battle cry "Kill the Jew," which we have been hearing daily for a decade, has led quite literally to a war of hundreds against one, the kind of war that used to be found only in Poland or Hungary. This is understandable, I think, only through the ancient and very deeply rooted anti-Semitic tradition in Germany, together with the political morality that Bismarck described as a lack of civil courage. That it is a basic characteristic of the German lifestyle—decidedly different from the political morality of, for example, the American or the Englishman—is something I myself learned to recognize only this year, although you have been telling me about it for a long time. . . .

I cannot imagine how a Jew is supposed to live a life in Germany at the present time that does justice to even the most primitive demands of truthfulness. While I was in Tokyo at a dinner that the Japanese-German Cultural Institute gave for me, a speech was addressed to me as the representative of German science. I, in turn, answered as a representative of German science. I was able to respond to the Japanese with a good conscience. But two minutes later I got the terrible feeling that I had just done something impossible. I knew that here I was speaking in the name of German science and here I was recognized by the German embassy, while in Germany at that very moment they were knocking my feet out from under me.

Am I supposed to speak as a representative of Germany again on my next trip abroad and "to counter the reports of atrocities," as is tacitly expected of every Jew? Or as who am I supposed to step forward? As a person deprived of the basic rights of a citizen, and who nevertheless continues, for a salary, to provide the children of this people with knowledge and with preparation for positions from which his own children are excluded?

Perhaps, like many other Jews, a cruel destiny will not spare me this fate. Certainly I have no reason to voluntarily relinquish any rights and thereby to enlarge the enormous spiritual and material damage committed against us daily. But even though it will tear my life apart, I hope you will understand and approve of my attempt to find a place for me and my children where we can live an honorable life.[6]

Wolfgang Köhler to Ralph Barton Perry, March 1934[7]

I am trying to build up a special position for myself in which I might stay with honour. As yet it seems to work, but the end may come [any] day. Quite exciting sometimes, not a life of leisure, occasionally great fun. The art is not to act in passion, but to make at once use of any occasion when the others make a mistake; then it is time to push a foot forward or to hit without serious danger for oneself. You will say that such is the method of cowards. But think of the difference in strength! . . .

Good work is being done in Berlin, as though we had to do what the emigrants are no longer able to do in Germany. Unfortunately my assistants have been in serious danger several times because of political denunciations—a denunciation a month is more or less our current rate; as yet, however, it has always been possible to save them.

Wolfgang Köhler to Ralph Barton Perry, May 21, 1934[8]

My resignation is most likely to be final. Since most of the serious workers in psychology had to leave before, and since my

---

6. Lewin, his wife, and their children emigrated to the United States in the fall of 1933 where he had a 2-year position at Cornell University. Lewin's mother and sister, who fled to Holland, were captured by the Nazis and sent to the death camps where they died.

7. Köhler wrote this letter while out of Germany on a brief trip to Norway. The Nazis were exerting greater and greater control over the activities of the universities, and Köhler was finding it increasingly difficult to remain in such an environment. But he continued to hold out for the sake of his student assistants and his concern for the welfare of Gestalt psychology and the course of Germany.

8. Köhler wrote to Perry from Scotland, where he was lecturing. For several months Köhler had been writing to the rector of the University of Berlin asking that commitments made to him regarding the Psychological Institute be honored. He indicated that without such action he would resign. In his final letter to the administration of the university he set a deadline for reply. When that date passed and Köhler had received no answer to his letter, he submitted his request for retirement.

excellent assistants would not stay without me, this means the abolition of German psychology for many years. I do not regard myself as responsible. If only 20 professors had fought the same battle, it would never have come so far with regard to German universities.

Kurt Koffka to Molly Harrower, November 13, 1934[9]

Now from here, Köhler's visit was absolutely magnificent. We had marvelous talks on psychology, physics and Germany. To begin with the last: I have changed my personal outlook a great deal after what he told me. I do not longer believe, as I did more or less, that a majority of Germans enjoy the Hitler regime. I see now utter chaos, the disunity, party strife, and chief and worst of all, the demoralizing influence which the regime exerts on the people. Köhler is furious with the slack attitude of American intel-lectuals—we had grand talks about tolerance in this connection. You may speak about this very freely provided you do not mention Köhler's name; as a matter of fact it would be good if you could influence public opinion in N.J.C. [New Jersey College for Women] in this direction. The present tolerance kills the efforts of all the decent people in Germany. They who want to be pro-German are really the worst enemies of the best German people. Köhler's own behavior is simply beyond praise. He does speak out to the man in power, and at the same time he does it diplomati-cally so that his actions have as much effect as they possibly can. I'll tell you more about it when we meet. To summarize: One can-not be sufficiently anti-Nazi! They are the enemies of all true morality, which they consider intellectualistic prejudice. Sneaking underhand creatures they are.

Wolfgang Köhler to Donald K. Adams, 1935[10]

I feel obliged to announce to all those who have taken a friendly interest in the Psychological Institute at Berlin that this

---

9. Koffka and Köhler met when the latter came to Cambridge to deliver the William James Lectures at Harvard University. While at Harvard, Köhler received a letter from the dep-uty rector at the University of Berlin asking him to sign an oath of loyalty to Adolf Hitler. He refused.

10. Adams, a professor of psychology at Duke University, was one of Köhler's closest American friends. Hans Rupp, a non-Jew, was the senior assistant in Köhler's institute.

institute does not exist any more—though the rooms and the apparatus and Mr. Rupp are still there. The government has decided in May to dismiss all the assistants who were trained by me and in June, during the term, they were suddenly forbidden to continue their work and their teaching: Duncker, von Lauenstein and von Restorff. Since, at my last visit in Berlin, I had expressly stated orally and in official documents that I could not possibly remain as director without the help of my young friends and since this is a clear case of their modern brutality (another man uses this method in order to push *me* out), the measure is morally equivalent to my own dismissal too. I shall have a last interview with the Nazi authorities in August. But there is not one chance in a hundred for my staying on in Germany. . . . We were depressed for some days but have come back to the fighting spirit once more. Personally, I shall be glad when I have no contact with the official Germany of today, and I have so many good friends in this country, more indeed than over there. My deepest anxiety refers to the assistants. I am not yet sure whether I shall be able to place them somewhere.

Kurt Koffka to Molly Harrower, September 9, 1938[11]

So much has happened. The days in Berlin were painfully exciting. It is much worse on the spot than outside. The war situation was critical although I was assured on my second day in Berlin that nothing would happen before the Partietag [Nazi party conference]. The Jewish situation is unbearable beyond words.

You know, I presume, that all Jews have to assume the names of Israel and Sarah respectively on January the first. They have special licensed numbers on their cars; they have to use yellow benches in public parks. All Jewish shops have to bear the name of the owners in large white letters on plate glass. This is already in existence. But they are afraid, based on leading Nazi papers, that they will be driven out of their apartments since Jews must not defile houses owned by Germans.

Under these conditions I could only confirm my mother and my brother in their respective resolutions to emigrate to America.

---

11. As the situation worsened in Germany, Koffka felt compelled to visit his family and assess the political events first hand.

This means new responsibilities for me. I must give them affida-vits, and must try to find some sort of employment for my brother. . . .

The news after a few days' respite was most alarming this morning. It is not impossible that the world will be aflame by the time I arrive back in New York. Although I cannot really believe it yet. However, my reason tells me that a catastrophe is bound to come sooner or later. Things cannot continue to go as they are at the moment. A new holocaust, much more terrible even than the last, may be necessary, and it is the most depressing part of the situation that such a new wholesale slaughter would probably lead to a peace even worse than the last one, and therefore breed new wars. Berlin has thoroughly discouraged me. I can't help agreeing with Gloucester in Shakespeare's King Lear when he says some-thing like this "what flies are to boys, we are to the Gods, they kill us for sport" you will know the quotation.

Gestalt Migration Bibliography

Ash, M. G. (1985). Gestalt psychology: Origins in Germany and reception in the United States. In C. E. Buxton (Ed.), *Points of View in the Modern History of Psychology*. Orlando, FL: Academic Press.

Of several excellent accounts of the Gestalt migration, this one provides the best description of the evolution of Gestalt psychology in Germany.

Ash, M. G. (1992). Cultural contexts and scientific change in psychology: Kurt Lewin in Iowa. *American Psychologist, 47,* 198–207.

An analysis of the change in cultural context for Lewin from Berlin to Iowa and the impact of that change on his theory and research.

Harrower, M. (1983). *Kurt Koffka: An Unwitting Self-portrait.* Gainesville, FL: University Presses of Florida.

This fascinating portrait of Koffka is largely based on excerpts from the more than 2,100 letters exchanged between Koffka and Harrower between 1930 and 1941. Some of the excerpts in this chapter are taken from this collection.

Henle, M. (1978). One man against the Nazis: Wolfgang Köhler. *American Psychologist, 33*, 939–944.

This is the dramatic account of the final days of the University of Berlin's Psychological Institute and Kohler's determined struggle to keep it going, independent of Nazi interference. Several letters in this chapter are taken from this article.

Henle, M. (1980). The influence of Gestalt psychology in America. In R. W. Rieber & K. Salzinger (Eds.), *Psychology: Theoretical-Historical Perspectives*, (pp. 177–190). New York: Academic Press.

This article focuses on misunderstandings of Gestalt psychology as cause and effect of the "less than overwhelming" influence that Gestalt psychology had in America. It provides a concise summary of the contributions of Gestalt psychology to contemporary psychology.

Köhler, W. (1947). *Gestalt Psychology: An Introduction to New Concepts in Modern Psychology*. New York: Liveright.

The most readable account of Gestalt psychology.

Lewin, K. (1986). "Everything within me rebels": A letter from Kurt Lewin to Wolfgang Köhler, 1933. *Journal of Social Issues, 42* (4), 39–47.

This article is the complete text of the Lewin-Köhler letter excerpted in this chapter.

Mandler, J. M., & Mandler, G. (1969). The diaspora of experimental psychology: The Gestaltists and others. In D. Fleming & B. Bailyn (Eds.), *The Intellectual Migration: Europe and America, 1930–1960* (pp. 371–419). Cambridge, MA: Harvard University Press.

An account of the migration of refugee psychologists from Europe to America, focusing on the Gestalt psychologists.

Marrow, A. J. (1969). *The Practical Theorist: The Life and Work of Kurt Lewin*. New York: Basic Books.

This biography of Lewin describes his social research agenda as an outgrowth of his all-too-real exposure to frustration, prejudice, authoritarianism, and hatred.

Sokal, M. M. (1984). The Gestalt psychologists in behaviorist America. *American Historical Review, 89*, 1240–1263.

This article argues that the Gestalt psychologists were treated better in America than other historical accounts would lead us to believe and that Gestalt psychology was quite successful in redirecting the mainstream of American psychology.

Chapter 14

A Social Agenda for American Psychology

By the beginning of the 1920s, much of the American public seemed convinced that the science of psychology held the keys to prosperity and happiness. Newspaper columnists urged the public to seek psychologists for advice about marriage, child rearing, and selection of a career; businesses were urged to consult psychologists about employee selection; and educators were encouraged to use psychologists to improve educational methods. One columnist told his readers, "You cannot achieve these things [effectiveness and happiness] in the fullest measure without the new knowledge of your own mind and personality that the psychologists have given us" (Wiggam, 1928, p. 13).

Public demand was high for psychological services, and because there were not enough psychologists interested in applying their science, many individuals with little or no training in psychology emerged to fill the void. When the stockmarket crashed in 1929, psychology's star fell with it. A 1934 *New York Times* editorial criticized psychology as a failed profession. The editorial reminded the public that in the good times of the 1920s, psychologists had ready answers for any questions, but now that the country faced serious economic and morale problems, psychologists were suddenly silent (Benjamin, 1986).

In the midst of the Great Depression a new psychological organization was formed, one that had a clear public agenda (and perhaps a private one). An extremely controversial organization, its founding represented an act of courage, because there were many, no doubt, who saw the society as a communist or socialist organization—psychologists promoting pinkism (indeed, the FBI established a file on the organization in the 1930s, see Harris, 1980). The organization was named the Society for the Psychological Study of Social Issues

(SPSSI), and it continues today as one of more than 40 divisions of the American Psychological Association.

The American Psychological Association (APA) was founded in 1892 and had always been dominated by psychologists in university settings. As opportunities for employment of psychologists outside of academic settings grew, there was pressure on APA to broaden its mission to serve the interests of these applied psychologists. In response to that pressure, an APA Division of Consulting Psychologists was founded in the 1920s but it was never able to do much for the applied psychologists. The APA leadership actively resisted the centrifugal forces that sought to extend psychology beyond the campus, including those voices that sought an application of psychological science to social problems. And in the 1930s there were plenty of social problems facing Americans and the rest of the world: unemployment, hunger, racism, labor-management disputes, and impending war.

The beginnings of SPSSI can be traced to 1935 when psychologists Ross Stagner (1909–) and Igor Krechevsky (later David Krech, 1909–1977) talked about common frustrations such as the unemployment faced by new psychologists, the avoidance of political questions by psychologists, and the lack of opportunity for psychology to contribute solutions to the social ills of the day (Stagner, 1986). Their conversation led to a plan of action to organize psychologists with similar interests. In February of 1936, Krechevsky wrote to a small number of psychologists he felt might be kindred spirits. Sixteen, in addition to Stagner and Krechevsky, agreed to be part of an organizing committee. Acting as secretary, Krechevsky mailed a letter in March to several hundred members of APA describing the plans for the new organization and asking for indications of interest.

The initial organizing meeting was held in September of that year in conjunction with the annual meeting of the APA. More than 100 psychologists attended a special meeting of the social issues group. Stagner chaired the meeting, and Krechevsky served as secretary. Krechevsky announced that he had already received over 200 expressions of interest in the society from his earlier mailing and had collected $63.13 in advance dues and assessments. "Those present readily agreed that $63.13 in the depression year of 1936 was sufficient evidence of interest to justify formalizing an organization" (Krech & Cartwright, 1956, p. 471). Goodwin Watson was elected the first chairperson of the organization and Krechevsky the first Secretary-Treasurer. Ten others were elected to the first Council of Directors, which included several distinguished psychologists of that time: Edward C. Tolman, Gardner Murphy, and Gordon Allport.

Following the meeting, a letter was mailed to the entire APA membership offering charter membership in SPSSI to anyone who joined before the end of 1936. The letter explained the two goals of the new society as follows:

> One is to encourage research upon those psychological problems most vitally related to modern social, economic and political policies. The second is to help the public and its representatives to understand and to use in the formation of social policies, contributions from the scientific investigation of human behavior. (Krech & Cartwright, 1956, p. 471)

That was the public agenda. The somewhat private agenda involved the problem of unemployment of psychologists, a problem exacerbated by the influx of European psychologists fleeing the Nazi regime (see Chapter 13). Some of the SPSSI organizers hoped to manufacture jobs for psychologists by creating a social agenda for behavioral research (see Finison, 1976, 1979).

In the years that followed, SPSSI encouraged research on social issues and even established its own journal, *The Journal of Social Issues*, to publish such research. It supported the application of psychological knowledge to social problems as diverse as divorce and war. It also acted to help psychologists who might be persecuted for their political beliefs or social activism. And it also helped to organize psychological support, including the APA, for various social issues.

The success of SPSSI is evidenced in part by the fact that the APA has amended its by-laws to include as one of its three goals, the promotion of human welfare. Today the APA is organized into four directorates, one of which is Public Interest. Such APA involvement is a direct result of the success of SPSSI in convincing the broader psychological community of the importance of a social agenda for psychology.

The letters that follow are taken from the SPSSI Papers, which are part of the Archives of the History of American Psychology at the University of Akron. They illustrate a great diversity of responses to

Krechevsky's March 1936 letter and tell part of the story of how this very important psychological society began.[1]

J. F. Brown [University of Kansas] to I. Krechevsky, February 26, 1936

I hasten to answer your letter of Feb. 24. You may count on me to support your society both with time and with somewhat paltry monetary donations. . . . As an earnest [sic] of my good intent I am enclosing my check for $5.00 and will try to send you more later. Also I will be glad to serve on the organizational committee.

My only suggestion is that we attempt to gain first support of the relatively few psychologists who are really politically literate rather than the wholesale support of the socalled socially minded. Secondly I suggest that the organization is in no way officially to be affiliated with the A.P.A. as the embarrassment might be mutual. Thirdly that the cooperation and membership of scientists in closely related fields like sociology and philosophy be asked and allowed.

Gordon Allport [Harvard University] to I. Krechevsky, March 6, 1936

I think I am willing to serve on your organizational committee. Certainly I am willing in principle. My only doubts come from the question of how pre-determined the policies are. Your letter is persuasive and for the most part unexceptionable. There is, however, a slightly over-emotional tone that might raise the question whether the committee itself is able to see issues clearly, and to pursue facts in an unbiased way.

In red I have made a few verbal suggestions for diminishing the excited tone of the letter. The passages in parentheses, might, for example, be deleted without loss of force and with a gain in dignity. . . .

It is necessary to postpone platforms, I think, until various regional meetings having been held. Most important of all it will be

---

1. Another organization of psychologists also formed in 1936: the American Association for Applied Psychology (AAAP). That group was concerned with improving the consulting and practice opportunities of psychologists, and not with the involvement of psychologists in social issues. When APA officially reorganized in 1945, AAAP and SPSSI merged with APA, becoming several of APA's divisions.

necessary to have answers to meet the coming ridicule and objections of the "pure" psychologists. Being a rather individualistic lot, I think the platform, to have any appeal, must be entirely unemotional, brief, and calculated to admit results and judgments that may in essence be non-socialistic. We would discredit social planning, the profession, and ourselves, if we prejudged the outcome of our respective researches. . . .

J. H. Elder [Yale University] to
I. Krechevsky, March 14, 1936

Considering my professional contacts your letter [of February 24] comes as a ray of promise that psychologists aren't all quite as hopeless as I have judged them. Several times I unhappily have concluded that no group of scientists could be as indifferent and provincial as psychologists. . . . I still don't see quite why psychological training shouldn't serve as a somewhat better than average scientific background for thinking about the world we live in. . . .

I do not feel that my name on your committee would strengthen it much. It looks good as it stands. Furthermore, I haven't any funds to spare at this time. But you must not take this as the usual liberal attitude of approval but no participation. I am as earnest about the proposition as anyone and I will give my services and money as soon as possible. . . .

I. Krechevsky and 17 other members of the Organizing Committee, including J. F. Brown and Gordon Allport, to Members and Associates of the American Psychological Association, ca. March, 1936

This letter is being sent to you by a group of associates and members of the A.P.A. which has organized itself as a temporary body to help express the attitudes of American psychologists on the important economic and political issues of today. We do not believe it at all necessary to belabor the fact that an economic depression exists in these United States and in the world around us. . . . Most of us have probably tried to do some hard-headed thinking about this situation and all of its implications. . . . Unfortunately, scientists in the past seemed to think that they had a very easy verbal way out of the necessity of thinking about these issues and of advising the rest of society on these important issues. All that was necessary was to repeat solemnly and gravely the magic phrase "pure science," and immediately, so it was believed, they had removed themselves from all environmental stimulation and influence! Certainly the psychologist should be the last scientist to rationalize his way out of the problem by postulating a sort of political-economic vaccum in which the scientist, *his theories and his work are supposed to exist.*

The group responsible for this letter was organized because its members believed that there are enough psychologists who are ready to translate some such "private feels" into behavior to justify an organized attempt to encourage this transformation. . . .

The present committee has no completed and "closed" program in mind. We want and need your help in formulating such a program. In general, we wish to establish an organization of accredited psychologists to promote specific research projects on *contemporary* psychological problems; to collect, analyze and disseminate data on the psychological consequences of our present economic, political and cultural crisis; to encourage the participation of psychologists *as psychologists* in the activities of the day. Society very definitely needs our aid. Economists, politicians, physicists, editorialists, munitions manufacturers and "philosophers" have not hesitated to advise society on problems of social motivation, the inevitability of war as "inherent in human nature" and the like. What psychologists have come forth to substantiate or refute these psychological "laws"? These are important psychological questions *per se;* that their answers may have important social implications does not make them any less so and should not frighten us away from them. There is, we believe, a definite need for an organization to encourage, promote and support (both financially and "morally") such research.

Before we can go ahead with any program, however, we must know how many other psychologists we can count on. Specifically, will you write us telling us that you are willing to help organize an agency for some such purpose? Will you include in your letter any general or specific suggestions? Will you also include an estimate of the probable attitude of your colleagues toward this work?

Raleigh M. Drake [Wesleyan College, Georgia] to I. Krechevsky, March 20, 1936

I like your idea very much and see much value in it. . . . The public does not have too much confidence in "psychology" now because psychologists have been so academic, impractical, theoritical [sic], and after all what have they contributed of an objective nature that the layman can observe? A committee, such as you suggest, might serve as a sieve to prevent unsound theories from reaching the public and thereby protect all psychologists, as well as to encourage the discovery and application of psychological laws which may be important for society. . . .

Ralph R. Brown [United States Public Health Service] to I. Krechevsky, March 20, 1936

I shall be very glad to cooperate in any possible way with your committee in its efforts to encourage, promote, and support psychological research on contemporary social problems. . . . Naturally, I am quite partial to the psychologist's standpoint in these matters, but I cannot help but see that the medical man has several good reasons for his attitude. Above all, the physician takes a practical attitude toward research and is most anxious to solve those problems which are directly concerned with human welfare. Only too often, however, the psychologist—safe in the confines of a university—is engaged in what I would call 'academic boondoggling'—research on insignificant problems. . . . Let the efforts of your committee be directed toward the promoting of a research problem to be worked out in collaboration with a medical group. This will necessitate a problem having a definite significance for human welfare. . . .

Ray Willoughby [Clark University] to I. Krechevsky, March 20, 1936

Sure, I'm with you "in principle"; but just to be ornery . . . I'm going to deny that you or anybody else, at least qua psychologists, can do a damned thing about it. . . .

And what research projects would you promote? Can you see anything in sight, in any direction, that you could do that would have any bearing on anything? I can't. The journals are crammed with tripe, in social as well as other fields, which no sensible

person bothers to read. Suppose you "collected, analyzed and dis-
seminated" data to your heart's content—to whom would it make
the slightest difference? . . . "What psychologists have come forth
to substantiate or refute these psychological 'laws'?" Well, I'll
bite—what psychologists *could* substantiate or refute them? And
how? By hollering louder than the propounders of the "laws"? Do
you know anybody that knows anything at all (relevant and beyond common sense, I mean) about these alleged laws? I don't.

Calvin Hall [University of Oregon] to I. Krechevsky, March 23, 1936

Of course you can count on me for any inflation of the ego of
homo psychologicus. Do we have to wave the red flag or is this
just a milksop, a parlor-pink organization? . . .

To be more serious however. . . . Care must be taken . . . not
to promise more than we can actually deliver. Just after the war
some psychologists sold aptitude testing "short" and we are only
now recovering from that period of exaggerated optomism [sic].
We ought to know, moreover, why some psychologists are unemployed. I am certainly in sympathy with the prospectus but I want
to emphasis [sic] again that I hope this can all be done through
the A.P.A. rather than through some independent organization.

Ralph White [Wesleyan University] to I. Krechevsky, March 23, 1936

I was delighted to find that psychologists were at last beginning to wake up, and particularly to find that you were one of the
wakers. . . . Suggestions for what could be done? Plenty: 1. Get
some non-A.P.A. members . . . 3. Get a representative cross-
section of the unemployed in the United States and make about a
hundred careful case studies, stressing infantilizing effects, ration-
alizations, paranoid trends, conscious explanations of the depression, and ideas about what is to be done about it . . . 5. Collect
case studies of strikers who are black-listed, and their families . . .
9. Catalogue the stereotypes of the American mind. Publicize the
fact that the same stereotypes are utilized by both left and right. . . .

A. T. Poffenberger [Columbia University]
to I. Krechevsky, March 23, 1936

I am heartily in favor of the ideas expressed in your circular letter. My views on the matters there discussed are expressed in my presidential address of last September before the American Psychological Association. It is my conviction that the A.P.A. should take the initiative in dealing with public questions either through a committee or through the machinery of a central office or preferably through a combination of these devices. I do not favor setting up a separate organization or an unattached or unofficial committee for purposes in mind. Such a move would, in my opinion, merely delay forcing the A.P.A. to become a more active public influence. . . .

William E. Walton [University of Nebraska]
to I. Krechevsky, March 26, 1936

I am in hearty accord with what your committee is trying to do to promote active research on contemporary psychological projects.

I feel there should be several functions of such a group: 1. We should educate the public concerning the contributions which psychology can make to its immediate problems . . . 2. We should create a market for our students . . . 3. We must educate the public against psychological quackery. In order that we may do this we should campaign for legal recognition of the term psychologist and limit its use to those qualified. . . .

J. M. Stephens [Johns Hopkins University]
to I. Krechevsky, March 27, 1936

. . . I belong to that group who have considerable faith in "pure science" and whose position is so illogical that to state it (with an exclamation mark) is to refute it. I doubt if the psychological information with which I am most familiar is clearly enough understood even by psychologists to be of much practical value. Furthermore I am afraid that a pre-mature attempt to apply our hypotheses to practical affairs may discredit psychology as a science in somewhat the same way that some aspects of economic theory and political science have been discredited. . . .

Ernest R. Hilgard [Stanford University]
to I. Krechevsky, March 30, 1936

I wish to express my interest in the proposal of your committee that psychologists concern themselves in an organized way
with regard to matters of public policy. . . . I have been teaching
industrial psychology for the first time this year, and I am amazed
to find that our textbooks are almost unaware of the fact that
labor unions exist. As though wage-incentives constitute motiva-
tional psychology, in complete disregard of the social realities
which labor is facing! The trouble as I see it is that in our deference to physiology and physics we have not taken seriously the
social sciences. . . .

Merrill Roff [Indiana University]
to I. Krechevsky, April 1, 1936

Your bulletins arrived and were properly dismissed. I have
talked enough about the whole thing to become rather a nuisance
to some of my associates, and since my status for next year is still
indefinite, I am pulling in my horns. The thing works this way:
any suggestion that psychologists take a look at the world is at
once interpreted as an advocacy of 'applied psychology', and dismissed summarily. . . .

James McKeen Cattell [Editorial Office, Science magazine]
to I. Krechevsky, April 4, 1936

I have read your memorandum with interest and am in full
sympathy with the objects of your committee. I am not convinced
that psychology as a science is in a position to supply adequate
guidance. There is consequently a danger that we may speak with
the authority of science when the value of what we advocate depends not on expert knowledge but on general intelligence.

G. H. Estabrooks [Colgate University]
to I. Krechevsky, April 10, 1936

With reference to your mimeographed sheets concerning the
participation of psychologists in the contemporary political world,
allow me to register my hearty dissent with approximately everything contained therein.

If psychologists, as individuals, wish to make themselves politically vocal on any topic-white, red, or pink-it seems to me that is wholly up to them. . . .

It seems to me that, as psychologists, our duties are pretty clear cut. If any group of us wish to organize as a "Committee for the Propagation of Mild Pinkism", for goodness sakes let us organize ourselves as such and not in camouflage under the protecting skirts of the American Psychological Association.

Robert B. MacLeod [Swarthmore College] to I. Krechevsky, April 14, 1936

. . . I feel the same way as you do about the present impotence of psychology and psychologists in the contemporary social crisis and I feel very strongly that we ought to do something about it. You can count on me to cooperate in any way possible in the realization of your program.

Just at present I feel myself somewhat restricted by the fact that I am not an American citizen and consequently would be chucked out of the country very quickly if I took part in any agitation. That would not interfere, however, with my contributing in any way possible to the organization of the group and to the research which it may undertake. . . .

Editor's Note: *As a result of the mailing, 333 of APA's nearly 2,000 members joined the new organization. A year later SPSSI requested formal identification with APA and was granted affiliate status by APA's Council of Directors.*

SPSSI Bibliography

Harris, B. (1980). The FBI's files on APA and SPSSI: Description and implications. *American Psychologist, 35,* 1141–1144.

    A description of the FBI files on SPSSI, obtained by Harris in the late 1970s through the Freedom of Information Act.

Finison, L. J. (1976). Unemployment, politics, and the history of organized psychology. *American Psychologist, 31,* 747–755.

    A history of the founding of two organizations, SPSSI and the Psychologist's League, both of which sought to force the APA to increase employment opportunities for psychologists.

Finison, L. J. (1979). An aspect of the early history of the Society for the Psychological Study of Social Issues: Psychologists and labor. *Journal of the History of the Behavioral Sciences, 15,* 29–37.

> Focuses principally on SPSSI's involvement with labor and trade unions during the Great Depression.

Krech, D., & Cartwright, D. (1956). On SPSSI's first twenty years. *American Psychologist, 11,* 470–473.

> A history of the founding and first 20 years of SPSSI whose senior author was the person most responsible for the establishment of the society.

Sargent, S. S., & Harris, B. (1986). Academic freedom, civil liberties, and SPSSI. *Journal of Social Issues, 42* (1), 43–67.

> A historical treatment of SPSSI's involvement in issues of academic and intellectual freedom from 1936 through 1970. Cases reviewed include: David Krech, Goodwin Watson, and Gardner Murphy.

Stagner, R. (1986). Reminiscences about the founding of SPSSI. *Journal of Social Issues, 42* (1), 35–42.

> A history of the founding of SPSSI by another of the most significant principals.

Note: For further information on SPSSI's history see two special issues of the *Journal of Social Issues,* 1986, Volume 42, Nos. 1 and 4.

Chapter 15

B. F. Skinner's Experimental Analysis of Behavior

✍🏻

The night before his death, Burrhus Frederic Skinner (1904–1990) made one final plea for psychology as a behavioral science. Within hours of his death, he completed an article for the *American Psychologist* that asked the question, "Can psychology be a science of mind?" (see Skinner, 1990). In this final attack on mentalism, that is, a cognitive approach to psychology, Skinner repeated his oft-stated concerns that psychology was abandoning its place among the natural sciences and, consequently, would forfeit its chance to improve the human condition.

Skinner's model for psychological science was revealed in his 1938 book, *The Behavior of Organisms*, a book that sold only 500 copies in its first 8 years. By contrast, Clark Hull's 1943 book, *Principles of Behavior*, sold more than 5 times as many copies in a 5-year period—more than 2,700 copies by 1948 (Knapp, 1986). Hull and his followers dominated American psychology, particularly learning theory, from the 1940s into the 1960s. However, in the 1960s, Skinner's star began to rise, partly because of the reception of his ideas in the field of education and partly because of the use of Skinnerian principles in the growing clinical field of behavior modification.

Skinner had always been interested in the application of behavioral principles. The experimental analysis of behavior, as he described his research program, sought to discover the contingencies governing behavior. Such an analysis maximized the prediction and control of behavior. Control of behavior offered a means to help individuals, companies, institutions, and even cultures (see Smith, 1992). Like other psychologists and philosophers before him, Skinner was interested in Utopian ideas, and he designed cultures that would achieve

such goals as maximizing happiness, and eliminating crime and pov-
erty (see Skinner's *Walden Two*).

Skinner believed in the power of the behavioral technology he
had developed. At its simplest level it was a system to strengthen desirable behaviors and reduce the occurrence of undesirable behaviors.
Skinner was dismayed with the treatment of psychological disorders,
with the education of children, and with the operating principles of
prisons. He developed techniques that dealt effectively with problems
in each of those areas, and then watched while his technologies were
abandoned. His frustration with society and with his colleagues in psychology increased in his later years and his writing took on a more
desperate character.

B. F. Skinner's faith in his science of psychology led him to apply
its principles to his own life as well. When he and his wife were planning for the birth of their second child, he invented the laborsaving
device that Skinner called a mechanical baby tender (Skinner, 1945).
When it was sold commercially it was called the "air crib," but to
much of the public it was known as the "baby box." The enclosed
chamber, the size of a regular crib, was soundproof and dustproof. It
maintained a constant temperature of 78 degrees (higher when the
baby was younger) and a humidity of 50%. The crib bottom was
tightly stretched canvas that was kept dry by warm air. Toys were sus-
pended from above and music was available for the infant's enjoyment. Despite its advantages, both for infant and parent, the baby box
was never a commercial success. Apparently many parents saw the en-
closure as inhumane when compared to the open-air crib or playpen.

An observation Skinner made in his daughter's fourth-grade classroom led him to design an electromechanical device—a teaching machine—that would teach new material, test the child's knowledge of
that material, and provide immediate feedback about the correctness
of the child's answer. These devices led to the teaching machine
movement that reached its peak in the mid-1960s with more than 200
companies manufacturing teaching machines for home and school use.
However, by the end of that decade teaching machines had largely
disappeared from the classroom, despite considerable scientific evidence supporting their effectiveness (see Benjamin, 1988).

Even with the rejections, Skinner was pleased that he was able to
use his science in solving everyday problems. He wrote:

> *I have, I think, made good use of my analysis of behavior in man-
> aging my own life. . . . Can the psychoanalysts and the cognitive*

*and humanistic psychologists say as much? Did Freud ever report
the use of his theory to influence his own thinking? Are cognitive
psychologists particularly knowledgeable about knowledge? Are humanistic psychologists more effective in helping other people because
of their theories? (Skinner, 1980, p. 75)*

Whether Skinner was better able to use his psychological approach when
compared to contrasting approaches is debatable. What is clear is that he
used the principles from his experimental analysis to observe and reflect
on the daily world of his experience. He recorded these observations and
reflections in a series of private notebooks begun in the 1950s. The excerpts that follow are taken from those notebooks (Skinner, 1980). These
entries have been selected, in particular, to illustrate citizen Skinner as a
psychological scientist. The titles of each entry are Skinner's and the
dates of the entries are included when known.

On Control:

Beyond "Beyond" (1976)

Beyond Freedom and Dignity[1] was a misleading title. It suggested that I was against freedom and personal worth. I did not
advocate imposing control; control existed and should be corrected. Only the complete anarchist refuses to recognize that the
individual must be restrained for the good of the group and, as we
now see, the species. But restraint is a threat to freedom only if it
is aversive. If acting for the good of the group is positively reinforced, people will feel as free and worthy as possible. I am in
favor of that. It is the best way to promote government by the
people for the people.

Loyalty (July 17, 1967)

A lawyer friend has been defending a teacher who refused to
sign a loyalty oath. I suggested that he argue that the man who is
forced to swear that he will behave loyally is robbed of the credit
he would otherwise receive for behaving loyally when not forced
to do so. My friend argued the point but got nowhere with it.

The marriage ceremony is composed of two loyalty oaths, as
young people today are discovering.

---

1. Skinner's 1971 best-selling book. See the reading list at the end of this chapter.

On the Science of Behavior:

Myth (October 31, 1976)

Someone at the London School of Economics asked me, "If mentalism is really so powerless, why has it held the field so long." I said that that was a question for the historian of ideas, and I mentioned Onians' *The Origins of European Thought* and Plato's "discovery" of nonphysical inner forces (I should also have mentioned Homer on μενος, ατε, etc.), and later physiologizing, such as the humors. I did not point to the difficulty in seeing the control exercised by the environment, especially selection by consequences, but I pointed to evolution. My questioner might have asked Darwin, "If natural selection is so powerful, why have people believed so long in the creation of species according to Genesis?" The myths that explain the origin of the universe and the existence of living things, especially man, have been extremely powerful and are not yet displaced by a scientific view. Mind is a myth, with all the power of myths.

Thinking (November 15, 1961)

Behavioral scientists are always competing with self-appointed lay experts. The political scientist must acknowledge the contributions of the success of the politician, the economist of the businessman. Every cattle breeder and animal trainer is an expert on the behavior of organisms. And everyone knows about the everyday behavior of everybody.

There is a special difficulty in talking about intellectual behavior because the people who know are famous as knowers. Mathematicians are likely to describe how mathematicians think. The distinguished chemist is an authority on scientific method.

Granted that such people are favorably placed to see intellect at work, it does not follow that they understand human behavior well enough to spot the relevant facts and formulate a general account of "thinking." The distinction between knowing *how* to behave and knowing *about* behaving is hard to make.

Dangerous Fiction (June 27, 1969)

An article on freedom begins: "You have chosen to read this sentence." A clever rhetorical device, but misleading. I was not reading the sentence when the author wrote it. He was predicting my behavior, not describing it. Even so, he had evidence for nothing more than: "You are reading this sentence." Perhaps the sentence "caught my eye" when I had nothing else to do—when there was no competing behavior. Perhaps I had been assigned the article by a teacher. Even under the "free" conditions assumed by the writer, my history and the current circumstances need to be taken into account. How important were earlier instances to which the title of the article, the name of the writer, and the layout of the page bore some resemblance? To bring my personal history, my present state, and the current situation all together in an act of choice is the kind of simplification that makes cognitive psychology so futile.

On Conditioning:

Teaching a Sheepdog (March 28, 1955)

A French woman who runs a restaurant in Vermont sold some young dogs to a farmer, who later complained that they had attacked, killed, and eaten a young lamb. She was sure this was because they were starving; they were given a commercial dog food and were too thin. Then she said that in France when a dog kills a sheep, all the other dogs are brought together around the dead sheep, and there the offending dog is "beaten to death and shot." And she insisted that the other dogs knew why it was being punished.

This desperate effort to teach animals, accentuating all the details of the human parallel, could at most have the effect of making a dead sheep a conditioned aversive stimulus. Would it work? I doubt it.

Why are people different? Or are they?

Tea and Madeleines (October 8, 1967)

This morning, washing my face in the bathtub, I felt an irregularity in a tooth and immediately concluded that a filling must have come loose. I had smelled oil of clove, which the dentist often uses. Then I realized that the oil of clove was in the soap, and immediately the filling went back into place. Neither the oil of clove nor the irregularity in the tooth alone would have suggested a dental problem. Combined, the conclusion was almost irresistible.

Nervousness (August 25, 1963)

A baseball pitcher who is "under pressure" is under aversive control. He must throw, but the behavior is likely to be punished (the ball may come straight back at him at great speed, or the batter may get a hit, possibly winning the game). Under these conditions, he is likely to show "nervous habits"—wiping his hands, adjusting his hat, tugging at his belt, and so on. Some of these are "superstitious"; any gesture adventitiously followed by a successful throw will acquire a slightly higher probability of emission. But many are simply ways of postponing a possibly punished act; a pitcher who stood stock still for a comparable period of time might be booed.

Bedside (November 14, 1976)

The argument that operant conditioning was "the best that nature could do," even though it made such things as superstition likely, can be extended to sexual behavior.

Heterosexual behavior is closely related to contingencies of survival, but nature could not be too specific. Strong personal affection, various forms of sexual stimulation, and possibly some built-in susceptibilities to particular visual forms and particular modes of stimulation—these are about the closest nature could come. But they produce homosexual and autosexual behavior, which are not otherwise related to survival.

For an anatomical parallel, compare the male breast. No great harm done and possibly safer in preserving the genes responsible for the female breast.

On Reinforcement:

Reinforcement Overlooked (early 1960s)

I once visited a laboratory in which a research assistant was taming a monkey. He sat in a small room with a handful of peanuts, a monkey far away on the floor. The assistant chirped, clicked his tongue, and talked in a soothing voice, more and more intensively as the monkey approached. Whenever the monkey took fright and turned away, he would throw it a peanut. He apparently did this to counteract escape, but the peanuts were actually reinforcing the very behavior he was trying to eliminate, and as a result, the monkey was approaching and turning away in a rather stereotyped pattern.

The same mistake is made by the teacher who offers a treat of some kind when the class is getting out of hand. If this behavior is a kind of aggression toward the teacher, the treat may have an opposing effect. But in the long run, the reinforcement of misbehavior will offset any gain. Unfortunately, the reduction in aggression is immediate but the effect of reinforcement apparent only later. Hence, the practice may be continued, even though in the long run misbehavior becomes even more serious.

Shall I Ever Learn? (March 20, 1976)

Yesterday Lisa, almost ten, was opening a new jar of mixed nuts. The metal cap was sealed with a tight plastic tape. She got a knife and began to pry one edge of the tape free of the glass on top. I was on the point of saying, "Here, let me help you," but I caught myself in time and she got the top off—and would no doubt do so even more effectively in the future because I stayed out of it.

Suppose now she had been frustrated, getting mad at the top, jabbing it ineffectively with the knife, muttering or swearing. Should I then have helped?

Definitely not! I should then have been teaching Lisa to display anger, to swear, and eventually to exaggerate these behaviors because someone then helps.

When *does* one help a child?

Pretty obviously: when the child *needs* help and before she displays behavior which, when reinforced by help from others, displaces effective behavior which might otherwise begin to be conditioned.

Don't give impossible assignments. If, by accident, one has been encountered, let any frustrated behavior extinguish before taking over and giving help.

Impressionism (January 24, 1970)

How much of the extraordinary productivity of the Impressionists was due to the quicker reinforcement and the reduction in aversive attention to detail which followed when photographic realism was abandoned? Cézanne worked hard, there is no question of that, but he could still produce a picture quickly. Could Picasso have done half of what he has done if he had done it "photographically?" Someone like Dali, who remains compulsive about details, has produced very little.

The startling discovery that detailed likeness was not necessary in a beautiful picture made a picture more immediately reinforcing and freed the artist from many hours of busy work.

Obeying a Rule (November 30, 1974)

The superiority of positive reinforcement is evident even in mediated consequences. I have trouble remembering to put drops in my eye, in part because they sting. If I forget them I may lose more of my field of vision, but even so I forget. The immediate aversive consequence is prepotent over the avoidance of loss in the future. The last time I was tested, however, I had a very *good* reading, an especially low intraocular pressure, and since then I have remembered much more easily to put in my drops. Why?

There is only a remote connection between putting a drop in my eye and a reading of reduced pressure. The behavior is rule-governed. The rule is laid down by my oculist, and I follow it either because he warns me that I may become blind or because he assures me that I will continue to have useful vision. The assurance appears to be more effective than the warning.

The Near Hit (June 6, 1963)

I suppose I mean the near miss—i.e., a miss but close enough to have some effect or at least to "arouse hope."

How reinforcing is it? The slot machine, the horse race, the Bingo game—all permit the player to come close without actually winning. There is a temporal element. One gets the first two bells, cherries, or bars on the slot machine but misses the third. One's horse is beaten in the stretch. The Bingo card shows four-in-a-row long before someone else gets five. (The slot machine and horse race offer consolation prizes: two cherries win, though much less than three; a horse may show or place.) A lottery ticket may be close to the winning number or may win a lesser prize. A sweepstakes ticket may draw a horse which almost wins the race.

There is undoubtedly something punishing in almost winning. An emotional component is clear: If there is a temporal pattern—if one loses at the very end of a contest—the effect is felt as *disappointment*, a *let down* from the elevation of impending reinforcement. But the net effect must be reinforcing, or the designers of gambling systems are wrong.

Those Who Gamble Punish Themselves (July 7, 1966)

Some schedules of reinforcement are aversive, and organisms escape from them when they can. Gamblers "know" that they are losing their fortunes, and accidents that interrupt their gambling may be looked back upon as good luck; yet if there is no interruption, they do not stop. A pigeon will peck a special key that turns off the whole experiment when comparable conditions prevail, although it will not stop responding if the experiment cannot be turned off.

Is it begging the question to say that the variable-ratio schedule is so powerful that it forces players to continue to play in spite of growing aversive stimuli? Certainly they continue to play, and certainly their condition becomes more and more painful. Escape should be strongly reinforced, yet they do not escape by stopping, evidently because playing is stronger.

An analysis of the contingencies, resulting in a rule (stop gambling if you do not want to lose), will have an effect only if (like all rules) there are special contingencies to maintain the rule-governed behavior.

Being Nice (March 25, 1972)

When a University of Texas student asked me "What is love?" I replied "mutual reinforcement." But I was uneasy about it, because when one does something nice to a person one loves, it is not done to reinforce. Now, however, it seems to me that a superstitious contingency may prevail. I originally felt that when one does something nice to another person, the other person is then emotionally disposed to do something even nicer in return, but adventitious reinforcement should be taken into account. If one is inclined to do something nice because another person has just done something nice, then what the other person has just done may be reinforced. There may be more of this than I had supposed in talking about an emotional disposition to be nice to others.

An emotional disposition to be nice to those who are nice to us is presumably part of a genetic endowment. But what were the contingencies of survival that selected that endowment? Could it not be that this is another example of ontogenic contingencies being taken over by a phylogenic mechanism? A built-in tendency to be nice to those who are nice to one would have survival value in increasing the number of nice things done. (I am assuming, of course, that by nice I mean ultimately biologically good.)

The 88-Lever Box (October 3, 1958)

A student at Hamilton College insisted that you must use punishment in raising children. He described an instance in which a mother and her small son came to call, and the boy immediately went to the piano and began to pound the keys. The mother frequently told him to stop but to no avail. The student insisted that he would have spanked a son of his, and justly, under such circumstances. I agreed that the mother should have backed up her first request, possibly by punishing or by separating the boy and the piano, or should not have made the request.

A piano is *designed* to make such behavior likely. Two centuries of skill and thought have gone into devising an instrument which provides reinforcing consequences when white and black keys are struck. Beautiful tones are ideally contingent upon striking. A piano is an 88-lever box.

Having provided such an instrument, it is foolish to allow a child to come into contact with it unless you wish to shape and sustain a great deal of behavior. Pianos can be locked; children can be left elsewhere; those are the simple solutions. The objectionable solution is to offset the reinforcement with punishment. It is objectionable because it has unwanted by-products.

On Contingencies:

Fault (December 23, 1977)

If students do not learn, is it their fault? No, their teachers have not arranged effective instructional contingencies. Is it then the teachers' fault? No, the culture has not arranged effective contingencies for them.

Is it then the fault of the culture? By the time we reach this question, the notion of fault is at fault. How shall we punish a culture? In moving from student to teacher to culture, we move steadily away from the feasibility of punitive measures—from the cane for the student, to dismissal for the teacher, to—what for the culture?

A culture could be said to be punished if it does not survive (this is the ultimate selective consequence), but we change it, if at all, through other means. We look for alternative measures. Similarly, we can look for other ways of improving the behavior of teachers and students—as by designing contingencies under which productive behaviors are reinforced.

Rules, Models, Contingencies (January 9, 1977)

The failure of many parents to have their children vaccinated shows the difference between rules and contingencies.

In the days when parents saw many children crippled by polio, they rushed for the new vaccine for their own children. Now that there are few cases, it is hard to get them to have their children vaccinated. Contingencies *grow* weak, and rules *are* weak.

What is to be done? Describe the epidemics which may come if the children are not vaccinated? Show crippled children on TV? In other words, reestablish modeling contingencies?

To what extent is one's own conduct changed upon seeing another person punished (by authorities or by nature, as in a car accident or a crippling disease)? Is nature's capital punishment a deterrent?

Puritan? (December 22, 1971)

Am I being a nineteenth-century prude in objecting to gambling? After all, isn't a national lottery a good way to make dull lives interesting? Think of the pleasure of looking at a ticket that may mean a fortune. And is not the same variable-ratio schedule at the heart of hunting, fishing, research, exploration, and writing?

Yes, but with a difference. In the contrived contingencies of a gambling enterprise, winning is not contingent on useful, let along ultimately useful, behavior. Gambling is wrong not because it ruins some people or is tabooed by a church, but because it commits a person to repetitious, stultifying behavior.

Editor's Note: *And finally, Skinner illustrates the reason for philosophical diversity in the science of psychology:*

Closure (December 23, 1967)

When Lisa was a year and a half old, she asked me to print A's. I printed several and then one with a small break in the horizontal line. She looked a little puzzled, and when I completed the letter by filling the gap she smiled. I did it again and she laughed. I did it again. Then I drew a larger A with a big gap, and she said "No!" quite vigorously. When I completed it, she laughed brightly.

How many systems of psychology might one found on such observations?

Skinner Bibliography

Benjamin, L. T., Jr., (1988). A history of teaching machines. *American Psychologist, 43,* 703–712.

A history of teaching machines in the classroom emphasizing the work of Sidney Pressey and B. F. Skinner.

Coleman, S. R. (1982, Spring/Summer). B. F. Skinner: Systematic iconoclast. *The Gamut,* pp. 53–75.

An excellent treatment of the complexity of Skinner as person and the place of his science in psychology.

Guttman, N. (1977). On Skinner and Hull: A reminiscence and projection. *American Psychologist, 32,* 321–328.

A comparison of the careers of Skinner and Hull that examines Skinner's greater popularity in contemporary psychology and projects the probable influence of both men in future centuries.

Skinner, B. F. (1938). *The Behavior of Organisms.* New York: Appleton.

Although pieces of his system of behavior had appeared in articles in the 1930s, this book marked the first comprehensive treatment of what would be the most radical of the various behaviorisms.

Skinner, B. F. (1945, October). Baby in a box. *Ladies' Home Journal,* pp. 30–31, 135–136, 138.

Skinner's original account of the rearing of daughter Debby in the (in)famous baby box. Also see his article in the March 1979 issue of *Psychology Today* (pp. 28–40) entitled "My experience with the baby-tender."

Skinner, B. F. (1948). *Walden Two*. New York: Macmillan
    Skinner's novel about a Utopian community founded on behavioral principles.

Skinner, B. F. (1971). *Beyond Freedom and Dignity*. New York: Alfred A. Knopf.
    This book topped the *New York Times* bestseller list. It argues that freedom is an illusion, that control (mostly haphazard) is a fact of life, and that cultures should structure contingencies (use control) to create desirable outcomes. Although many nonreaders of this book labeled Skinner a fascist, his humanitarian goals were recognized by the American Humanist Association that gave him its Humanist of the Year Award in 1972.

Skinner, B. F. (1976, 1979, 1983). *Particulars of My Life. The Shaping of a Behaviorist. A Matter of Consequences*. New York: Alfred A. Knopf.
    Skinner's three-volume autobiography. The first volume, which covers Skinner's life through his undergraduate days at Hamilton College, is especially good reading.

Skinner, B. F. (1980). *Notebooks*. (Edited and with an introduction by R. Epstein). Englewood Cliffs, NJ: Prentice-Hall.
    The entries in this chapter are taken from this book, which is a compilation of excerpts from Skinner's notebooks.

Skinner, B. F. (1990). Can psychology be a science of mind? *American Psychologist, 45,* 1206–1210.
    This was Skinner's final published work, an article that he finished writing the night before he died. It attacks cognitive psychology as a kind of pseudoscience and argues that the experimental analysis of behavior has yet to be given a full and fair trial in psychology.

Note: *A special issue of the* American Psychologist *devoted to Skinner is to be published in February 1993.*

Chapter 16

Abraham Maslow's Research on Good Human Beings

In the 1940s, two views dominated the study of human behavior. One, behaviorism, was strongly environmentalistic, emphasizing the control of human behavior by punishment and reinforcement. The other, psychoanalysis, emphasized unconscious motives, mostly sexual and aggressive, as the agents controlling behavior. Both systems of thought were extremely deterministic, leaving little opportunity for individuals to be seen as having control over their lives. Humanistic psychology, sometimes referred to as "the Third Force," arose in opposition to those two systems.

Psychologists espousing this alternative view emphasized the goodness of human nature and that individuals could take responsibility for their personal growth. They were concerned with topics such as love, creativity, the nature of self, autonomy, and transcendental experiences. Humanistic psychologists sought to study the healthy personality, in contrast to the neurotic personalities that were the substance of psychoanalysis and the mechanistic actions that characterized behaviorism.

Although humanistic psychology has roots in the philosophies of Soren Kierkegaard and Jean-Paul Sartre, its formation as an identifiable system of psychology began with Abraham H. Maslow (1908–1970). In 1954 he invited some like-minded friends—Gordon Allport, Erich Fromm, Kurt Goldstein, Karen Horney, and Carl Rogers—to begin an organization to promote a humanistic view. That led to the founding, in 1962, of the American Association for Humanistic Psychology, and a decade later, to the establishment of a division within the American Psychological Association (Stagner, 1988).

In the fall of 1943, with the United States and much of the rest of the world engaged in war, Maslow published the most influential work of his career, an article entitled "A Theory of Human Motivation." This theory had grown from his need to understand people. Why do people behave the way they do? Why do people behave in admirable ways? Why do they behave badly? Why would they follow a dictator like Adolf Hitler? Maslow believed in the inherent goodness of people, and it was difficult for him to understand the horrors of war. He hoped that a better understanding of human needs might lead to the elimination of such tragedies.

Maslow hypothesized that human motives existed in a hierarchical arrangement with physiological needs such as hunger and thirst at the bottom and the need for self-actualization at the top. This hierarchy meant that needs were pursued in a particular order, starting at the bottom. If an individual's physiological needs were satisfied, then the individual would pursue those needs at the second level: security needs—that is, needs associated with safety. When physiological and security needs were met, then the individual pursued love and belongingness, followed by a fourth level labeled "self-esteem needs," and finally the fifth and highest level, self-actualization.

For Maslow, people were seen as having a vast capacity for expressing kindness and love. But in order for people to display such kindness to others, their physiological needs must be met, and they must be free of the negative emotions of fear and uncertainty that cause people to aggress against others. Once all lower needs were satisfied, individuals would be capable of self-actualizing, an achievement that would create inner peace for the individual and, indeed, peace for the world. A fuller statement of this theory appeared a little more than a decade later in Maslow's 1954 book, *Motivation and Personality*.

Maslow had begun his study of psychology at the City College of New York, transferred to Cornell University in 1927, where he took a course from E. B. Titchener and transferred again the following year to the University of Wisconsin, where he eventually received his doctorate in psychology in 1934. His dissertation research on social dominance in rhesus monkeys was conducted under the guidance of Harry Harlow.

Edward L. Thorndike was so impressed by that research that he invited Maslow to come to Columbia University to work with him. Maslow spent the next 2 years there as a Carnegie Fellow. While at Columbia, Maslow met the two people who were most responsible for his eventual research on self-actualization: Ruth Benedict and Max Wertheimer. Benedict was an anthropologist on the faculty at Columbia;

and Wertheimer, the founder of Gestalt psychology, was on the faculty of the New School for Social Research, where he arrived in 1935 having fled the growing Nazi menace in Germany.

In a book published shortly after his death, Maslow (1971) relates the impetus for his study of self-actualization:

> My investigations on self-actualization were not planned to be research and did not start out as research, [but] as the effort of a young intellectual to try to understand two of his teachers whom he loved, adored, and admired, and who were very, very wonderful people. I could not be content simply to adore, but sought to understand why these two people were so different from the run-of-the-mill people in the world. (p. 40)

Maslow began to study these two special people, keeping a notebook about them. Exactly when these personal studies began is not known but certainly no later than the early 1940s (Lowry, 1973). During his study of Benedict and Wertheimer he got the idea for the concept of self-actualization. About this insight he wrote:

> I realized in one wonderful moment that their two patterns could be generalized. I was talking about a kind of person, not about two incomparable individuals. There was wonderful excitement in this. I tried to see whether this pattern could be found elsewhere, and I did find it elsewhere, in one person after another. (pp. 41–42)

The term "self-actualization" was actually used earlier by Kurt Goldstein, a member of the Gestalt psychology group, to connote an innate desire for individuals to achieve their full potential. However, Maslow used the concept in a very different way. Self-actualization was not something to be achieved; it was the natural state. Those who were not self-actualized had been hindered in some way by society or by their own unfortunate circumstances. Through his research he settled on certain characteristics that seemed shared by people who were self-actualized: (a) caring for all living things, (b) dedication to their work, (c) clear perception of reality, (d) accepting of their own behavior and resisting conformity, (e) a need for privacy, (f) creativity, (g) spontaneity, (h) a democratic outlook, (i) a kind sense of humor, and (j) occasional peak experiences of great awe or ecstasy. For Maslow, self-actualization meant being possessed of the greatest psychological health.

Maslow's studies of Benedict and Wertheimer expanded to others. He began to ask his students at Brooklyn College to write about the most self-actualized person they had known. As he developed an idea of the traits associated with self-actualization he sought to gain empirical evidence of his views through psychological testing. Not surprisingly, such empirical measures were not easily obtained. Yet Maslow persisted, enlarging his vision of what characterized a self-actualized person. Subsequent research by others has mostly failed to support a trait cluster for self-actualizers.

Despite the lack of empirical support for the concept of self-actualization as defined by Maslow, the concept continues to stimulate research and discussion in the fields of motivation, personality, and clinical psychology. The concept enjoys some applied use today in business and industry for purposes of employee motivation and job satisfaction.

As Maslow began his work on self-actualization in the 1940s, he kept a notebook from 1945 through 1949, which he called his "GHB" notebook, describing his observations and testing of "Good Human Beings." The excerpts that follow are taken from that notebook. They provide a glimpse of Maslow's early thinking about this concept that is so central to his humanistic psychology.

May 6, 1945

After fussing along for some years, I have decided to dig into GHB research and do it more formally and rigidly. It's all very difficult though. Lots of problems. As things stand now, I try to be as conscious as possible of insurmountable difficulties, and then I go ahead anyway.

The layout now is to collect students who look like potential GHB and then go through several sieving processes, keeping records all the way. (1) Pick them just by looking at them in class. (2) Then look up their security scores.[1] (3) Then interview them for about an hour. (4) Ask them to write me a memorandum of the interview to the best of their memory for my records. (5) Rorschach test. That's as far as it's gone so far.

Problems. Practically all I've picked show poor Rorschachs. Can't get any satisfaction on this from the experts. What's a good

---

1. The security scores referred to a test of self-esteem that Maslow developed in 1940.

Rorschach [test result] anyway? *Must* study Rorschach [test] in future. Don't know enough about it. . . .

It would seem that ultimately a full psychoanalysis is the only valid technique for picking. And then, since everyone would show up with some neurotic trends, what degree is necessary for inclusion as GHB?

Also, how about picking apart various qualities I have lumped together? The very sweet and kind, the strong, the creative, the clear-in-mind-about-goals-and-life-in-general? . . .

Another thought. The whole concept has to be defined operationally anyhow. Otherwise I find myself looking for some essence or Platonic idea which may not exist anywhere but in my own mind. Perhaps a whole series of operational researches. Good adjustment according to Rorschach test. . . . according to psychiatric interviews, according to psychoanalysis, according to TAT, according to degree of satisfaction of basic needs, according to degree and quality of achievement. All of these groups would simultaneously overlap to some extent and *not* overlap to some extent. Maybe study at *that* point could really get someplace.

Maybe anyway we'll have to speak of different types of GHB rather than just one type. Maybe they won't be similar in many respects. Maybe they will.

Question: who should do the picking? The picker's values will certainly get in the way. Ought he to be GHB himself? A study of the different people whom different investigators would pick might tell more about the choosers than the chosen.

Anyway there can be at least a minimum requirement. No neurosis, psychosis, psychopathic personality, or obviously psychosomatic diseases. While this will exclude *some* very fine people, it should let most of them through. While it should let through some stinkers, it should exclude most of them.

Also, maybe should use as criterion followups after a certain number of years. Seeing them under *various* circumstances would help, maybe even be necessary. Is it *possible* in our culture for a twenty-year-old to be GHB? With only superficial techniques at my disposal, how can I talk about character structure—the presumably unchangeable part of the person? Maybe they should be married and bear babies before I can judge.

Actually what I've been doing is studying self-actualized adults over fifty or sixty and then getting a list of their common characteristics and then picking youngsters[2] who seemed to me to look like them and show in some degree these same characteristics. But such youngsters might be standing on their ears at age of twenty. Maybe *just* because they're essentially fine people in a cockeyed world?

May 14, 1945

Have completed very interesting research on 4 classes. It's somewhat vitiated because I spoke of some students publicly, but not enough to damage the results. Students in general voted for those I had selected. Also, those I selected had somewhat higher security scores. Those whom the students selected had *much* higher security scores. Apparently they picked for security. But I see quite clearly now that security and GHB are different. High security scorers seem to be sometimes quite smug, self-content, cocky in an unpleasant way. . . .

Then so many that I pick as GHB have average or fairly low security scores. And still this doesn't make me change my mind about their futures. Again I get the impression that the security test taps only superficial consciousness which is sometimes contradicted by deeper more unconscious security feelings. If we define security as love for others, then it's possible to have such a difference between conscious and unconscious feelings. . . .

September 8, 1945

It finally becomes unmistakably clear that my subjects won't cooperate as they have in other studies. I learned long ago that the older GHBs had an awfully strong sense of privacy, as Ruth Benedict tried to explain to me long ago. She as a matter of fact spoke more freely than any of them about personal things. There was no difficulty about impersonal things, and they would go on at length about their ideas or theories. I don't even dare approach Köhler. Same for Wertheimer. Levy hasn't refused but tends to

---

2. According to Richard Lowry (1973), Maslow choose to study college students because they were available, not because he believed there would be a high proportion of self-actualizers in that population. However, because he had access to so many students, he felt sure he would find at least a few who reached his criteria for self-actualization.

change the subject.[3] . . . They all seemed uneasy when I told them what I thought of them and what I wanted of them.

Now, to a lesser extent, I find the same with my college students, though probably for different reasons. They just seem bored or evasive or merely polite. I think all the talk and probing just bores them. It's a chore. If I get them in a corner they'll kick through. They won't protest *against* it or refuse; they just don't show up or come late or postpone. . . . . So far no one has refused to fill out blanks. Apparently they can do this on their own time and so mind it less.

It's got so that I think of all this as a GHB characteristic and suspect anyone who cooperates eagerly.

What's the difference between these and those in dominance-sex research and all the insecure and neurotic people? They cooperated eagerly. Must be because they could get something out of it. And my present GHB subjects don't get anything out of it. It's pure and simple doing me a favor with little or no return to the subject. It's not personal distaste, because they turn to me easily for help and they like to call socially.

October 20, 1945

I suppose a necessary control would be to rely not alone on my impressions from appearance—which may let many slip through—but also on selection by class elections, by Bertha's[4] judgments, and by security test scores and other scores which sample everyone in class. I think I must start that this semester.

I must list separately all those students selected from classes last semester and this. All others were chosen unsystematically and can't be described in terms of the sampling by which they were chosen. It was mostly from going back over all my records and picking the ones who seemed to me in retrospect to have been GHB.

---

3. Wolfgang Köhler (1887–1967) was professor of psychology at Swarthmore College, (see chapter 13) and David Levy (1892–1977) was a child psychiatrist who introduced the Rorschach ink blot test in the United States. He was one of Maslow's closest friends.

4. Bertha Goodman immigrated to New York City from Russia in 1922. She and Maslow met shortly after that, and he began to tutor her in English. They were married in 1928. They enjoyed a close relationship, and Bertha Maslow was a frequent sounding board for her husband's ideas and one who shaped those ideas.

November 11, 1945

Today I went through my old classbooks collecting dominance and security scores from my GHB subjects. The general finding is that either the security test is no good at correlating with GHB or else the concept of GHB is quite different from the concept of security. Generally I had not picked, either from appearance or after knowing security scores, those who had the highest security scores. Most of my people had *moderately* high security scores, *not* very high ones. There were also a few with security scores *below* the median.

Upon examining all these data, I came to the conclusion that I've been picking "fine" people whom I could respect and in whom I saw some sort of promise. But many high security scorers are just opposite of this—smug, self-satisfied, "lumpish" in the sense of just not doing much or wanting much, almost torpid. Some seem to me to be stolid. I think this semester I'll examine more carefully the high security scores.

December 17, 1945

I have been thinking for some time that an especially important characteristic of my GHBs is their ability to see reality more clearly. This showed itself in my security studies, especially among the Blackfoot Indians.[5] It showed itself most, or at least first, in the ability to judge character. They could spot a phony a mile away.

Maybe I should have them try to distinguish fine shades of color. Try Seashore's record on tone differences. Maier test of art judgment. Spot phony poems. Tests of reasoning a la Sell's atmosphere effect experiment. Also suggestion experiments with odors, electricity, etc.

December 28, 1945

. . . Borrowed various books on theology, saints, etc. Talked of Tillich, Niebuhr, Augustine. Borrowed Cheney and Meihlin. He told me of Boehme. I asked him about concept of original sin. He told me only Catholics and fundamentalists take it seriously as

---

5. As part of his anthropological studies, Maslow spent some time in the late 1930s with the Blackfoot Indians in Canada.

sects. Unitarians broke away on this question. Parker said "Our disagreement is not so much on the nature of God but on the nature of Man." Other Protestant sects are not for or against it—not fashionable to talk about it.

But the next movement among highbrow theologians in line from Augustine, Kierkegaard, Tillich, and Niebuhr came back to this notion in the form of sin or evil inhering in human nature itself—as part of it.

But I objected. I don't see it. Most of what we call evil or nastiness is a *product*—of frustration, crippling, misery, etc. As for children, they are neither good nor evil. We mustn't use adult terms for them, no more than we should for animals. We can't study the problem, then, because it cannot be seen in children and because the sin of adults is mostly not original. This argument is, we cannot prove "original goodness," but also we see no evidence for "original sin."

The big point is that we just can't find in ordinary mankind the answer to the question.

But what if we study *extra*ordinary people? Certainly a visitor from Mars descending upon a colony of birth-injured cripples, dwarfs, hunchbacks, etc., could not deduce what they *should* have been. But then let us study *not* cripples, but the closest approach we can get to whole, healthy men. In them we find qualitative differences, a different system of motivation, emotion, value, thinking, and perceiving. In a certain sense, only the saints *are* mankind. Others are sick, twisted cripples.

Do we find sin and evil in them? I don't think so. We find neutral equipment which under certain circumstances can make trouble, under other circumstances not. Original sin can be attributed to them only by prejudging the case, e.g., by defining pride as sin and then finding the sin. *Ergo* original sin.

January 13, 1946

So uncertain about my choices, and so many of them turn out badly or doubtful, that I've decided to use the Rorschach as screening device. Until now, I've been taking Rorschachs as the dependent variable and using my judgment as the independent variable. But now will have to add Rorschach to the list of independent variables, which also includes (1) my judgment, (2) security test scores, and (3) self-judgment of subjects.

Mostly this is because I hesitate to plunge into the full study of any individual until I'm fairly sure he's well adjusted. Too much investment of time involved. Does no harm anyway to have a finer screen for selection. Will be convincing to more people. . . .

Also I've decided, for next semester, to rely on security test scores a little more for selection of subjects. I can record my intuitive judgments before I get these scores. I'll keep a running record of students who seem to me to be GHB, but I won't select them for interview until I get security scores too, about middle of semester. Can use first half of semester in catching up with this semester's batch. . . .

The notion I am working toward is of some ideal of human nature, closely approximated in reality by a few "self-actualized" people. Everybody else is sick in greater or lesser degree it is true, but these degrees are much less important than we have thought. The self-actualized person is so different from all others that we need a different theory of motivation, perception, emotion, thinking, values, humor, personality, psychopathology, etc.

We may use these people as synonymous with human nature in general because there seems to be no *intrinsic* reason why everyone shouldn't be this way. Apparently every baby has all possibilities for self-actualization, but most all of them get it knocked out of them.

Also have to start writing eventually about the relation of these people to "mystic experiences." Any naturalistic definition of a mystic would be close to a definition of the self-actualized person. Also the fact is that these people (or most of them) have many so-called mystic experiences only never call them that.

Werner[6] suggested that the perception experiments I had thought of would show differences in favor of GHB because others got more easily frustrated and therefore tense and anxious. But I said that could be precisely the point. It is not that I think the perceptual or cognitive apparatus of the neurotic is bad—it is just tempered, inhibited, shackled, blinded by anxiety, rigidity, conventionalization, egocentricity.

I think of the self-actualizing man not as an ordinary man with something added, but rather as the ordinary man with nothing

---

6. Heinz Werner was a psychologist on the faculty at Clark University.

taken away. The average man is a full human being with damp-
ened and inhibited powers and capacities. . . .

January 18, 1946

Notes on J. Brooks Atkinson, *Henry Thoreau: The Cosmic Yan-
kee.* In general it is as if Thoreau is *trying* to be a mystic, a self-
actualized man, but succeeding more in his writing than in his life.
Unmarried, practically no friends, not really liberal, definitely maladjusted in college, quite sour in many of his judgments. Emerson:
"Henry is—with difficulty—sweet." Considered a crank and a boor
by many of his townsfolk.

Also a Yogi. Supported by his friends mostly. "Sauntering
through life" is impossible with wife and children and with ordinary obligations to friends, family, and society. One who does this
is likely to be parasitic. Not that he was a primitive. He approved
of railroads, commerce, ships. Nonetheless, "he scorned science,
because it ignored the 'higher law' ".

January 19, 1946

Trying to clear up notions of self-actualization. I have the idea
of using the concept of "ideal" or even "typical type" of the species. Thoreau points out that the eagle has to do what he does,
like any other animal, because he is "eagle-like." No animal is
cruel or kind or cowardly, etc. These are all human terms and suggest decision at the voluntary, thoughtful level. But animal behavior is determined almost entirely by instincts, by a fate inherent
almost entirely in the simple fact of being a member of one species rather than another. The type "instinct" tells the animal
(1) when to feel a craving and under what circumstances, (2) *what*
to look for to satisfy the craving, and (3) how to behave while
looking for his goal object. Thus it's fair to say that the drive, the
motivated behavior, and the goal object are largely or primarily
determined by heredity.

But it is still possible to make value judgments upon tigers,
ants, or oak trees, and *not* on an anthropocentric basis. It need
have nothing to do with human values.

To start with the crudely obvious—a lion with no eyes, a tiger
with no claws, a deer that can't run, an oak tree without leaves,
etc. All these are "bad" or atypical or abnormal or unsuitable.

Better to say "deviant" because that is value*less*. For the same reason, we should not use "average," "nonaverage," "extreme," etc.

Of course the obvious universal criterion here would be "survival" viability, or at least the ability to mate and reproduce. But in the long run, this too would be weak because it invokes some value external to the data, to the species. Furthermore, either deviation or lack of it might have survival value. Thus, all tigers without teeth or claws might be allowed to live by the hunter, while other average or "normal" tigers would die. Or, in time of depression, feebleminded children might live better than the average (unemployed) man.

Even so, such biological criteria would still be better than what is available now, by way of countering complete relativity.

But what I think I can really stand on is the notion taken from the biological taxonomists of the "type specimen." This is supposed to be perfect in its own kind, to be standard and typical. And therefore it can be used as an absolute or fixed or constant or invariant (something like the standard foot, pound, quart, etc., of the Bureau of Standards). . . .

The type-specimen is the most perfect-in-its-own-kind rather than the most average. It would be the one who had most developed or actualized the unique potentialities of the species—the *finest* specimen of its type.

What does this mean for human beings? That a neurotic is less "good" because he isn't human enough? Because he falls short of the type-specimen? Because he doesn't fit the definition of the species "human being" (like an imperfectly pronounced word, an ungrammatical sentence)?

In any case we can be sure that defining the human species would be a supracultural affair, for it would have to be the *species* that we define.

January 21, 1946

It becomes apparent that I must allow for *various* types of good health, just as there are various syndromes of maladjustment. This is seen especially in my student subjects. There is extroverted and introverted health. There is creativeness, both theoretically minded and practically minded. They are ambitious and contented. Also there are those who seem to me *essentially* and deeply sound, but who are at the moment in trouble. Their symptoms and troubles seem to be superficial, perhaps only situationally produced. There are those with strong sex drive and those without.

I have so many poor Rorschachs among my selectees that it looks as if I can cull only three or four or five clear cases out of my forty or fifty selectees. I won't bother going into extensive interviewing until I am convinced they're OK. . . .

February 9, 1946

Have spent last two weeks studying Rorschach. Feel fairly competent now to judge them. Can easily reject *bad* ones. . . . But still have not run across one that looks very good, let alone perfect. But can spot *relatively* good ones. . . . Of course, must check my impression with those of an expert. . . .

Meanwhile I've learned not to trust my security test too far. It's good enough for screening out those who admit themselves to be maladjusted, but those who score high may still not amount to much by the Rorschach test or even by observations. . . .

Additional men to study: Whitman, Emerson, James, Dewey, Spinoza, Channing, Pascal, Jakob Boehme, Goethe.

May 22, 1946

Stopped work for a while. Interested in other things. Also rather puzzled and discouraged by developments in GHB research. . . .

Have decided to continue with at least *some* of the prospects whom I rejected after interview. They will be told they are GHB, well adjusted, etc., and followed up as a control group. This certainly can't do any harm—only good (by suggestion). I think I'd better be careful about picking *only* those who wouldn't be hurt by being lied to.

June 21, 1946

. . . Definitely my impressions about people and their Rorschach's don't agree very well. . . . The ones I have picked were often not supported by the Rorschach, and the ones the Rorschach picked haven't impressed me much. David Levy, when I asked him, said the independent variable *must* be the psychiatric interview, behavior, etc. The Rorschach makes mistakes except in the very best hands, and even then it does. . . . Anyway I can't lean on the Rorschach as much as I would have liked to—but it will certainly be OK to pick as cases those who pass *all* criteria, including the Rorschach.

Editor's Note: *There are 19 more entries in Maslow's GHB Notebook after the above entry, the last of those dated December 20, 1949. None offer any new insights on GHB or the methods to select them. Partly this lessened activity was due to poor health, started with a heart attack in late 1946. Maslow's principal treatment of the concept of self-actualization appeared in a 1950 article (see bibliography for this chapter). Lowry (1973) has written, "Passing from Maslow's GHB notebook to his published paper of 1950 is like going from a diamond mine to Cartier's: one has the impression that somewhere along the way there has been a great deal of shaping, polishing, and setting. The vision of self-actualization that appeared in the notebook was groping and tentative, to say the least. . . . In sharp contrast, the vision presented in the published paper was finely cut, polished, and set. Also, notwithstanding Maslow's apologies for methodological shortcomings, it was presented with a confidence that could scarcely be described as groping or tentative" (p. 39). Maslow wrote that paper in the middle of 1949. Lowry suggests that the 2 years of illness may have served as a period of incubation that brought clarity to the concept that was meant to define good human beings.*

Abraham Maslow Bibliography

Bugental, J. F. T. (Ed.) (1967). *Challenges of Humanistic Psychology.* New York: McGraw-Hill.

    A collection of articles describing the past, present, and future of what its authors hoped would be a third force in psychology.

Caffrey, M. M. (1989). *Ruth Benedict: Stranger in This Land.* Austin: University of Texas Press; Modell, J. S. (1983). *Ruth Benedict: Patterns of a Life.* Philadelphia: University of Pennsylvania Press.

    Two biographies of anthropologist Ruth Benedict, one of the two individuals responsible for Maslow's interest in self-actualization.

Hoffman, E. (1988). *The Right to Be Human: A Biography of Abraham Maslow.* Los Angeles: Jeremy Tarcher.

    An excellent biography and the most extensive treatment of Maslow's life and career to date. It includes a glossary and a complete bibliography of Maslow's publications.

Lowry, R. J. (1973). *A. H. Maslow: An Intellectual Portrait*. Monterey, CA: Brooks/Cole Publishing Company.

    Lowry, a former student of Maslow's, is arguably the most authoritative source. This small book provides excellent coverage of Maslow's views on human motivation with special emphasis on self-actualization and peak-experience. An appendix to the book includes the only published version of the GHB notebook. The excerpts in this chapter were reprinted from that book.

Lowry, R. J. (Ed.) (1979). *The Journals of A. H. Maslow*. 2 volumes. Monterey, CA: Brooks/Cole Publishing Company.

    These two volumes comprise more than 1,300 pages and contain Maslow's previously unpublished private journals, covering the years 1959 to 1970.

Maslow, A. H. (1943). A theory of human motivation. *Psychological Review*, 50, 370–396.

    Maslow's important article that described his hierarchical theory of human motivation.

Maslow, A. H. (1950). Self-actualization: A study of psychological health. In *Personality Symposia*. New York: Grune & Stratton, pp. 11–34.

    This article marked Maslow's first comprehensive treatment of the concept of self-actualization. It grew out of the GHB research.

Maslow, A. H. (1954). *Motivation and Personality*. New York: Harper & Brothers.

    Maslow's most complete treatment of his views on psychology. In this book he attacked psychology for focusing on the shortcomings of humanity and called for a new psychology that would focus on the positive qualities of humankind. The book clearly established an agenda for humanistic psychology.

References

Benjamin, L. T., Jr. (1986). Why don't they understand us? A history of psychology's public image. *American Psychologist, 41*, 941–946.

Benjamin, L. T., Jr. (1988). A history of teaching machines. *American Psychologist, 43*, 703–712.

Benjamin, L. T., Jr. (1991). *Harry Kirke Wolfe: Pioneer in psychology*. Lincoln, NE: University of Nebraska Press.

Benjamin, L. T., Jr., Durkin, M., Link, M., Vestal, M., & Acord, J. (1992). Wundt's American doctoral students. *American Psychologist, 47*, 123–131.

Boring, E. G. (1938). The Society of Experimental Psychologists, 1904–1938. *American Journal of Psychology, 51*, 410–423.

Boring, E. G. (1950). *A history of experimental psychology* (2nd ed.). New York: Appleton-Century-Crofts.

Boring, E. G. (1967). Titchener's Experimentalists. *Journal of the History of the Behavioral Sciences, 3*, 315–325.

Buckley, K. W. (1989). *Mechanical man: John Broadus Watson and the beginnings of behaviorism*. New York: Guilford Press.

Burkhardt, F., Smith, S., Kohn, D., & Montgomery, W. (Eds.) (1985). *The correspondence of Charles Darwin, Volume 1, 1826–1831*. New York: Cambridge University Press.

Cadwallader, T., & Cadwallader, J. (1990). Christine Ladd-Franklin. In A. N. O'Connell & N. F. Russo (Eds.), *Women in psychology: A bio-bibliographic sourcebook* (pp. 220–229). Westport, CT: Greenwood Press.

Calkins, M. W. (1930). Autobiography. In C. Murchison (Ed.), *A history of psychology in autobiography* (Vol. 1) (pp. 31–62). Worcester, MA: Clark University Press.

Capshew, J. (1992). Psychologists on site: A reconnaissance of the historiography of the laboratory. *American Psychologist, 47*, 132–142.

Cocks, G. (1988). *Psychotherapy in the Third Reich: The Goring Institute*. New York: Oxford University Press.

Coon, D. J. (1992). Testing the limits of sense and science: American experimental psychologists combat spiritualism, 1880–1920. *American Psychologist, 47*, 143–151.

Cranston, M. (1957). *John Locke: A biography*. Boston: Longmans, Green.

Danziger, K. (1990). *Constructing the subject: Historical origins of psychological research*. Cambridge: Cambridge University Press.

Darwin, C. R. (1859). *On the origin of species*. London: John Murray.

Finison, L. J. (1976). Unemployment, politics, and the history of organized psychology. *American Psychologist, 31*, 747–755.

Finison, L. J. (1979). An aspect of the early history of the Society for the Psychological Study of Social Issues: Psychologists and labor. *Journal of the History of the Behavioral Sciences, 15*, 29–37.

French, F. C. (1898). The place of experimental psychology in the undergraduate course. *Psychological Review, 5*, 510–512.

Freud, S. (1901). *The psychopathology of everyday life*. In *Standard Edition* (Vol. 6). London: Hogarth Press.

Freud, S. (1910). *Five lectures on psychoanalysis*. In *Standard Edition* (Vol. 2). London: Hogarth Press.

Furumoto, L. (1990). Mary Whiton Calkins (1863–1930). In A. N. O'Connell & N. F. Russo (Eds.), *Women in psychology: A bio-bibliographic sourcebook* (pp. 57–65). Westport, CT: Greenwood Press.

Gay, P. (1988). *Freud: A life for our time*. New York: Norton.

Goodwin, C. J. (1990). The Experimentalists and the APA: The Round Tables of the 1920s. Paper presented at the annual meeting of the American Psychological Association, Boston, Massachusetts.

Griffith, C. R. (1926). *Psychology of coaching*. New York: Scribners' Sons.

Griffith, C. R. (1928). *Psychology and athletics*. New York: Scribners' Sons.

Griffith, C. R. (1930). A laboratory for research in athletics. *Research Quarterly, 1*, 34–40.

Hale, N. G., Jr. (1979). Freud's Reich, the psychiatric establishment, and the founding of the American Psychoanalytic Association: Professional styles in conflict. *Journal of the History of the Behavioral Sciences, 15*, 135–141.

Harris, B. (1979). Whatever happened to little Albert? *American Psychologist, 34*, 151–160.

Harris, B. (1980). The FBI's files on APA and SPSSI: Description and implications. *American Psychologist, 35*, 1141–1144.

Hayek, F. A. (1951). *John Stuart Mill and Harriet Taylor: Their friendship and subsequent marriage*. Chicago: University of Chicago Press.

Heidbreder, E. (1933). *Seven psychologies*. New York: Appleton-Century.

Helson, H. (1925). The psychology of Gestalt, Parts I and II. *American Journal of Psychology, 36*, 342–370, 494–526.

Helson, H. (1926). The psychology of Gestalt, Parts III and IV. *American Journal of Psychology, 37*, 25–62, 189–223.

Henle, M. (1978). One man against the Nazis: Wolfgang Köhler. *American Psychologist, 33,* 939–944.

Heyd, T. (1989). Mill and Comte on psychology. *Journal of the History of the Behavioral Sciences, 25,* 125–138.

Hull, C. L. (1943). *Principles of behavior.* New York: Appleton-Century-Crofts.

James, W. (1890). *The principles of psychology* (Vols. 1–2). New York: Henry Holt.

James, W. (1892). *Psychology: A briefer course.* New York: Henry Holt.

Jones, E. (1953, 1955, 1957). *The life and work of Sigmund Freud* (Vols. 1–3). New York: Basic Books.

Jones, M. C. (1924). A laboratory study of fear: The case of Peter. *Pedagogical Seminary, 31,* 308–315.

Jung, C. G. (1961). *Memories, dreams, reflections.* New York: Random House.

Knapp, T. J. (1986). Contributions to psychohistory: XI. "The Behavior of Organisms" and "The Principles of Behavior": Note on a technique of historical analysis. *Psychological Reports, 59,* 1293–1294.

Koffka, K. (1922). Perception: An introduction to Gestalt-theorie. *Psychological Bulletin, 19,* 531–585.

Krech, D., & Cartwright, D. (1956). On SPSSI's first twenty years. *American Psychologist, 11,* 470–473.

Leahey, T. H. (1981). The mistaken mirror: On Wundt and Titchener's psychologies. *Journal of the History of the Behavioral Sciences, 17,* 273–282.

Leahey, T. H. (1987). *A history of psychology: Main currents in psychological thought* (2nd ed.). Englewood Cliffs, NJ: Prentice Hall.

Locke, J. (1689). *Two treatises on government.* Cambridge: Cambridge University Press (1960 printing).

Locke, J. (1690). *An essay concerning human understanding.* Oxford: Clarendon Press (1975 printing).

Locke, J. (1693). *Some thoughts concerning education.* Woodbury: Barron's Educational Series (1964 printing).

Lowry, R. J. (1973). *A. H. Maslow: An intellectual portrait.* Monterey, CA: Brooks/Cole.

Malthus, T. (1789/1914). *Essay on the principle of population.* New York: Dutton.

Maslow, A. H. (1954). *Motivation and personality.* New York: Harper.

Maslow, A. H. (1971). *Farther reaches of human nature.* New York: Viking Press.

Mill, J. (1829). *Analysis of the phenomena of the human mind.* London: Baldwin and Cradock.

Mill, J. S. (1843). *A system of logic, ratiocinative and inductive.* London: Longmans, Green.

Mill, J. S. (1859). *On liberty.* New York: Henry Holt (1885 reprint).

Mill, J. S. (1869). *The subjection of women.* London: Longmans, Green.

Mill, J. S. (1873). *Autobiography*. Boston: Houghton Mifflin (1969 printing).

Moore, R. L. (1977). *In search of white crows: Spiritualism, parapsychology, and American culture*. New York: Oxford University Press.

Moore-Russell, M. E. (1978). The philosopher and society: John Locke and the English revolution. *Journal of the History of the Behavioral Sciences, 14*, 65–73.

Morawski, J. G. (Ed.) (1988). *The rise of experimentation in American psychology*. New Haven: Yale University Press.

Murray, F. S., & Rowe, F. B. (1979). Psychology laboratories in the United States prior to 1900. *Teaching of Psychology, 6*, 19–21.

Napoli, D. S. (1981). *Architects of adjustment: The history of the psychological profession in the United States*. Port Washington, New York: Kennikat Press.

O'Donnell, J. M. (1985). *The origins of behaviorism: American psychology, 1870–1920*. New York: New York University Press.

Packe, M. (1954). *The life of John Stuart Mill*. New York: Macmillan.

Perry, R. B. (1935). *The thought and character of William James* (Vols. 1–2). Boston: Little Brown.

Richards, R. J. (1983). Why Darwin delayed, or interesting problems and models in the history of science. *Journal of the History of the Behavioral Sciences, 19*, 45–53.

Ross, D. (1972). *G. Stanley Hall: The psychologist as prophet*. Chicago: University of Chicago Press.

Russell, B. (1921). *The analysis of mind*. London: George Allen & Unwin.

Samelson, F. (1981). Struggle for scientific authority: The reception of Watson's behaviorism. *Journal of the History of the Behavioral Sciences, 17*, 399–425.

Scarborough, E., & Furumoto, L. (1987). *Untold lives: The first generation of American women psychologists*. New York: Columbia University Press.

Skinner, B. F. (1938). *The behavior of organisms*. New York: Appleton-Century.

Skinner, B. F. (1945, October). Baby in a box. *Ladies' Home Journal*, pp. 30–31, 135–136, 138.

Skinner, B. F. (1948). *Walden two*. New York: Macmillan.

Skinner, B. F. (1971). *Beyond freedom and dignity*. New York: Alfred A. Knopf.

Skinner, B. F. (1980). *Notebooks*. Englewood Cliffs, NJ: Prentice-Hall.

Skinner, B. F. (1990). Can psychology be a science of mind? *American Psychologist, 45*, 1206–1210.

Smith, D. J. (1985). *Minds made feeble: The myth and legend of the Kallikaks*. Rockville, MD: Aspen.

Smith, L. D. (1992). On prediction and control: B. F. Skinner and the technological ideal. *American Psychologist, 47*, 216–223.

Sokal, M. M. (1981). *An education in psychology: James McKeen Cattell's journal and letters from Germany and England, 1880–1888.* Cambridge, MA: MIT Press.

Stagner, R. (1986). Reminiscences about the founding of SPSSI. *Journal of Social Issues, 42,* (1), 35–42.

Stagner, R. (1988). *A history of psychological theories.* New York: Macmillan.

Titchener, E. B. (1901–1905). *Experimental psychology* (Vols. 1–4). New York: Macmillan.

Watson, J. B. (1910, February). The new science of animal behavior. *Harper's,* pp. 346–353.

Watson, J. B. (1913). Psychology as the behaviorist views it. *Psychological Review, 20,* 158–177.

Watson, J. B. (1919). *Psychology from the standpoint of a behaviorist.* Philadelphia: Lippincott.

Watson, J. B. (1928). *Psychological care of infant and child.* New York: Norton.

Watson, J. B. (1936). Autobiography. In C. Murchison, (Ed.), *A history of psychology in autobiography* (Volume 3) (pp. 271–281). Worcester, MA: Clark University Press.

Wiggam, A. E. (1928). *Exploring your mind with the psychologists.* New York: Bobbs-Merrill.

Wolfe, H. K. (1895). The new psychology in undergraduate work. *Psychological Review, 2,* 382–387.

Worcester, E. (1932). *Life's adventure: The story of a varied career.* New York: Scribner's.

Credits

The following sources are credited for granting permission to reprint the letters and other copyrighted materials used in this book.

Chapter 1: Oxford University Press 1976–1989. Reprinted from *The Correspondence of John Locke* edited by E. S. de Beer (1976–1989) by permission of Oxford University Press.

Chapter 2: Reprinted from *The Correspondence of Charles Darwin* edited by F. Burkhardt, S. Smith, D. Kohn, & W. Montgomery (1985–) by permission of Cambridge University Press.

Chapter 3: Mill-Taylor letters by permission of Stephen Kresge, Editor of the collected works of F. A. Hayek and by permission of the University of Chicago Press.

Chapter 4: Reprinted from *An Education in Psychology: James McKeen Cattell's Journals and Letters from Germany and England, 1880–1888* edited by M. M. Sokal (1981), by permission of M. M. Sokal and MIT Press.

Chapter 5: Letters and reports reprinted by permission of Harry Kirke Wolfe, II.

Chapter 6: Letters of Mary Whiton Calkins by permission of the Wellesley College Archives.

Chapter 7: Reprinted from *The Letters of William James* (2 vols.) edited by H. James (1920) by permission of Alexander James.

Chapter 8: Letters of E. B. Titchener from the Edward Bradford Titchener Papers, collection #14/23/545, Department of Manuscripts and University Archives, reprinted by permission of the Cornell University Library.

Chapter 9: John Watson letters reprinted by permission of James B. Watson.

Chapter 10: H. H. Goddard letters reprinted by permission of the Archives of the History of American Psychology, University of Akron, John Popplestone, Director.

Chapter 11: Freud-Jung letters reprinted from *The Freud-Jung Letters: The Correspondence between Sigmund Freud and Carl Jung* edited by W. McGuire (1974) by permission of Princeton University Press. Carl

Jung-Emma Jung letters reprinted from *Memories, Dreams, Reflections* by C. G. Jung (1961) by permission of Random House, Inc.

Chapter 12: C. R. Griffith letters from Coleman R. Griffith Papers, RS 5/1/21, by permission of University of Illinois Archives.

Chapter 13: Wolfgang Köhler letters by permission of the American Philosophical Society. Molly Harrower-Kurt Koffka letters from *Kurt Koffka: An Unwitting Self-Portrait* (1983) by permission of M. Harrower. Kurt Lewin letter reprinted by permission of Miriam Lewin. Previously published as "Everything within me rebels: A letter from Kurt Lewin to Wolfgang Köhler, 1933." *Journal of Social Issues*, 1987, *42* (4), 39–47.

Chapter 14: Letters from the Society for the Psychological Study of Social Issues Papers, by permission of the Archives of the History of American Psychology, University of Akron, John Popplestone, Director. Permission from Ernest R. Hilgard and Ralph K. White for reprinting their letters.

Chapter 15: Excerpts from B. F. Skinner's *Notebooks* edited by R. Epstein (1980) reprinted by permission of Julie Skinner Vargas for the B. F. Skinner Foundation and Robert Epstein.

Chapter 16: Excerpts from A. H. Maslow's "Good Human Being Notebook" in *A. H. Maslow: An Intellectual Portrait* edited by R. J. Lowry (1973) by permission of Brooks/Cole Publishing Company, Pacific Grove, CA 93950.

Index

Adams, D. K., 161–62
Adams, F. W., 126–27
Air crib, 178, 188
Albert B., 110, 119
Allen, J., 33
Allport, G. W., 166, 168, 169, 190
American Association for Applied
    Psychology (AAAP), 167
American Association for
    Humanistic Psychology, 190
American Journal of Psychology, 140,
    153
American Philosophical Association,
    65
American Psychological Association,
    55, 65, 77, 94, 95, 97, 98,
    103–104, 105, 123, 140, 143,
    155, 165–69, 172–75, 190
American Society for Psychical
    Research, 77–78, 79, 80, 82, 85,
    89
Amherst College, 66
Analysis of Mind, The (Russell), 114
*Analysis of the Phenomena of the
    Human Mind* (Mill, J.), 26
Angell, F., 54, 67, 93, 94, 100
Angell, J. R., 108, 112
Angier, R. P., 105–106
Animal research, 108
Apparatus, 45, 56, 60, 122
Archives of the History of American
    Psychology (Akron), 123, 167
Aristotle, 1
Association, 48, 49, 72, 75
Athletics. *See* Sport psychology.

Atkinson, J. B., 200
Atmosphere effect, 197
Augustine, St., 197–98
Automatograph, 122
Bain, A., 34
Baird, J. W., 100, 101
Baldwin, J. M., 87, 108, 110
Bearg, E., 151
Behavior of Organisms, The (Skinner),
    177, 188
Behavioral technology, 177–89
Behaviorism, 108–20, 154, 177–89
Benedict, R., 191, 195, 203
Bentley, M., 55, 100
Berger, G. O., 42, 43, 45, 49
Berkeley, G., 1
Berlin, University of, 54–55, 80, 153,
    160–63
Bessey, C. E., 56–57, 59, 60–61
Beyond Freedom and Dignity (Skinner),
    179, 189
Binet, A., 122
Blackfoot Indians, 197
Boas, F., 132
Boehme, J., 202
Bolton, T. L., 62–63
Boring, E. G., 95, 102, 105
Brill, A. A., 131, 140
British Psychological Association, 65
Brooklyn College, 193
Brown, J. F., 168, 169
Brown, R. R., 171
Bryan, W. L., 63
Bryn Mawr College, 101
California, University of, 54

Calkins, M. W., 65–76
  Graduate study of, 65–76
Cambridge University, 161
Campbell, C. M., 126–27
Carlyle, T., 38
Carnegie Institution, 126
Catholic University, 54
Cattell, J. McK., 39–52, 54, 55, 77,
    87, 94, 100, 102, 126, 132, 174
  Autobiography, 51
  Editorship of *Science*, 39, 41, 52,
    78, 88
  On psychic phenomena, 85–86
  Relationship with Wundt, 41–52
  Research on speed of mental
    processes, 41, 42, 46–47, 48–49,
    51
Cattell, W., 41, 43–45
Channing, W. E., 202
Chicago, University of, 108
Child psychology, 110
Child rearing, 3–12, 110, 115–18
  Uncontrollable child, 116–17
City College of New York, 191
Clark University, 57, 67, 74, 127,
    128
  Anniversary conference of 1909,
    131–42
Clarke, E., 2
Clarke, M. J., 2
Clothes psychosis, 125
Coaching. *See* Sport psychology.
Cognitive psychology, 154
Columbia University, 39, 54, 102,
    110, 113, 115, 191
Comte, A., 28, 31–32, 54
Conditioning, 181, 183–87
  of fear, 110, 117, 118, 120
Control, 177–79
Cook, H. D., 102
Cornell University, 54, 67, 93–94,
    153, 154, 191
Cruelty in children, 11
Culture, 186–87
Curiosity in children, 9–11
Dallenbach, K., 95, 105
Darwin, C. R., 14–25
Darwin, E., 17
Davidson, T., 79

Deconditioning of fear, 118
Decroly, O., 122
Dewey, J., 108, 202
Division of Consulting Psychologists, 166
Dodge, R., 94, 95, 100, 103–104,
    105–106
Dominance, 191, 196, 197
Donaldson, H. H., 108
Downey, J. E., 96
Drake, R. M., 171
Duke University, 161
Duncker, K., 162
Ebbinghaus, H., 55
Elder, J. H., 169
Eliot, C., 70
Emerson, R. W., 200, 202
Emotional reactions, 117, 125
Empiricism, 1, 3, 53
*Essay Concerning Human Understanding,
    An* (Locke), 1
Estabrooks, G. H., 174
Ethics, 47, 56
Evolution, 14
Experimental Psychology (Titchener), 94
Experimentalists, The. *See* Titchener.
Faribault, Minnesota, 121
Fear, 110, 117
Federal Bureau of Investigation (FBI),
    165, 175
Feeblemindedness. *See* Mental
    retardation.
Ferenczi, S., 131–32, 137
Fernberger, S., 95
Fitzroy, R., 15
Fliess, W., 142
Flournoy, T., 89, 91
Football, 144, 145–47, 149–50
Franck, J., 156
Frankfurt, University of, 153
Freiberg, University of, 67
Freud, S., 131–42
Fromm, E., 190
Functionalism, 109
Furman University, 108
Furumoto, L., 65
Gamble, E., 102
Gardiner, H. N., 66, 70
Garman, C. E., 66, 68–70
Germany, 153–64

Gestalt psychology, 153–64, 192
Goddard, H. H., 121–30
Goethe, J. W., 156, 202
Goldstein, K., 190, 192
Good human beings (Maslow),
     190–204
Goodman (Maslow), B., 196
Göttingen, University of, 156
Gould, S. J., 16
Gravity chronometer, 45
Gray, A., 20, 21, 22
Griffith, C. R., 143–52
Gruber, H., 16
Gurney, E., 77, 79
Guthrie, E. R., 55
Hall, C., 172
Hall, G. S., 39, 42, 44, 53–54, 62,
     63, 70, 101, 108, 121, 124–25,
     127–28, 131–34, 136–42
Harlow, H., 191
Harrower, M., 155, 161, 162–63
Harvard University, 54, 60, 66, 67,
     68, 69, 70, 72, 73, 74, 140, 155,
     161
Heider, F., 157
Henslow, J. S., 15
Hertz, H., 156
Hilgard, E. R., 174
Hill, P. S., 115–18
Hitler, A., 154–64, 167, 191, 192
Hodgson, R., 86, 89
Hodgson, S., 79
Hollingworth, H. L., 39
Hooker, B. (Mrs.), 36
Hooker, J. D., 15, 17, 20, 21, 22
Horney, K., 190
Huff, G., 145, 146, 148
Hull, C. L., 177, 188
Humanistic psychology, 190–204
Hume, D., 1
Idiot, 123, 124, 127
Illinois, University of, 144
Imbecile, 123, 126
Incontinence, 117
Indiana University, 57, 60, 63
Instincts, 117, 125, 200
Intelligence, 122–23, 129, 130
Iowa, University of, 154
Irwin, A., 74

James, H., 78
James, W., 54, 66, 70, 71, 72–73,
     77–92, 132, 161, 202
   Views on psychology, 78–79
Jennings, H. S., 132
Jenyns, L., 15, 18–19
Jews, 154, 156–60, 162–64
Johns Hopkins University, 39, 42, 44,
     54, 108, 112, 113, 123
Johnstone, E., 121
Jones, E., 134, 140
Jones, M. C., 118
Jordan, M. A., 66, 68
Journal of Philosophy, 73
Journal of Social Issues, 167
Judd, C., 94, 100
Jung, C. G., 131–42
Jung, E., 137–39
Kallikak family, 129
Kant, I., 1
Kierkegaard, S., 190, 198
Kirschmann, A., 95
Koffka, K., 153, 155, 157, 161–63
Köhler, W., 153, 154, 156, 160–62,
     164, 195
Krech, D., 166–76
Krechevsky, I. *See* Krech, D.
Külpe, O., 94
Ladd-Franklin, C., 80, 101–102
Lafayette College, 39
Language, 125
Leipzig, University of, 40–52, 53, 67,
     131
Lessing, G. E., 156
Letters on Tolerance (Locke), 2
Leuba, J. H., 101
Levy, D., 195–96, 202
Lewin, G. W., 157
Lewin, K., 153, 154, 157–60, 163, 164
Linnean Society (London), 21
Locke, J., 1–13, 26
   Nature of ideas, 1–2
Loeb, J., 108
Logic, 56, 61
London, University of, 155
Lotze, R., 42, 43
Love, 185
Loyalty, 179
Ludwig, C., 54

Lyell, C., 15, 18, 19, 20, 21, 22, 23
McCosh, J., 53
Maclean, G., 62
MacLeod, R. B., 175
Malthus, T., 15
Maslow, A. H., 190–204
    Theory of motivation, 190–93,
        204
Masturbation, 117
Medium, 77, 81–84, 85–88
Memory, 55, 65, 75
Mental retardation, 121–30, 201
Mental test, 39
Mentalism, 108–109, 180
Meyer, A., 123–24, 132
Michigan, University of, 60, 64, 93
Miles, W., 144
Mill, J., 26
Mill, J. S., 26–38, 54
    Views on marriage, 29, 32–33,
        35, 37
Mitchell, S. W., 87
Monroe, W. S., 121
Moral philosophy, 53–54
Moron, 123
Motivation, 190, 204
Motivation and Personality (Maslow),
    191
Münsterberg, H., 67, 77, 94, 98, 100,
    101
Murphy, G., 166, 176
Murray, J., 23
Myers, F. W. H., 77, 79, 84–85
Myers, W. H., 81
National Academy of Sciences, 39,
    77
Natural selection, 15, 19, 22
Nazi Germany. *See* Hitler.
Nebraska, University of, 54
New Jersey College for Women, 161
New Jersey Training School for
    Feebleminded Girls and Boys.
    See Vineland Training School.
New School for Social Research
    (New York City), 110, 154, 192
Nichol, J., 35
Niebuhr, R., 197–98
Norsworthy, N., 126
Notre Dame, University of, 149–50

Nuremberg Laws, 154
Oaths, 179
On Liberty (Mill, J. S.), 28
On the Origin of Species (Darwin), 14, 22
Original sin, 197–98
Oxford University, 2, 93
Pace, E. A., 54, 100
Paired-associate technique, 65
Pascal, B., 202
Patrick, G., 144
Pedagogy, 59, 60
Pennsylvania State Teachers College
    (West Chester), 121
Pennsylvania, University of, 39, 54, 57,
    100, 124
Perry, R. B., 155–56, 160–61
Perry, T. S., 90
Phi phenomenon, 153
Philosophische Studien, 48, 50, 56
Phipps Clinic (Johns Hopkins
    University), 113
Physics, 161
Pierce, J. M., 87
Pillsbury, W. B., 55, 64, 93, 100
Piper, L., 77–78, 81–84, 85–88, 89
Plato, 68
Poffenberger, A. T., 173
Popularization of psychology, 110, 111
Porter, N., 53
Princeton University, 53, 96, 106
Principles of Behavior (Hull), 177
Principles of Psychology (James), 54,
    66–67, 72, 77
Psychical research, 77–92
Psychoanalysis, 131–42, 194
Psychological Care of Infant and Child
    (Watson), 111, 120
Psychological Corporation, 39
Psychological Review, 108, 113
Psychological Round Table (PRT),
    106–107
Psychology: A Briefer Course (James), 72
*Psychology from the Standpoint of a
    Behaviorist* (Watson), 113
Psychology laboratories, 54–64
Psychopathology of Everyday Life, The
    (Freud), 132
Psychophysics, 58
Public policy, 165–76

Punishment, 9, 185
Putnam, J. J., 140, 141
Radcliffe College, 68, 74
Rayner, R., 110, 118
Reaction time, 41, 42, 46–47, 48–49,
  58
Reasonableness of Christianity, The
  (Locke), 2
Reinforcement, 182–87
Richards, R. J., 16
Robertson, G. C., 35–36, 80
Rockefeller, L. S., 110
Rockne, K., 149–50
Roff, M., 174
Rogers, C., 190
Rorschach test, 193, 194, 196, 198,
  202, 203
Royce, J., 66, 70–71, 71–72, 73
Rupp, H., 161, 162
Russell, B., 113–15
Sanford, E. C., 67, 73–74, 98, 100,
  125–26
Santayana, G., 67
Sartre, J. P., 190
Schiller, F. C. S., 89
Science, 39, 52, 63, 78, 88
Scripture, E. W., 54, 73, 144
Seashore, C. E., 100, 197
Security, 195, 197, 199, 202
Self-actualization, 191–94, 199–200,
  203
Self-esteem, 193
Sells, S. B., 197
Sex differences, 7–9, 30–31, 33–36
Sex drive, 202
Shaler, N. S., 87
Sidgwick, H., 77
Sidis, B., 140
Skinner, B. F., 177–89
Slatterly, C. L., 89
Smith College, 65, 66, 68, 153, 155
Smith, T. L., 127
Spinoza, B., 156, 202
Social issues, 165–76
Society of Experimental
  Psychologists, 96. *See* also
  Titchener's Experimentalists.

Society for Psychical Research (Boston).
  See American Society of Psychical
  Research.
Society for Psychical Research
  (London), 77–78, 79, 80
Society for the Psychological Study of
  Social Issues (SPSSI), 165–76
Sokal, M. M., 41, 51, 52
Some Thoughts Concerning Education
  (Locke), 3
Spiritualism, 90
Sport psychology, 143–52
Stagner, R., 166
Stanford University, 54, 123, 150, 157
Stephens, J. M., 173
Sterile insects, 16, 23
Stern, W., 132
Stratton, G. M., 54, 100
Structuralism, 93, 109
Stumpf, C., 80
Swarthmore College, 154, 196
Subjection of Women, The (Mill, J. S.), 28
System of Logic, A (Mill, J. S.), 28
Tabula rasa, 1
Taylor, H., 27–33
Taylor, J., 27
Teaching machines, 178
Terman, L., 123
Thematic Apperception Test (TAT),
  194
Thinking, 180
Thompson, J. Walter, Advertising, 110
Thoreau, H. D., 200
Thorndike, E. L., 39, 191
Thumb sucking, 116
Tillich, P. J., 197–98
Titchener, E. B., 77, 93–107, 112, 123,
  129, 132, 191
  The Experimentalists, 93–107
  Organization of The
  Experimentalists, 99–100
Tobin, L. M., 147, 148
Tolman, E. C., 166
Toronto, University of, 95
Trance, 83
Transference, 117–18
Trowbridge, J., 87
Two Treatises on Government (Locke), 2
Type specimen, 201

Vassar College, 93, 96
Vineland Training School, 121–30
von Lauenstein, 162
von Restorff, 162
Walden Two (Skinner), 177, 189
Wallace, A. R., 16, 19–20, 21
Walton, W. E., 173
Warren, H., 94, 100, 102–103, 106
Washburn, M. F., 93, 96, 102, 118
Watson, G., 166, 176
Watson, J. B., 102–103, 108–20
Weber's Law, 58
Wedgwood, H., 17
Wellesley College, 65, 66, 67, 68,
    71, 75
Werner, H., 199
Wertheimer, M., 153, 154, 157, 191,
    195
West Chester State College. *See*
    Pennsylvania State Teachers
    College.
West, T. F., 151
White, R., 172
Whitman, W., 202
Willoughby, R., 171

Wisconsin, University of, 57, 60, 153,
    191
Witmer, L., 94, 99, 100, 124, 126
Wolfe, H. K., 54–64
Women,
    and The Experimentalists, 95–96,
        97–102, 107
    and graduate education, 65–76
    and marriage, 29–30, 32–33, 35–37
Woodworth, R. S., 39
Word association method, 141
World War I, 155
World War II, 154–64
Wundt, W., 28, 40–52, 53, 55, 67, 93,
    131, 139
    American students of, 40, 51, 54–64,
        73, 124
    As teacher, 40
Wylie, A. R. T., 121, 125
Wyoming, University of, 96
Yale University, 53, 54, 73, 105–106,
    144, 150–51
Yerkes, R. M., 102, 108, 111–12, 118–19
Zuppke, R., 145, 146, 147

3. http://strikemag.org/bullshit-jobs/
4. https://www.theguardian.com/technology/2016/may/20/silicon-assassins-condemn-humans-life-useless-artificial-intelligence
5. https://www.bbvaopenmind.com/en/articles/the-crisis-of-social-reproduction-and-the-end-of-work/
6. "The theory of the leisure class: An economic study of institutions", by Thorstein Veblen, Aakar Books, 1899
7. http://www.sociology.ox.ac.uk/materials/papers/wp20143.pdf
8. http://www.sociology.ox.ac.uk/materials/papers/wp20143.pdf (page 8)
9. "The Time Bind: When home becomes work and work becomes home", by Arlie Russel Hochschild, CA Henry Holt, 2009
10. https://hbr.org/2012/03/tackling-the-trauma-of-unemplo
11. https://www.nytimes.com/2018/05/02/opinion/universal-basic-income-finland.html
12. https://www.reddit.com/r/science/comments/3nyn5i/science_ama_series_stephen_hawking_ama_answers/cvsdmkv/
13. https://qz.com/911968/bill-gates-the-robot-that-takes-your-job-should-pay-taxes/
14. https://www.wsj.com/articles/why-a-universal-basic-income-would-be-a-calamity-1502403580; https://www.independent.co.uk/voices/don-t-fall-for-universal-basic-income-it-s-a-utopian-fiction-that-wastes-public-money-on-the-rich-a6945881.html

14. https://agency.reuters.com/en/insights/articles/articles-archive/reuters-news-tracer-filtering-through-the-noise-of-social-media.html
15. https://www.cjr.org/analysis/cyborg_virtual_reality_reuters_tracer.php
16. https://www.techemergence.com/companies/narrative-science/
17. https://www.digitaltrends.com/cool-tech/japanese-ai-writes-novel-passes-first-round-nationanl-literary-prize/
18. http://www.thestartupofyou.com/about-the-book/
19. http://gizmodo.com/lyft-thinks-its-exciting-that-a-driver-was-working-whil-1786970298
20. https://www.theguardian.com/commentisfree/2018/may/24/deliveroo-couriers-dystopia-union
21. https://www.buzzfeed.com/johanabhuiyan/what-uber-drivers-really-make-according-to-their-pay-stubs?utm_term=.hlW3oL6xl#.vdZDazlPn
22. https://www.ridester.com/how-much-do-uber-drivers-make/
23. https://www.theguardian.com/technology/2018/mar/01/uber-lyft-driver-wages-median-report
24. https://www.theguardian.com/business/2018/may/16/gig-economy-union-seeking-to-raise-cash-to-fund-deliveroo-fight-legal-action
25. https://www.theguardian.com/business/2017/nov/14/deliveroo-couriers-minimum-wage-holiday-pay
26. https://www.theguardian.com/business/2018/jun/15/union-wins-first-round-in-deliveroo-high-court-employment-challenge
27. https://www.theguardian.com/business/2018/jun/18/deliveroos-hiring-conditions-to-face-scrutiny-by-mps
28. https://www.bls.gov/news.release/conemp.nr0.htm
29. http://money.cnn.com/2018/03/14/news/economy/handy-gig-economy-workers/index.html
30. http://thehill.com/opinion/finance/383334-gig-economy-is-no-excuse-for-lax-protections-for-american-workers
31. https://theoutline.com/post/1417/we-listened-to-every-episode-of-uber-s-anti-union-propaganda-podcast?zd=1&zi=bzwvgc7r; https://www.opensecrets.org/lobby/firmsum.php?id=D0000 67336&year=2017; https://www.theguardian.com/technology/2016/may/09/uber-lyft-austin-vote-against-self-regulation

Chapter 14

1. https://roarmag.org/2016/06/03/david-frayne-refusal-of-work-excerpt/
2. https://www.indy100.com/article/this-is-how-anarchists-welcomed-us-back-to-work--g1We1j9Lcl

Chapter 12

1. The Believing Brain, Michael Shermer.
2. http://www.michaelshermer.com/the-believing-brain/
3. http://bigthink.com/going-mental/the-neurological-origins-of-religious-belief
4. https://www.ncbi.nlm.nih.gov/pubmed/14594742?dopt=Abstract
5. http://www.thebookoflife.org/the-duty-trap/
6. https://www.amazon.com/Coherence-Thought-Action-Life-Mind/dp/0262201313/
7. http://www.attn.com/stories/10520/joe-biden-memo-employees-spend-time-with-family

Chapter 13

1. US Patent Number: US20170278051
2. https://www.channel4.com/news/anger-at-amazon-working-conditions
3. https://static1.squarespace.com/static/5a3af3e22aeba59a4ad56d8cb/t/5ad098b356f2a7b8c9od5e1b/1523652002069/Amazon+Warehouse+Staff+Survey+Results.pdf
4. https://www.theverge.com/2018/4/16/17243026/amazon-warehouse-jobs-worker-conditions-bathroom-breaks
5. https://www.salon.com/2014/02/23/worse_than_wal_mart_amazons_sick_brutality_and_secret_history_of_ruthlessly_intimidating_workers/
6. https://www.independent.co.uk/news/uk/home-news/amazon-workers-working-hours-weeks-conditions-targets-online-shopping-delivery-a8079111.html
7. https://www.bbc.com/news/uk-england-37708996
8. https://www.businessinsider.my/how-whole-foods-uses-scorecards-to-punish-employees-2018-1/
9. https://www.salon.com/2014/02/23/worse_than_wal_mart_amazons_sick_brutality_and_secret_history_of_ruthlessly_intimidating_workers/
10. https://sites.google.com/site/thefaceofamazon/
11. https://www.nytimes.com/2015/08/16/technology/inside-amazon-wrestling-big-ideas-in-a-bruising-workplace.html
12. https://medium.com/@nickciubotariu/an-amazonian-s-response-to-inside-amazon-wrestling-big-ideas-in-a-bruising-workplace-b06ca4f6d53a
13. https://www.geekwire.com/2015/full-memo-jeff-bezos-responds-to-cutting-nyt-expose-says-tolerance-for-lack-of-empathy-needs-to-be-zero/